Blackstone's
Police Q& A

General Police Duties 2008

Blackstone's
Police Q&A

General Police Duties 2008

Sixth Edition

Huw Smart and John Watson

OXFORD
UNIVERSITY PRESS

OXFORD

UNIVERSITY PRESS

Great Clarendon Street, Oxford OX2 6DP

Oxford University Press is a department of the University of Oxford.
It furthers the University's objective of excellence in research, scholarship,
and education by publishing worldwide in

Oxford New York

Auckland Bangkok Buenos Aires Cape Town Chennai
Dar es Salaam Delhi Hong Kong Istanbul Karachi Kolkata
Kuala Lumpur Madrid Melbourne Mexico City Mumbai Nairobi
São Paulo Shanghai Taipei Tokyo Toronto

With offices in

Argentina Austria Brazil Chile Czech Republic France Greece
Guatemala Hungary Italy Japan Poland Portugal Singapore
South Korea Switzerland Thailand Turkey Ukraine Vietnam

Published in the United States
by Oxford University Press Inc., New York

British Library Cataloguing in Publication Data

Data available

Library of Congress Cataloging in Publication Data

Data available

Typeset by Laserwords Private Limited, Chennai, India
Printed in Great Britain
on acid-free paper by
Ashford Colour Press Limited, Gosport, Hampshire

ISBN 978-0-19-922920-8

10 9 8 7 6 5 4 3 2 1

Contents

Contents

Introduction

Before you get into the detail of this book, there are two myths about multiple-choice questions (MCQs) that we need to get out of the way right at the start:

1. that they are easy to answer;
2. that they are easy to write.

Take one look at a professionally designed and properly developed exam paper such as those used by the Police Promotion Examinations Board or the National Board of Medical Examiners in the US and the first myth collapses straight away. Contrary to what some people believe, MCQs are not an easy solution for examiners and not a 'multiple-guess' soft option for examinees.

That is not to say that *all* MCQs are taxing, or even testing — in the psychometric sense. If MCQs are to have any real value at all, they need to be carefully designed and follow some agreed basic rules.

And this leads us to myth number 2.

It is widely assumed by many people and educational organisations that anyone with the knowledge of a subject can write MCQs. You need only look at how few MCQ writing courses are offered by training providers in the UK to see just how far this myth is believed. Similarly, you need only to have a go at a few badly designed MCQs to realise that it is a myth nonetheless. Writing bad MCQs is easy; writing good ones is no easier than answering them!

As with many things, the design of MCQs benefits considerably from time, training and experience. Many MCQ writers fall easily and often unwittingly into the trap of making their questions too hard, too easy or too obscure, or completely different from the type of question that you will eventually encounter in your own particular exam. Others seem to use the MCQ as a way to catch people out or to show how smart they, the authors, are (or think they are).

There are several purposes for which MCQs are very useful. The first is in producing a reliable, valid and fair test of knowledge and understanding across a wide range of subject matter. Another is an aid to study, preparation and revision for such examinations and tests. The differences in objective mean that there are slight differences in the rules that the MCQ writers follow. Whereas the design of fully validated MCQs is to be used in high stakes examinations which will effectively determine who passes and who fails have very strict guidelines as to construction, content and style, less stringent rules apply to MCQs that are being used for teaching and revision. For that reason, there may be types of MCQ that are appropriate in the latter setting which would not be used in the former. However, in developing the MCQs for this book, the authors have tried to follow the fundamental rules of MCQ design but they would not claim to have replicated the level of psychometric rigour that is — and has to be — adopted by the type of examining bodies referred to above.

These MCQs are designed to reinforce your knowledge and understanding, to highlight any gaps or weaknesses in that knowledge and understanding and to help focus your revision of the relevant topics.

I hope that we have achieved that aim.

Good luck!

Blackstone's Police Q&As — Special Features

References to Blackstone's Police Manuals

Every answer is followed by a paragraph reference to Blackstone's Police Manuals. This means that once you have attempted a question and looked at an answer, the Manual can immediately be referred to for help and clarification.

Unique numbers for each question

Each question and answer has the same unique number. This should ensure that there is no confusion as to which question is linked to which answer. For example, Question 2.1 is linked to Answer 2.1.

Checklists

The checklists are designed to help you keep track of your progress when answering the multiple-choice questions. If you fill in the checklist after attempting a question, you will be able to check how many you got right on the first attempt and will know immediately which questions need to be revisited a second time. Please visit www.blackstonepolicemanuals.com and click through to the Blackstone's Police Q&As 2008 page. You will then find electronic versions of the checklists to download and print out.

Acknowledgements

This book has been written as an accompaniment to *Blackstone's Police Manuals*, and will test the knowledge you have accrued through reading that series. It is of the essence that full study of the relevant chapters in each *Police Manual* is completed prior to attempting the Questions and Answers. As qualified police trainers we recognise that students tend to answer questions incorrectly either because they don't read the question properly, or because one of the 'distracters' has done its work. The distracter is one of the three incorrect answers in a multiple-choice question (MCQ), and is designed to distract you from the correct answer and in this way discriminate between candidates: the better-prepared candidate not being 'distracted'.

So particular attention should be paid to the *Answers* sections, and students should ask themselves 'Why did I get that question wrong?' and, just as importantly, 'Why did I get that question right?' Combining the information gained in the *Answers* section together with re-reading the chapter in the *Police Manuals* should lead to greater understanding of the subject matter.

The authors wish to thank all the staff at Oxford University Press who have helped put this publication together. We would also like to show appreciation to Alistair MacQueen for his vision and support, without which this project would never have been started; also Fraser Sampson, consultant editor of Blackstone's Police Manuals, whose influence on these Q&As is appreciated.

Huw would like to thank Caroline for her constant love, support and understanding over the past year — and her ability to withstand the pressures of being the partner to a workaholic! Special thanks to Lawrence and Maddie — two perfect young adults. Last but not least, love and special affection to Haf and Nia, two beautiful young girls.

John would like to thank Sue, David, Catherine and Andrew for their continued support, and understanding that 'deadline' means 'deadline'.

1 | Police

QUESTIONS

Question 1.1

Constable KERSLAKE is an undercover officer working for the drug squad. Constable KERSLAKE has recently been working on a case which involved working closely with the Serious Organised Crime Agency (SOCA). The officer enjoyed working with SOCA and is wondering whether police officers can be seconded to work with the agency on attachment.

Considering that members of SOCA are not police officers, in respect of second-ments, which of the following statements is correct?

A A police officer cannot be seconded; they would have to permanently resign from the police service and apply for a post in SOCA.

B A police officer can be seconded; they would have to resign temporarily as a constable and would be re-appointed on their return to the police service.

C A police officer can be seconded; they would not have to resign and would be treated as having been suspended until they return to the police service.

D A police officer can be seconded; they would remain a constable until they return to the police service.

Question 1.2

Special Constable PATTERSON is an officer with Northshire Constabulary. SC PATTERSON's home force has a Football League Club in its own area and SC PATTERSON works regularly with the police spotters' team, identifying football hooligans. SC PATTERSON has developed an expertise in this area and has been asked to attend away matches to assist regular police officers with preventing crowd trouble.

Would SC PATTERSON enjoy the powers and privileges of a special constable, when working in other police areas?

A Yes, SC PATTERSON would enjoy the powers and privileges of a special constable when working in any police area.

B No, SC PATTERSON would only enjoy the powers and privileges of a special constable when working in an adjoining area, on mutual aid.

C Yes, but SC PATTERSON would only enjoy the powers and privileges of a special constable when working in an adjoining area.

D No, SC PATTERSON would only enjoy the powers and privileges of a special constable when working on mutual aid, but this may be in any police area.

Question 1.3

MANGLEY has recently been promoted to the rank of chief inspector. MANGLEY has a child under the age of 5 and is considering asking for flexible hours, to work part-time, due to family commitments.

Would the Police Regulations 2003 allow MANGLEY to work part-time as a chief inspector?

A Yes, any officer below the rank of superintendent may work part-time.

B No, only officers below the rank of inspector may work part-time.

C Yes, officers of any rank may work part-time.
D No, only officers of the rank of inspector or below may work part-time.

Question 1.4

Sergeant GUNNEY has been a part-time worker for two years. Due to a change in personal circumstances, Sergeant GUNNEY has submitted a report asking to return to full-time working within two weeks as a matter of urgency.

Would the Police Regulations 2003 allow Sergeant GUNNEY to return to full-time working within this time period?
A Yes, if it is considered reasonably practicable to do so.
B No, Sergeant GUNNEY should return to full-time working within 1 month.
C No, Sergeant GUNNEY should return to full-time working within 3 months.
D Yes, an officer can return to full-time duties at any time provided a request is made in writing.

Question 1.5

The Public Interest Disclosure Act 1998 deals with 'protected disclosures' made by employees of wrongdoings at their place of work.

To whom should disclosures be made, under the Act?
A To any person, including persons outside the employee's own organisation.
B Only to the person's employer.
C Only to a responsible or prescribed person, within the employee's own organisation.
D To any person, provided he or she is within the employee's own organisation.

Question 1.6

The procedures for evaluating and addressing performance of police staff are set out in the Police (Efficiency) Regulations 1999 (SI 1999/732).

To whom do the Regulations apply?
A A probationary constable.
B An assistant chief constable/commander.
C A chief inspector.
D A civilian enquiry officer.

Question 1.7

SMITHSON has written a letter of complaint to the police regarding Constable BRANDRICK and her investigation of a burglary. The letter outlines that the officer did not make any local enquiries, or call a scenes of crime officer (SOCO) to examine the scene. The letter raises SMITHSON'S concerns about the officer's ability. Constable BRANDRICK has 4 years' police service.

How should BRANDRICK'S sergeant deal with the letter?

A It must be investigated as a complaint against police only.
B It must be forwarded to the complaints department for investigation.
C It must be dealt with as 'unsatisfactory performance' only.
D It can be dealt with either as unsatisfactory performance, or as a complaint.

Question 1.8

Constable DOUGHTY has been served with a notice requiring him to attend a first interview in relation to unsatisfactory performance. He wishes to take someone with him to the interview to advise him.

Who can the officer take with him to the interview?

A Anyone who is a serving officer in any police force.
B Anyone who is a serving member of his own police force.
C Anyone at all, provided they are not a solicitor.
D Anyone at all, including a solicitor.

Question 1.9

Constable DOUGHTY is now at his first hearing and is accompanied by his friend, Constable GRIFFITHS.

Who is entitled to make representations at this hearing?

A Only Constable DOUGHTY may make representations.
B Only Constable GRIFFITHS may make representations.
C Both of them may make representations.
D Both of them must make representations.

Question 1.10

An officer subject to unsatisfactory performance, following formal interviews, is subject to a 'reasonable period' under which they must improve their performance.

How long is this 'reasonable period' normally?

A No less than 2 months and no more than 6 months.

B No less than 3 months and no more than 6 months.

C No less than 3 months and no more than 8 months.

D No less than 2 months and no more than 8 months.

Question 1.11

Constable FRAZER is the subject of an initial action plan due to previous incidents of unsatisfactory performance. One month into the action plan, the reporting officer dealing with Constable FRAZER's case is concerned that there has been no improvement in the officer's performance.

What further evidence would the reporting officer require, in order to invite Constable FRAZER to a first interview, under the Police (Efficiency) Regulations 1999?

A The reporting officer must be 'of the opinion' that there has been no improvement in performance.

B The reporting officer must have 'reasonable cause to suspect' that there has been no improvement in performance.

C The reporting officer must have 'sufficient grounds to believe' that there has been no improvement in performance.

D The reporting officer must show 'on the balance of probabilities' that there has been no improvement in performance.

Question 1.12

Constable SPIERS has been issued with a fixed penalty notice for disorderly behaviour while drunk in a public place. The incident occurred when Constable SPIERS was off duty and out drinking with friends. Constable SPIERS intends to contest the penalty notice.

Does Constable SPIERS have to report the matter to the police service, under sch. 1, para. 9 of the Police (Conduct) Regulations 2004?

A No, as Constable SPIERS has not been convicted of, or cautioned for a criminal offence.

B Yes, as proceedings have been issued against Constable SPIERS for a criminal offence.

C No, as Constable SPIERS was issued with a penalty notice and not arrested for a criminal offence.

D Yes, the police are obliged to report being arrested, or receiving a fixed penalty notice for *any* offence.

Question 1.13

HOLLINS is a serving uniformed police constable. A complaint has been made to the inspector that HOLLINS frequently turns up for duty in an inebriated state and that members of the public have also noticed, a fact that brings discredit to the service.

Given that a lack of sobriety whilst on duty may give rise to a reasonable suspicion of substance abuse, could HOLLINS be asked to give a sample under reg. 19A of the Police Regulations 2003?

A No, the Regulations only cover occasions where a member of the force is suspected of drug misuse.

B Yes, HOLLINS may be asked to provide a sample of breath in these circumstances.

C No, screening is only allowed in respect of officers working in specialist or critical roles, such as firearms officers.

D Yes, HOLLINS may be asked to provide a sample of breath or urine in these circumstances.

Question 1.14

Drug squad officers were conducting surveillance on PASSMORE, a suspected drug dealer. During the operation, PASSMORE was picked up several times in a vehicle, which was registered to HUTTON, a serving police constable in the firearms department. At the conclusion of the operation, PASSMORE was arrested and during interview claimed that HUTTON was a casual drug user, who was not involved in supplying drugs. HUTTON was also arrested, but there was insufficient evidence to charge for the offence of possession of controlled drugs. The information was passed on to the Professional Standards department and HUTTON was interviewed in respect of the association with PASSMORE and suspected misuse of drugs.

Given that the Professional Standards officers might suspect that HUTTON was involved in misusing substances, what sample would they be entitled to ask for, under reg. 19A of the Police Regulations 2003?

A HUTTON may be asked to supply a sample of saliva or urine.

B HUTTON may be asked to supply a sample of saliva.

C HUTTON may be asked to supply a sample of saliva, blood or urine.

D HUTTON may be asked to supply a sample of blood or urine.

Question 1.15

Constable EVERITT is being investigated for a misconduct offence, and has been given notice to appear before a disciplinary hearing.

Which of the following statements is correct, in relation to whether Constable EVERITT is entitled to legal representation at the hearing?

A She has an absolute right to be legally represented in any discipline hearing.

B She has no right to be legally represented as this is not an efficiency hearing.

C She has the right to be legally represented only where the supervising officer has given written notice of that right.

D She has the right to be legally represented only where the supervising officer has given oral notice of that right.

Question 1.16

Constable FREEMAN works for a non-metropolitan police force and has been warned to attend a conduct hearing. He has been the subject of a complaint for an offence of assault and the investigation is being supervised by the Independent Police Complaints Commission.

Who will be the presiding officer at the hearing, and who will he or she be assisted by?

A The presiding officer will be a superintendent, accompanied by another superintendent and a member of the police authority.

B The presiding officer will be an assistant chief constable, accompanied by a superintendent and a member of the police authority.

C The presiding officer will be an assistant chief constable, accompanied by two members of the police authority.

D The presiding officer will be a superintendent, accompanied by two members of the police authority.

Question 1.17

Inspector BERRY was investigating a complaint made by AICHESON against a constable who worked in her sector. AICHESON had previously made several complaints against other officers in the sector, and on each occasion the complaints were found to be malicious. Inspector BERRY believed that this particular complaint was also malicious, because of the previous complaints. The inspector requested that an application be made to the Independent Police Complaints Commission (IPCC) for the complaint to be dispensed with, because of the previous complaints. However, the application was rejected by the IPCC.

Under what circumstances, if any, could a further application be made for the complaint to be dispensed with?

A An appeal may be made to the IPCC, provided the application is made within 28 days.

B No further applications may be made to the IPCC in relation to this complaint.

C An appeal may be made to the IPCC, provided the application is made within 21 days.

D An appeal may be made to the IPCC, provided the application is made within 14 days.

Question 1.18

FENTON is a member of the British National Party (BNP), although she does not actively take part in politics herself. She is considering joining the police force, but is unsure as to the regulations in relation to the political party she is affiliated to.

In relation to Sch. 1 to the Police Regulations 2003 (SI 2003/527) (restrictions on the private lives of officers) could FENTON be a member of the BNP, as a police officer?

A Yes, she may be a member of this political party, provided she does not take an active part in politics.

B No, she may not be a member of any political party under this schedule.

C No, she may not be a member of this particular party.

D Yes, she may be a member of any political party, provided she does not take an active part in politics.

Question 1.19

Constable PURSEY creates a false piece of intelligence as a joke relating to a male believed to be in possession of a firearm. As a result of this a member of the public is stopped by the local Armed Response Vehicle and challenged with live police firearms. The member of the public is not happy and wishes to take action against the police for misconduct in a public office.

Which of the following is correct?

A The officer's actions amount to a tort (civil wrong) only and action in the High Court should be commenced.

B The officer's actions amount to a criminal offence only and criminal proceedings should be started.

C The officer's actions amount to a tort (civil wrong) and a criminal offence and both criminal and civil proceedings can be started.

D The officer's actions amount to a tort (civil wrong) and a criminal offence, however only civil *or* criminal proceedings can be started, not both.

Question 1.20

The common law offence of misconduct in public office, deals with an abuse of public power.

In relation to police officers and the actions they take, which of the following is correct?

A An abuse of power can only relate to conduct, i.e. actual actions an officer took.

B An abuse of power can relate to omissions, i.e. a failure to act where they should have.

C An abuse of power can include *any* action taken by an officer whilst off duty.

D An abuse of power can include actions where an officer has acted inadvertently.

Question 1.21

FARR is aware that special constables are entitled to free travel on the local buses. FARR makes a false warrant card with the term 'Special Constable' on it and a picture of himself. Every day he travels on the bus and produces this card to obtain free rides. He never states he is a special constable; he merely shows the bus driver his card.

Has FARR committed an offence of impersonating a police officer contrary to s. 90(1) of the Police Act 1996?

A No, as he did not say he was a special constable.

B No, as the legislation does not apply to impersonating special constables.

C Yes, provided his intention was to deceive.

D Yes, provided his intention was to obtain an advantage.

ANSWERS

Answer 1.1

Answer **C** — Members of the Serious Organised Crime Agency (SOCA) are not police officers (although they may be endowed with the powers of a constable). A constable may be seconded to SOCA without resigning from the police service (answers A and B are incorrect). Where a constable is seconded to SOCA, s. 43(6) of the Serious Organised Crime and Police Act 2005 states that if the constable does not resign from the police service, they will be treated as having been suspended from that office until they return to the police service. Answer D is therefore incorrect.

General Police Duties, para. 4.1.2.3

Answer 1.2

Answer **A** — The terms under which special constables may be appointed and deployed are set out in s. 30 of the Police Act 1996. Previously, special constables would only have powers and privileges in their own areas or adjoining police areas, unless they were used in mutual aid schemes, when they would enjoy the powers of a special constable in the area they were providing mutual aid.

However, the Police and Justice Act 2006 introduces significant amendments: para. 21 of sch. 2, will allow special constables to use their constabulary powers in forces throughout England and Wales, regardless of the duties they are performing. Answers B, C and D are therefore incorrect.

General Police Duties, para. 4.1.2.10

Answer 1.3

Answer **C** — Regulation 5 of the Police Regulations 2003 allows a chief constable, after consultation with local representatives of the staff associations, to appoint an officer to perform part-time service *in any rank*. Answers A, B and D are therefore incorrect.

General Police Duties, para. 4.1.7.1

Answer 1.4

Answer **A** — The Police Regulations 2003 set out the required notice period for part-time workers who wish to return to full-time duties. Part-time officers may give notice in writing of their intention to be re-appointed as a full-time member and will be appointed within:

- one month of the date the notice is received by the police authority, where the authority has a suitable vacancy, or
- when 3 months have elapsed since the day the notice was received, or
- from an earlier date if reasonably practicable.

Therefore, the normal time period would be one month; if there is no suitable vacancy, this may be extended to three months. However, the police authority may allow such a change in duties from an earlier date if it is considered reasonably practicable to do so. Answers B, C and D are therefore incorrect.

General Police Duties, para. 4.1.7.1

Answer 1.5

Answer **A** — The Public Interest Disclosure Act 1998 refers to 'protected disclosures', which employees may make for a number of reasons, including where they have information which leads them reasonably to believe that a colleague has committed a criminal offence or a miscarriage of justice, or has failed to comply with a legal obligation which he or she is obliged to comply with.

Disclosure should generally be made to the employer, or other reasonable or prescribed persons within the employee's own organisation where the person reasonably believes that he or she will be subject to a detriment if the disclosure is made to his or her employer (answer B is incorrect, as this disclosure may be made to other persons, and not just to the employer).

The Act also allows for disclosure to be made to an external person, if the relevant disclosure is of an exceptionally serious nature and the employee reasonably believes that the information is substantially true, and he or she is making the disclosure in good faith and not for personal gain. Answers C and D are incorrect, as disclosure is not always limited to people within the employee's own organisation.

General Police Duties, para. 4.1.8.1

Answer 1.6

Answer **C** — The Police (Efficiency) Regulations 1999 do not apply to officers above the rank of chief superintendent (therefore answer B is incorrect), probationers (therefore answer A is incorrect) or civilian staff (therefore answer D is incorrect).

All these members of staff have their own procedures, but they are not covered by the above Regulations. Note that the Police Reform Act 2003 has introduced new measures for the removal, suspension and discipline of officers above the rank of chief superintendent, but the Police (Efficiency) Regulations still do not apply.

General Police Duties, para. 4.1.10.1

Answer 1.7

Answer **D** — SMITHSON, a member of the public, is complaining about the performance of the officer's duty. This is part of the misconduct procedures, which the sergeant may investigate without forwarding to the complaints department, and therefore answer B is incorrect. However, it is clearly evidence of unsatisfactory performance, and although the procedures for performance improvement and the investigation of complaints are quite separate, there may be cases, as here, where they overlap. In deciding which course of action to take, the sergeant can consider both procedures and is not mandated to use either one, and therefore answers A and C are incorrect.

General Police Duties, para. 4.1.10.2

Answer 1.8

Answer **A** — Constable DOUGHTY is entitled to be accompanied only by another police officer, so answers C and D are incorrect. That officer may be from any police service, not necessarily the officer's own force, and so answer B is incorrect. In relation to solicitors, at this stage of the proceedings the officer is not entitled to be legally represented in any case.

General Police Duties, para. 4.1.10.5

Answer 1.9

Answer **C** — Part of the procedure under the Police (Efficiency) Regulations 1999 is to allow the member concerned, or the member of the police force who has accompanied him or both of them, an opportunity to make representations. As both are given the opportunity, answers A and B are incorrect. However, it is not mandatory for them to make these representations, which makes answer D incorrect.

General Police Duties, para. 4.1.10.5

Answer 1.10

Answer **B** — The 'reasonable period' is normally not less than 3 months and no more than 6 months, and therefore answers A, C and D are incorrect.

General Police Duties, para. 4.1.10.6

Answer 1.11

Answer **A** — Regulation 8 of the Police (Efficiency) Regulations 1999 states:

(1) Where the reporting officer *is of the opinion* that a member of a police force who was warned under regulation 6(3)(b) that he was required to improve his performance or attendance has, at the end of the period specified by the interviewing officer under regulation 6(3)(c), failed to make a sufficient improvement in his performance, or, as the case may be, in his attendance, he may refer the case to the countersigning officer.

The requirement under reg. 8 is fairly broad and requires a lower standard of proof than 'reasonable cause to believe or suspect', (referred to in answers B and C above) and at this stage there is no burden of proof for either party. Answers B, C and D are therefore incorrect.

General Police Duties, para. 4.1.10.9

Answer 1.12

Answer **B** — Sch. 1, para. 9 of the Police (Conduct) Regulations 2004, requires a constable to report any proceedings which have been instigated against him or her for a criminal offence, rather than a conviction or caution. Answer A is therefore incorrect. This will include being issued with a penalty notice for disorder (answer C is therefore incorrect).

Sch. 1, para. 9 only requires the reporting of criminal proceedings, which means that an officer does not need to report being issued with a fixed penalty notice for a non-criminal offence, such as a parking ticket. Answer D is therefore incorrect.

General Police Duties, para. 4.1.11.4

Answer 1.13

Answer **B** — The Police (Amendment) Regulations 2005 (SI 2005/2834) inserted reg. 19A into the Police Regulations 2003. Under this regulation, the chief officer of a police force (in accordance with procedures determined by the Secretary of State) may require any member of the force to give a sample of breath to be tested for alcohol (or a sample of saliva or urine to be tested for evidence of controlled drugs). Since only a sample of breath may be requested in respect of alcohol abuse, answer D is incorrect.

The testing for drugs or alcohol may be carried out where there is reasonable suspicion of substance abuse, or during pre-employment screening, testing in the probationary period, and screening in specialist and safety critical areas, such as firearms officers. Answers A and C are therefore incorrect.

General Police Duties, para. 4.1.11.4

Answer 1.14

Answer **A** — The Police (Amendment) Regulations 2005 (SI 2005/2834) inserted reg. 19A into the Police Regulations 2003. Under this paragraph, the chief officer of a police force (in accordance with procedures determined by the Secretary of State) may require any member of the force to give a sample of saliva or urine to be tested for evidence of controlled drugs (or a sample of breath to be tested for alcohol).

The testing for drugs or alcohol may be carried out where there is reasonable suspicion of substance abuse, or during pre-employment screening, testing in the probationary period, and screening in specialist and safety critical areas, such as firearms officers. The Regulations also cover where a member gives the chief officer reasonable cause to suspect that he or she has used a controlled drug (which would certainly be the case in this question). Since the Regulations only allow for either a sample of saliva or urine when drug misuse is suspected, answers B, C and D are incorrect.

General Police Duties, para. 4.1.11.4

Answer 1.15

Answer **C** — Under reg. 17 of the Police (Conduct) Regulations 2004, where the supervising officer of a disciplinary hearing is of the opinion that the officer attending the hearing is likely to face sanctions of dismissal, requirement to resign or reduction in rank, he or she must give written notice to the officer concerned that he or she is entitled to have legal representation at the hearing and that the above sanctions may not be imposed unless he or she has been given the opportunity to elect such representation. Answer B is incorrect.

The right to have legal representation applies only where one of the above sanctions is being considered, therefore answer A is incorrect (for example, if the supervising officer is of the opinion that the officer may be given a reprimand, legal representation will not be required). Since the officer attending the hearing must be given written notice of his or her right to legal representation (and not oral), answer D is incorrect.

General Police Duties, para. 4.1.11.12

Answer 1.16

Answer **B** — Generally, a hearing in relation to a complaint or conduct matter against a constable will be presided over by an assistant chief constable (or commander in the case of an officer from the Metropolitan or City of London Police), who will be accompanied by two assisting officers of at least the rank of superintendent (reg. 19(4) of the Police (Conduct) Regulations 2004). However, under reg. 19(5), where a hearing arises out of a complaint or conduct matter which has been the subject of an investigation supervised by the Independent Police Complaints Commission, the presiding officer (an assistant chief constable) will be accompanied by an officer of at least the rank of superintendent and a person selected by the police authority for the force concerned. Answer B is the only one with the correct combination, therefore answers A, C and D are incorrect.

General Police Duties, para. 4.1.11.13

Answer 1.17

Answer **B** — An appropriate authority may apply to the Independent Police Complaints Commission (IPCC) for permission to have a complaint dispensed with for several reasons, including where the appropriate authority believes that the complaint is vexatious, oppressive, repetitious or otherwise an abuse of the procedures for dealing with complaints. The IPCC must inform the appropriate authority of its decision; however, if permission is not granted, no further applications can be made in respect of that particular complaint and the appropriate authority must decide whether to investigate the complaint, or deal with it by way of local resolution. Answers A, C and D are therefore incorrect.

General Police Duties, para. 4.1.12.20

Answer 1.18

Answer **C** — Schedule 1 provides that a member of a police force:

- shall at all times abstain from any activity which is likely to interfere with the impartial discharge of his/her duties or which is likely to give rise to the impression amongst members of the public that it may so interfere;
- shall in particular —
    - (a) not take any active part in politics;
    - (b) not belong to any organisation specified or described in a determination of the Secretary of State.

For this purpose, the Secretary of State has determined that no member of the police force may be a member of the British National Party (BNP), Combat 18 or the National Front. Answers A and D are therefore incorrect. The wording of sch. 1 does not actually prohibit police officers from being members of other political parties; they are merely prevented from taking an active part in politics, which means that a police officer *could* be a member of any other party, and answer B is incorrect.

General Police Duties, para. 4.1.15.1

Answer 1.19

Answer **C** — Misconduct in a public office is defined by common law as follows:

It is a misdemeanour at common law for the holder of a public office to do anything that amounts to a malfeasance or a 'culpable' misfeasance (*R v Wyatt (1705)* 1 Salk 380).

This primordial common law idiosyncrasy is both a tort and a criminal offence, which could give rise to litigation in both the criminal and civil courts. Answers A, B and D are therefore incorrect.

Misfeasance can cover many misdemeanours committed by police officers from deliberately mistreating prisoners to improper use of the National Intelligence Model.

General Police Duties, para. 4.1.16.1

Answer 1.20

Answer **B** — A death in police custody has led to a clarification as to the nature of the criminal common law offence of misconduct in public office (see *Attorney*

General's Reference (No 3 of 2003) [2004] EWCA Crim 868). The elements of the offence were summarised by the Court of Appeal (Criminal Division) as follows:

A public officer acting as such [who]:

- wilfully neglects to perform his duty and/or wilfully misconducts himself, (this requires 'an awareness of the duty to act or a subjective recklessness as to the existence of the duty')
- to such a degree as to amount to an abuse of the public's trust in the office holder
- without reasonable excuse or justification [may be guilty of the criminal offence.]

The Court of Appeal also held that there must be a serious departure from proper standards before the criminal offence is committed; and a departure not merely negligent but amounting to an affront to the standing of the public office held. The threshold is a high one requiring conduct so far below acceptable standards as to amount to an abuse of the public's trust in the office holder. A mistake, even a serious one, will not suffice; answer D is therefore incorrect.

The conduct must have been by a public office holder acting as such, in this case a police constable. Note that this offence will also apply to omissions as well as conduct; answer A is therefore incorrect. A purely personal matter whilst the officer was off duty would not normally fit these criteria; answer C is therefore incorrect. There will no doubt be occasions where off-duty malpractice will be covered (for a good example see *Weir* v *Chief Constable of Merseyside* [2003] ICR 708).

In the civil setting, even though there might be circumstances where officers could be criticised for failures including incompetence, excess of zeal and even serious negligence, the absence of bad faith or deliberate misuse of power would generally mean that there is not enough to support an allegation of misfeasance (see *Ashley & others* v *Chief Constable of Sussex* [2005] EWHC 415).

General Police Duties, para. 4.1.16.1

Answer 1.21

Answer **C** — Impersonating a police officer is defined in the Police Act 1996. Section 90(1) states:

Any person who with intent to deceive impersonates a member of a police force or special constable, or makes any statement or does any act calculated falsely to suggest that he is such a member or constable shall be guilty of an offence...

As can be seen from the definition, the legislation applies to special constables, and therefore answer B is incorrect. The offence includes not only statements but also acts that suggest the person is a special constable. Such acts would include producing a false warrant card, and therefore answer A is incorrect. This is a crime of 'specific' intent and intention to deceive must be proved, not just an intention to gain an advantage, and therefore answer D is incorrect.

General Police Duties, para. 4.1.16.2

2 | Extending the Policing Family

STUDY PREPARATION

This chapter deals with the legislation contained in the Police Reform Act 2002. The 2002 Act introduces powers to groups of people who are either directly employed by police authorities, or who work in close liaison with the police. Under Part 4 of the Act, the following people may be employed by police authorities, and be 'designated' by the relevant chief officer:

- police community support officers (PCSOs);
- investigating officers;
- detention officers;
- escort officers.

The chapter deals with the powers conferred on the above groups of people, who are known as designated police employees. Their powers are allocated according to the roles they are likely to perform: for example, PCSOs have powers to deal with community issues and anti-social behaviour; investigating officers have powers to interview suspects and conduct searches; detention officers and escort officers have powers to deal with custody-related matters.

A further extension of the policing family comes in the form of accredited employees. Chief officers, in consultation with police authorities and local authorities, may establish a Community Safety Accreditation Scheme (CSAS). This allows members of the public who are not employed by the police to be accredited with certain policing powers, such as confiscating alcohol in public places or from people under 16. Many of the powers given to an accredited employee are similar to those given to PCSOs.

The Police and Justice Act 2006 further extends the powers given to PCSOs and is tested in this chapter.

QUESTIONS

Question 2.1

Whilst on patrol in a local park, PCSO HILLIER spoke to BARTON, who was responsible for a dog which had fouled in a children's play area. PCSO HILLIER was designated to issue a fixed penalty notice for this offence. BARTON demanded to know what authority PCSO HILLIER had to issue such a notice.

Is PCSO HILLIER obliged to produce any documentary evidence of his authority, in these circumstances?

A No, provided PCSO HILLIER was in uniform.

B Yes, PCSO HILLIER must produce evidence of his designation as a PCSO.

C Yes, PCSO HILLIER must produce details of all the standard and non-standard powers he has as a PCSO.

D Yes, PCSO HILLIER must produce evidence of his designation as a PCSO and any non-standard power he has.

Question 2.2

PCSO BURTON was on patrol and saw HAINES cycling on a footpath. PCSO BURTON has received the appropriate designation and approached HAINES, intending to issue a fixed penalty notice for the offence. However, HAINES refused to provide a name and address and started walking away.

What powers, if any, are available to PCSO BURTON to detain HAINES in these circumstances?

A PCSO BURTON may detain HAINES at the scene until a police officer arrives.

B PCSO BURTON has no power to detain HAINES; a PCSO's powers are restricted to issuing fixed penalty notices.

C PCSO BURTON may detain HAINES for up to 30 minutes until a police officer arrives.

D PCSO BURTON may arrest HAINES and call for transport to the station.

Question 2.3

PCSO REGAN was on foot patrol in uniform one day. As PCSO REGAN was passing a local off-licence the manager came outside with WALKER, asking for help. The manager had refused to sell 4 cans of lager to WALKER, who admitted to being under 18.

Does PCSO REGAN have the power to detain WALKER, in these circumstances?

A Yes, WALKER may be detained for the offence until a police officer arrives.

B No, this power does not extend to licensing offences.

C Yes, but only if WALKER refuses to provide a name and address, or provides details which PCSO REGAN has reasonable grounds for suspecting to be false.

D No, this power does not extend to this particular licensing offence.

Question 2.4

PCSO BECKER was assisting at the scene of a road traffic collision by directing traffic. PETERS was walking along the pavement, which was blocked by one of the cars involved in the accident. PCSO BECKER asked PETERS to wait on the pavement until it was safe to walk in the road. Being in a hurry, PETERS refused to do so and walked out into the road, nearly causing another accident.

Assuming that the collision occurred in a relevant police area for the application of such powers, did PCSO BECKER have the authority to demand PETERS' name and address in these circumstances?

A No, the power to direct vehicles and pedestrians is restricted to police officers or traffic wardens.

B Yes, PETERS has failed to comply with a direction given to stop.

C No, a PCSO's power to request a name and address is restricted to giving directions to vehicles and not pedestrians.

D Yes, a PCSO's power to request a name and address is restricted to giving directions to pedestrians and not to vehicles.

Question 2.5

FEEHAN is a retired police officer, having been an experienced detective before his retirement. He is now employed by a police force as a designated investigating officer. FEEHAN is currently attached to an enquiry team, investigating persons accessing child pornography from the Internet. FEEHAN was interviewing HEALEY, who was suspected of such an offence. HEALEY admitted his involvement in the offences; however, towards the end of the interview, he also confessed to having intercourse with his 11-year-old step-daughter.

Would FEEHAN have the power to arrest HEALEY for further offences in these circumstances?

A No, investigating officers may not arrest for an offence of this nature.

B Yes, he may arrest HEALEY, where necessary, for a further offence and carry on with the interview.

C No, investigating officers are not empowered to arrest persons in any circumstances.

D Yes, investigating officers have the same powers of arrest as a constable in any circumstances.

Question 2.6

LAWDAY worked in a large store on a retail park on the outskirts of a town. He had recently been accredited under the Community Safety Accreditation Scheme, by the chief officer of police in his designated area. LAWDAY conducted patrols in his lunch break in the vicinity of his employer's shop, where recent problems had occurred with young people drinking in the car park. One day, LAWDAY approached a group of youths who were drinking lager from cans, and confiscated alcohol from several of them. However, one of the youths, who admitted he was 16, failed to surrender a can of lager from which he was drinking.

What powers, if any, would LAWDAY have to detain the youth under the Confiscation of Alcohol (Young Persons) Act 1997, in these circumstances?

A None, an accredited employee has no power of arrest in these circumstances.

B He may arrest the person for failing to surrender the alcohol.

C He may detain the person and call the police to the scene to arrest him.

D He may arrest the person for failing to surrender the alcohol, but only if the person refuses to give his name and address.

Question 2.7

Section 42(3) of the Police Reform Act 2002 outlines how an accredited employee's designation or accreditation may be withdrawn in certain circumstances.

Which of the following statements is correct, in relation to withdrawing an accredited employee's designation or accreditation?

A It may be withdrawn only where the person's conduct becomes an issue.

B It may be withdrawn only either where a person's conduct becomes an issue, or where the person is under-performing.

C It may be withdrawn for any reason, and is not restricted to a person's conduct or performance.

D It may be withdrawn only either where a person's conduct becomes an issue, or where the person is under-performing, provided he or she is given the opportunity to improve performance.

Question 2.8

Section 42(3) of the Police Reform Act 2002 outlines how an accredited employee's designation or accreditation may be withdrawn in certain circumstances.

Who has the authority to withdraw such a person's designation or accreditation?
A The chief officer of police, in consultation with the police authority.
B The chief officer of police, in consultation with the police authority and the local authority.
C The chief officer of police, in consultation with the police authority, the local authority and the person's employer.
D The chief officer of police, who may make the decision without consultation.

Question 2.9

HANSEN has been appointed as an accredited employee in her local policing area. A complaint has been made against her by ADEDEYO, that she unlawfully detained him while acting in her capacity as an accredited employee.

If ADEDEYO were to make a civil claim for unlawful detention, against whom should the claim be made?
A Either the police authority, or HANSEN, or HANSEN's employer.
B Both the police authority and HANSEN.
C Both the police authority and HANSEN's employer.
D The police authority, HANSEN and HANSEN's employer.

Question 2.10

MOHAMED and BEVAN are retired police officers, having both been experienced detectives before their retirement. They are now employed by a police force as designated investigating officers, and are currently attached to an enquiry team investigating a murder. The team have arrested a suspect for the offence, and MOHAMMED and BEVAN have been sent to his home address to conduct a search, under s. 18(1) of the Police and Criminal Evidence Act 1984, for material relevant to the murder.

2. Extending the Policing Family

If necessary, would MOHAMMED and BEVAN be entitled to use force to enter the suspect's home in these circumstances?

A Yes, but only if they are accompanied by, and under the supervision of, a police officer.

B Yes, they have the power to use force on their own in these circumstances.

C No, they have no power to use force in any circumstances.

D No, they may use force in order to enter premises only to save life or limb, or to prevent serious damage to property.

ANSWERS

Answer 2.1

Answer **D** — Section 9 of the Police and Justice Act 2006 introduces sch. 5 which makes various amendments to provisions in the Police Reform Act 2002. Paragraph 3 of the schedule amends s. 42 of the 2002 Act so that PCSOs, when exercising powers or duties, must produce on demand evidence of their designation as a CSO and of any non-standard power which they exercise that has been conferred on them by their Chief Officer under s. 38. Answer A is incorrect as evidence must be produced. Answer B is incorrect as the evidence must include any non-standard powers the PCSO has.

PCSOs will not have to carry with them details of *all* the standard powers which have been conferred upon them by an order under s. 38A. The requirement to produce evidence of a designation could be satisfied by production of the designation itself, but could also be satisfied by something less, such as some form of document or card. Answer C is therefore incorrect.

General Police Duties, para. 4.2.3.1

Answer 2.2

Answer **C** — Under Part 1 of sch. 4 to the Police Reform Act 2002, where a police community support officer (PCSO) has reason to believe that any individual has committed a relevant fixed penalty offence, he or she has the powers of an authorised police constable to issue a fixed penalty notice in respect of the offence (para. 1(a)). Under para. 1(b), the PCSO may issue a fixed penalty notice to a cyclist under s. 54 of the Road Traffic Offenders Act 1988 (fixed penalty notices) in respect of an offence under s. 72 of the Highway Act 1835 (riding on a footway).

Where a PCSO has reason to believe that another has committed a relevant offence (such as the one above) the PCSO may require the other person to give his or her name and address (para. 2(2)). Where the person fails to give his or her name and address, or where the PCSO has reasonable grounds for suspecting that the name and address given is inaccurate, the PCSO may require the other person to wait with the PCSO for a period not exceeding 30 minutes, for the arrival of a constable (para. 2(3)). The PCSO may use reasonable force in order to prevent the person from making off (para. 4). Answers A and B are consequently incorrect.

Although there is power of arrest granted to persons other than a constable, they only apply to indictable offences; answer D is therefore incorrect.

General Police Duties, para. 4.2.4

Answer 2.3

Answer **C** — Under para. 1A of sch. 4 to the Police Reform Act 2002, where a PCSO has reason to believe that another person has committed a relevant offence in their own police area, or a relevant licensing offence in any police area, he or she may require that person to give their name and address (para. 1A(3)). Failure to comply with this requirement is a summary offence (para. 1A(5)). A relevant licensing offence includes some, but not all, offences under the Licensing Act 2003.

Paragraph 2(3) of the Act states that where a person has been required to provide their name and address under para. 1A(3) above and they either refuse, or they provide details which the PCSO has reasonable grounds to suspect are false or inaccurate, the PCSO may detain the person for a period not exceeding 30 minutes. PCSOs are not given the power to detain people for the actual offence committed. The power to detain kicks in when the person either fails to provide details, or gives those which are reasonably suspected to be false. Answer A is therefore incorrect.

The power to detain a person, as described in para. 2(3) above, will apply to certain, relevant licensing offences — answer B is incorrect.

A person under 18 attempting to buy alcohol would commit a relevant licensing offence for the purposes of this paragraph; therefore, answer D is incorrect.

(It is worth noting that the relevant licensing offences to which the power of detention applies appear to be restricted to offences committed by people other than the licensee or their employees. This means that a PCSO may demand a licensee's name when such an offence is committed, but they would not be entitled to detain that person if the details are refused. Presumably this is because such people will be easy to trace through their licences).

General Police Duties, para. 4.2.4

Answer 2.4

Answer **B** — A police officer in uniform engaged in the regulation of vehicular traffic in a road has the authority to stop pedestrians from proceeding (s. 37 of the Road Traffic Act 1988) — this power is also given to traffic wardens (s. 96 of the 1988 Act). Paragraph 11B of sch. 4 to the Police Reform Act 2002 states that a PCSO will, within the relevant police area, have the same powers as a police officer to direct vehicles (s. 35 of the 1988 Act), and direct pedestrians (s. 37 of the 1988 Act). Answer A is therefore incorrect.

Paragraph 3A of sch. 4 to the Police Reform Act 2002 states that a PCSO will, within the relevant police area, have the powers of a constable to require the name and address of a person who has committed an offence under s. 35 or s. 37 above. Answers C and D are therefore incorrect.

General Police Duties, para. 4.2.4

Answer 2.5

Answer **B** — Under Part 2 of sch. 4 to the Police Reform Act 2002, an investigating officer will have the same power of arrest at any police station in the relevant police area in any case where an arrest is required to be made under s. 31 of the Police and Criminal Evidence Act 1984 (arrest for a further offence of a person who is already at a police station) (para. 21). Answer C is incorrect. No mention is made in this paragraph of the nature of the offence — an investigating officer may make an arrest for any offence, where appropriate. Answer A is therefore incorrect. An investigating officer will not enjoy the same powers as a constable to arrest a person in any circumstances and will only be able to exercise the power in a police station, under s. 31 above. Answer D is therefore incorrect.

General Police Duties, para. 4.2.5

Answer 2.6

Answer **A** — Chief officers, in consultation with police authorities and local authorities, may establish a Community Safety Accreditation Scheme. Under s. 41 of the Police Reform Act 2002, members of the public who are not employed by the police may be accredited with certain policing powers.

An accredited employee may be given the power to confiscate alcohol either under the Confiscation of Alcohol (Young Persons) Act 1997 (confiscation of alcohol from persons under 18), or under the Criminal Justice and Police Act 2001 (confiscation of alcohol from people in designated public places). Schedule 5 to the Police Reform Act 2002 lists the powers that may be conferred on an accredited employee, and para. 5 states that such a person may require a person under the age of 18 to surrender intoxicating liquor when in possession of it in a public place, and to state his or her name and address. However, para. 5 specifically states that an accredited employee may not arrest a person who fails to comply with a requirement made under the 1997 Act. Answers B and D are therefore incorrect.

Although many of the powers given to an accredited employee are similar to those conferred on a police community support officer (PCSO), an accredited employee does not have the same powers to detain a person until a police officer arrives at the scene in these circumstances. Answer C is therefore incorrect.

Note that if the area had been designated by the local authority under the Criminal Justice and Police Act 2001, the accredited employee in this scenario would have had powers to deal with the youth, however, this question specifically deals with powers under the 1997 Act.

General Police Duties, paras 4.2.4, 4.2.6.2, 4.11.9.14, 4.11.10.1

Answer 2.7

Answer **C** — Section 42(3) of the Police Reform Act 2002 allows an accredited employee's designation or accreditation to be withdrawn at any time simply by giving the employee notice of this fact. The power is absolute and there is no requirement for any misconduct or poor performance. Answers A, B and D are therefore incorrect.

General Police Duties, para. 4.2.6.3

Answer 2.8

Answer **D** — Section 42(3) of the Police Reform Act 2002 allows an accredited employee's designation or accreditation to be withdrawn at any time by a chief officer of police. There is no requirement to consult with the local authority, the police authority or the person's employer; therefore, answers A, B and C are incorrect.

General Police Duties, para. 4.2.6.3

Answer 2.9

Answer **D** — Under s. 42 of the Police Reform Act 2002, any liability for civil wrongs arising out of conduct in the course of an employee's accreditation or designation will be apportioned jointly between the police authority, the employer and the individual (therefore answers B and C are incorrect). Answer A is incorrect, as the claim should be made against all three.

General Police Duties, para. 4.2.6.3

Answer 2.10

Answer **A** — Under s. 38(6) of the Police Reform Act 2002, a designated employee is able to exercise the same powers as a constable to use reasonable force, if a constable were entitled to use force in the circumstances. Answer C is therefore incorrect. Section 117 of the Police and Criminal Evidence Act 1984 would allow a constable to enter premises in these circumstances, using force if necessary; therefore the designated investigating officers in the question are also entitled to do so.

However, s. 38(9) of the 2002 Act allows designated employees to use force to enter premises only either if they are in the company and under the supervision of a constable, or to save life or limb, or to prevent serious damage to property. Answer D is incorrect, as the power may be used in both these circumstances. Since there is no suggestion that there is a danger to any person or their property, the investigating officers would be able to enter the premises only when accompanied by a constable, so answer B is incorrect.

General Police Duties, para. 4.2.7

3 | Human Rights

STUDY PREPARATION

It is generally accepted that the introduction of the Human Rights Act 1998 (which incorporates the European Convention on Human Rights into our domestic law) has had the largest effect on the use of police powers since the Police and Criminal Evidence Act 1984 came into being. Many of the questions contained in this chapter are based on decisions made in the European Court of Human Rights. It remains to be seen how quickly such decisions will continue to be interpreted in England and Wales, as no doubt they will be challenged and developed regularly. Under s. 2 of the Human Rights Act 1998, courts and tribunals are under an obligation to take such decisions into account. However, it is important to remember that the Convention, as a 'living instrument', is constantly evolving.

When looking at the Convention rights in detail, it is also important to recognise the difference between an *absolute* right under the Convention (such as the right to freedom from torture under Art. 3), and a *qualified* or *restricted* right (such as Art. 5, the right to liberty). Probably, the most important consideration is to recognise how the 1998 Act sets out to *balance* the rights of the individual against the needs of a democratic society.

The 'three tests' must be learned, namely 'prescribed by law', 'legitimate objective' and 'proportionality', as well as who will be a 'victim' and who may be in breach of the Act.

Lastly, there are several Articles contained in the Convention which directly affect the police, such as the right to life, freedom from torture, right to liberty and security, right to a fair trial and right to respect for private life. Other Articles, such as right of freedom of expression and freedom of assembly, also have a significant effect on everyday policing.

Human rights law does not exist in isolation. Therefore, although it is specifically addressed in this chapter, every aspect of the law contained in this book should be viewed with the 1998 Act in mind.

QUESTIONS

Question 3.1

Section 2 of the Human Rights Act 1998 outlines the duty of domestic courts in England and Wales to take into account decisions made in the European Court of Human Rights (ECHR).

In relation to whether courts in England and Wales should follow decisions made in the ECHR, which of the following statements is correct?

A Any decision made in the ECHR must be followed by courts in England and Wales.

B Courts in England and Wales need only take into account past cases from the ECHR.

C Courts in England and Wales need not take into account past cases from the ECHR.

D Courts in England and Wales must take into account cases from the ECHR, but they need not follow them.

Question 3.2

Where the European Convention on Human Rights gives individuals a particular right, any interference with that right must be done so with care.

In relation to a person's human rights being infringed, which, if any, of the following statements are correct?

A Any interference with a Convention right must be traceable to a clear legal source which has to be primary legislation.

B Any interference with a Convention right must be traceable to a clear legal source, primary or secondary.

C Any interference with a Convention right only has to be proportionate and necessary.

D Any interference with a Convention right only has to be proportionate and have a legitimate aim.

Question 3.3

HART works as a prison officer in a private prison. On several occasions GRANGER, a prisoner, had been rude to her. In order to teach GRANGER a lesson, HART made GRANGER stand in the shower for a whole hour while she looked on.

Have GRANGER's rights been breached under Art. 3 of the European Convention on Human Rights (right to freedom from torture)?

A No, because HART does not work for a public authority.

B Yes, because HART's employer performs a public function.

C No, because HART does not work for a government authority.

D Yes, regardless of the employer that HART works for.

Question 3.4

The police are conducting observations near a lay-by, which is a meeting place for gay men. They are seeking to detect offences of homosexual activity in public, under the Sexual Offences Act 1956. DANE regularly frequents the area, and is also a member of a gay and lesbian group. He has sought legal advice in order to challenge police action under the Human Rights Act 1998.

In relation to whether DANE may use the Act to challenge the police activity, which statement is correct?

A He may do so as an individual only, whether he has been arrested or not.

B He may do so as part of a group, but only if he has been arrested for an offence.

C He may do so as part of a group, or as an individual, whether he has been arrested or not.

D He may do so as an individual only if he has been proceeded against for an offence.

Question 3.5

Section 7(1) of the Human Rights Act 1998 outlines the circumstances in which a person may bring proceedings against a public authority, and the time limits that are placed on such proceedings being brought.

How long does a person normally have in which to bring proceedings against a public authority under s. 7(1)(a)?

A 1 year from the date on which the act took place.

B 2 years from the date on which the act took place.

C 3 years from the date on which the act took place.

D 5 years from the date on which the act took place.

Question 3.6

Before a person can bring proceedings under the Human Rights Act 1998, he or she must be a 'victim' for the purposes of the Act.

The Office of Constable

The bedrock of modern day British policing

Foreword

by Jan Berry, Chairman of the Police Federation of England and Wales

The Office of Constable has evolved over the centuries and the 'British Bobby' is recognised across the world, but what is it that makes it so special, so endearing, so different?

There is, as this pamphlet seeks to set out, a legal status, being the holders of an Office, the coercive powers that come with that Office. There are also the high standards and restrictions placed on our professional and private lives.

But what is at its heart, and why does it remain a recognised and trusted brand leader around the world? Why does it conjure up feelings of safety and security, and why do the public want to see more 'bobbies'? Why do those of us who hold this proud Office of Constable go forward into dangers when others go back?

The answer is simple; it's about integrity, impartiality, and most importantly, political independence. It is the tie breaker, the ultimate check and balance in our democracy to protect against a tyrannical abuse of power.

The imposition of targets and the employment of non-sworn staff in operational policing roles are slowly eroding the Office of Constable. It is a proud and honourable Office and one which I have had the honour to hold for 35 years.

"Where is this Offic

The above quotation is not made up. It was actually said by a Member of Parliament upon hearing the term the Office of Constable.

The Police Federation is always quick to raise the merits of the Office of Constable. But in view of the above quote, what does it mean to those outside the police service? Where does the Office of Constable originate from, and is it as important today as it was two centuries ago?

This pamphlet takes a look at the Office of Constable – what it is, what its values are, what it means for the police service today, and gives a summary history which shows how the Office of Constable is not only the bedrock of traditional policing but also the platform for any change required for modern day policing.

The independent Office of Constable operates within, and is accountable to, the rule of law. The rule of law is the principle that no one is above the law. Perhaps the most important application of the rule of law is the principle that government authority is legitimately exercised only in accordance with written, publicly disclosed laws adopted and enforced in accordance with established procedural steps. The principle of the rule of law is intended to be a safeguard against arbitrary governance. The law must be accessible, intelligible, clear and predictable and must apply equally to all. It must also afford adequate protection of fundamental human rights. It is the independent and impartial holder of the Office of Constable who is tasked with upholding and enforcing the law.

Whilst the rule of law binds our society together, of equal importance is the separation of power, which prevents over-concentration of power in any one institution. At one level this reflects the legislature, the executive, the judiciary. In the case of policing, politicians – democratically elected – make the laws, police officers enforce them, and the judiciary decides on the outcome post-charge. However, we are each independent and separately accountable. Operational independence is a guiding principle of policing.

Whilst this may be understood by some, the thirst and struggle for power needs to be balanced and controlled. During a Parliamentary debate on policing in July 2002, Nottingham North MP Graham Allen made the following observation: "Home Secretaries of all political colours will not only set targets, but will ensure that money is allocated to meeting them, so it is almost inevitable that chief constables and local police officers will have to pursue those targets. In that way there is interference, almost by stealth, in the operational objectives of local police forces."

It was in the words of Lord Denning, in his judgement in the case of *R v. Metropolitan Police Commissioner ex parte Blackburn* in 1968, that the doctrine of police independence found its most expansive and most often quoted modern expression:

"I have no hesitation… in holding that, like every constable in the land, the Commissioner should be, and is, independent of the executive. He is not subject to the orders of the Secretary of State, save that under the Police Act 1964 the Secretary of State can call on him to give a report, or to retire in the interests of inefficiency.

"I hold it to be the duty of the Commissioner of Police, as it is of every chief constable, to enforce the law of the land. He must take steps so to post his men that crimes may be detected; and that honest citizens may go about their affairs in peace.

"He must decide whether or not suspected persons are to be prosecuted; and, if need be, bring the prosecution or see that it is brought; but in all these things he is not the servant of anyone, save of the law itself.

"No Minister of the Crown can tell him that he must, or must not, keep observation on this place or that; or that he must, or must not, prosecute this man or that one. Nor can any police authority tell him so. The responsibility for law enforcement lies on him. He is answerable to the law and to the law alone."

(R v. Metropolitan Police Commissioner at 769)

Why now?

For the first time since 1919 police officers are talking of industrial action, and the Police Federation of England and Wales has recently held a poll of its membership on the important subject of industrial rights. What has become abundantly clear during that process is that many of the politicians and opinion formers who have a direct interest and influence on policing do not understand what the Office of Constable is, its history, meaning and purpose.

The police service is undoubtedly more accountable now than it ever has been, and to that end, faces far greater public scrutiny than it has to date. No-one is suggesting that has a negative impact on policing, but there does seem to be a greater degree of accountability based on quantitative assessment (such as the satisfaction of national targets) rather than based on the quality of service provided. This is having a negative impact on the independent and impartial Office of Constable, as decisions which should be based on discretion and common sense are often now determined by targets for which officers are held accountable to achieve.

The Tripartite relationship

In England and Wales there exists a tripartite arrangement in policing, which provides checks and balances between the Home Office, police forces and police authorities. This means that no one part has complete and overall control and power over the others. The roles of each element of the tripartite arrangement are as follows:

1) The Home Secretary is answerable to Parliament and the public for the provision of an efficient and effective police service. The Home Secretary sets out annual strategic policing priorities, and a statutory performance framework against which police performance will be measured and compared.

Assessments of Policing and Community Safety (APACS) is a performance assessment framework for policing and community safety. It is being developed by the Home Office and its partners, including; the Association of Chief Police Officers, the Association of Police Authorities, Communities and Local Government, the Audit Commission, the Local Government Association and Her Majesty's Inspectorate of Constabulary.

2) Chief officers retain overall operational independence. The chief officer is responsible for the direction and control of the force, including civilian staff and delegated financial management.

3) Police authorities have a statutory duty to maintain an efficient and effective police force for the area and to hold the chief officer to account for the exercise of their functions and those of persons under their direction and control.

> Constables use their discretion superbly, with compassion and commonsense. The office of constable can never – and must never – be just about targets. It is much more important than that and the British public knows it.
>
> **David Ruffley MP, Shadow Police Minister**

Change, change and more change

Since the turn of the Millennium the policing structure, processes and workforce has experienced constant change on an unprecedented level. All of this change has been in a piecemeal way, without any overview of the long term impact it will have on the structure of the service, the resilience of police forces and the roles and purpose of police officers and police staff.

Whilst recognising the need for specialist police officers and police staff, the Office of Constable must be the bedrock of modern day policing. It provides the most flexibility and resilience to the police service. As well as the day to day policing required, you only have to look back at recent examples of flooding or terrorist attacks to see first hand how police officers have the skills and abilities to be used wherever and whenever required.

Worldwide the British police constable is a recognisable and respected figure, but has any government ever seriously examined why this is so? Taking it apart piece by piece through ill conceived reform risks destroying the value of, and deskilling, the Office of Constable by separating the component parts that make it work. The Office of Constable provides impartiality, stability and accountability in the legal and constitutional framework, as well as resilience and flexibility for frontline operational practical policing.

The demands upon policing are constantly changing. We didn't have drug squads until the government focus was tackling the growing drugs problem, or robbery squads until that became a core objective to focus on. By having multi-skilled police officers with a full range of powers, training, knowledge and experience, the service has been able to respond appropriately to the needs of the day. Current workforce modernisation plans are creating a greater number of specialist non-sworn police staff in operational roles. This will limit the resilience and capability of the police service to be able to respond appropriately to the many unknown demands suddenly placed upon it, and reduce the opportunity for police officers to become proficient and gain experience.

> The Office of Constable bestows upon an ordinary citizen an extraordinary range of powers. The impartial execution of these powers, free from political interference, is the cornerstone of the criminal justice system and the non-negotiable key to maintaining any civilised democracy. We change this at our peril.
>
> **Clive Chamberlain, Chairman, Dorset Police Federation**

Demands on the frontline

The number of 999 calls to the police service increases year on year. Whilst Police Community Support Officers (PCSOs) may have a role supporting their frontline police officer colleagues, this must not be at the expense of police officer numbers.

PCSOs are the most visible providers of the non-sworn operational functions. In the last year many Chief Officers have openly stated that they will be increasing PCSO numbers and not police officer numbers. This cannot be right and will weaken the protection the public can be afforded. The public too are clearly opposed to replacing constables with PCSOs, as they recognise this reduces flexibility and resilience. If money was not an issue then the additional resource would be welcome, but not when it replaces rather than compliments police officers on the street.

Greater numbers of PCSOs and falling numbers of constables will impact on the service frontline officers, whether that be uniform or CID, can provide. Research conducted by the Police Federation of England and Wales has clearly demonstrated that both frontline uniform officers and their CID colleagues are run ragged with increasing demands, many generated by PCSOs who do not have the powers, training or equipment to deal with them. Both reports are available to read or download on the Police Federation website at www.polfed.org.

Police officers, as Office holders, are accountable for their actions or inactions 24/7 – they are involved in off duty interventions and arrests every day. They do not have the option of turning a blind eye, otherwise they may face criminal charges. They cannot refuse to work extra hours; they are the most flexible workforce the service could have. While it is right that police officers have increasingly needed specialist skills to deal effectively with changing demands, all require a basic foundation of skills they get as a constable upon which to build their specialist expertise, such as patrol, interview and statement taking. These are extremely valuable attributes that will be lost if workforce modernisation plans to reduce police officer numbers and roles continues.

Swearing allegiance to the Crown

In England and Wales those who decide to become police officers take an oath at the point of becoming a constable. The oath, or attestation, is set within the legislation of this country, and is as follows:

"I do solemnly and sincerely declare and affirm that I will well and truly serve the Queen in the office of constable, with fairness, integrity, diligence and impartiality, upholding fundamental human rights and according equal respect to all people; and that I will, to the best of my power, cause the peace to be kept and preserved and prevent all offences against people and property; and that while I continue to hold the said office I will to the best of my skill and knowledge discharge all the duties thereof faithfully according to law."

What is the Office of Constable?

Every sworn police officer in England and Wales is a 'Constable', irrespective of rank. It is from the Office of Constable that each officer derives their powers.

On appointment each police officer makes a declaration to "faithfully discharge the duties of the Office of Constable". In England and Wales, police officers swear an oath of allegiance to the monarch; this is to ensure the separation of power and political independence of the Office of Constable.

The Office of Constable means a police officer has the additional legal powers of arrest and control of the public given to him or her directly by a sworn oath and warrant. These are not delegated powers simply because they have been employed as an officer. Police officers are not employees.

Each sworn constable is an independent legal official; they are not agents of the police force, police authority or government. Each police officer has personal liability for their actions or inaction. The chief officer of the force to which the constable is attached also has a level of corporate responsibility.

Those who hold the Office of Constable are servants of the Crown, not employee. Police officers have access to most statutory employment rights afforded to employees, but it is a criminal offence for police officers to take industrial action.

> A citizen appointed to police a given area with impartiality and without political persuasion. Fully accountable to the public they serve, which they police with their full consent and trust.
> **PC 360 Ingram, Lancashire Constabulary**

What it means to hold the Office of Constable

Holding the Office of Constable means a police officer executes their duty independently, without fear or favour.

With the Office of Constable comes personal accountability and responsibility for the protection of life and property, the prevention and detection of crime, the maintenance of law and order and the detection and prosecution of offenders.

Police officers must be allowed to police using common sense, free from political preference and political targets. Again, the Office of Constable and the rule of law protect this.

The Constable must be at the heart of policing communities, ensuring cohesion and security at a local, national and international level.

Those holding the Office of Constable do so in full knowledge of the increasing dangers they face, the accountability both on and off duty and the restrictions placed on their family lives (see Restraints upon the Office of Constable).

The strengths of th

Sometimes you never know what you have until it has gone. There is a very real danger this will happen with the Office of Constable – we know the price of everything but the value of nothing.

- Police officers must be allowed to police with discretion. Discretion is the bedrock of policing; it allows reasoned and fair decisions based on experience to be taken by police officers without the need to take a course of action merely to satisfy targets. The drive to satisfy targets has resulted in the many ludicrous arrests that make a splash in the tabloid newspapers.

- Police officers cannot legally be instructed to arrest a person. It is a decision they must take for themselves, using their experience, knowledge and discretion to take the most appropriate course of action to fulfil their function as officers of the Crown.

- Police officers have authority under the Crown for the protection of life and property, maintenance or order, prevention and detection of crime and prosecution of offenders against the peace. With the imposition of central and politically set targets there are dangers that officers' discretion and operational independence is being compromised.

- Police officers must be apolitical, impartial and accountable for their actions. If not, how and what we police will become subject to political whim and electioneering. The operational independence of our police service comes with the Office of Constable.

- The Office of Constable ensures the integrity, impartiality and accountability of operational policing.

ffice of Constable

- If we value the rule of law, we must protect the Office of Constable and through increased training and skills convert PCSOs into sworn apolitical, impartial, independent, accountable police constables.

- A fragmented workforce becomes disjointed, lacks cohesion and a sense of purpose.

- Non-sworn police staff should be recruited into non-operational roles to support and assist those who hold the Office of Constable.

- Police officers must gain a foundation of knowledge and experience in the execution of duty according to the rule of law, the use of authority and discretion, core skills and the practicalities and reality of policing. This must gained via entry to the police service at the rank of Constable.

- Government must provide the resources to ensure sufficient numbers of multi-skilled sworn officers that can be called upon whatever the demands.

- The government should, as a matter of urgency, undertake a full, independent and holistic review of policing examining role, structure, governance, function and accountability. Otherwise there is a genuine fear that the current workforce modernisation programme could destroy the Office of Constable by default.

- The Police Federation of England and Wales will resist any moves to introduce non-sworn officers into operational policing roles.

A brief history of the Office of Constable

- In England the office of constable was in existence during Henry I's reign – the principal duty of the constable, which was a military term at this stage, being to command of the army.

- The term constable first appeared on the scene after the Norman conquest, and towards the end of the 12th century acquired the local significance it has held ever since.

- *The Statute of Westminster 1285* enshrined the principles of two high constables appointed in every hundred with responsible for suppressing riots and violent crimes and for the arming of the militia to enable them to do so.

- The Statute was the only general public measure of any consequence enacted to regulate the policing of the country between the Norman Conquest and *The Metropolitan Police Act 1829*.

- By the end of the 13th century the constable acquired two distinct characteristics; the executive agent of the parish and an officer recognised by the Crown for keeping the King's peace.

- This system reached its height under the Tudors and progressively disintegrated during the 17th and 18th centuries. Nothing replaced it until the Victorian era.

- As more laws were passed to protect property and the person, the Office of Constable becomes more established.

- In 1798, Patrick Colquhoun convinced wealthy merchants to set up and fund a police service in the Port of London. It had 60 salaried officers, with Colquhoun as its superintending magistrate.

- Following this, a number of police forces were established:
  - the Thames River Police in 1799.
  - Royal Irish Constabulary in the first decades of the 19th century by Robert Peel; they were an armed force whose primary role was the maintenance of order.
  - Peel's attempts to introduce a similar model in mainland Britain failed.

- In the early 18th century, the Bow Street police office, under the chief magistrate, operated a rudimentary police force – most famously the Bow Street Runners of Henry and John Fielding – but they were short-lived because of a lack of Government funding.

- Robert Peel pushed through the *Metropolitan Police Act* in 1829 to create the Metropolitan Police, who had just over 1,000 officers.

- Peel created a police office under the direction of the Home Secretary. Specifically appointed magistrates should be in charge of the police, with costs met by the Government and the Metropolitan ratepayers. The Bill was passed with very little debate and no opposition, mainly because the City of London retained its own police.

> The Office of Constable is the very bedrock of an independent police service. The ability to take decisions, based on an officer's individual discretion, within the bounds of the law, is a principle that must be maintained. Police officers must remain independent of government, of party politics and be totally unbiased in their approach to the public.
>
> Nick Clegg, Leader, Liberal Democrats

- Peel was determined to establish professional policing in the rest of England and Wales. The Special Constables' Act 1831 allowed JPs to conscript men as special constables to deal with riots

- The outbreak of serious disorder in many towns over Parliamentary reform led to a sudden expansion of provincial policing during the 1830s.

- *The Municipal Corporations Act 1835* established regular police forces under the control of new democratic 178 boroughs town councils:
  - many boroughs simply appointed the old watchmen to implement the Act as cheaply as possible.
  - some ignored the Act completely, without reproach or penalty.
  - therefore the Act's good intentions were nullified.

- A 1839 Royal Commission proposed that there should be a single police force for the whole of the country (including Wales) outside London, controlled by local magistrates rather than the local authorities, but the idea was rejected.

- In the 1850s, the Government attempted to reform provincial policing, but faced furious opposition from the local authorities. Finally, despite the resistance of local authorities, it passed the *County and Borough Police Act 1856:*
  - a rural police force was to be created in all counties, and county policemen would have the same powers in the boroughs that borough policemen had in the counties.

- the major issue in this debate was, who controlled or – ought to control – the police?
- The Government was forced to make concessions to the local authorities, including dropping a proposed power to enable Home Secretaries to decide the size of a county force.

- In the early 20th century, the police service was "a collection of Victorian bric-a-brac", with little co-operation between forces and no common standards of pay or conditions of service.

- In 1919 the Desborough Committee recommended that the pay and conditions of service of all police officers should be improved, standardised, and placed under the control of the Home Secretary.

- Desborough rejected "nationalisation" of the service and increased a constable's pay to that of a semi-professional worker, rather than an agricultural labourer or unskilled worker.

- Local authorities protested about the extent of central government control, especially the new pay scales. Protests were ignored, and the Home Office began to exercise a measure of control over the police for the first time, designed to bring uniformity to policing throughout the country.

- The 1929 Royal Commission seemed to reject the unique status of the constable, stating: *"A policeman, in the view of the common law, is only a person paid to perform, as a matter of duty, acts which if he were so minded, he might have done voluntarily."*

- However, the next year a judge restated the importance of the office of constable:

"The powers of a constable, whether conferred by statute law or common law, are exercised by him by virtue of his office, and cannot be exercised on the responsibility of any person but himself. A constable, therefore, when acting as a peace officer, is not exercising a delegated authority, but an original authority."

- It was not until the *Police Act 1964* that the chief officer was liable for the wrongful acts of a constable of his force. This was so that a citizen with a justifiable complaint could obtain financial redress. It did not affect the doctrine of a constable's individual responsibility for his actions.

- In 1955, the Judicial Committee of the Privy Council stated: *"(The constable) is an officer whose authority is original, not delegated, and is exercised at his own discretion by virtue of his office: he is a ministerial officer exercising statutory rights independently of contract."*

- The 1931 and 1955 judgements came to be relied upon by chief constables who wished to assert their independence of their police authorities when it came to the exercise of police powers.

Historic policing pictures courtesy of Simon Dell

Are there any restraints upon the Office of Constable?

Police officers terms and conditions are laid out in Police Regulations. There are not many employment rights that police officers don't have that ordinary employees do. However, holding the Office of Constable and being a sworn officer of the Crown does mean there are some restraints upon action that the individual can take:

- Section 91(1) of the Police Act 1996 provides: "Any person who causes, or attempts to cause, or does any act calculated to cause, disaffection amongst the members of any police force, or induces or attempts to induce, or does any act calculated to induce, any member of a police force to withhold his services, shall be guilty of an offence…"

- There is also a common law criminal offence of misconduct in a public office where an officer wilfully neglects to perform a public duty or misconducts themselves to such a degree as to amount to abuse of the public's trust and without reasonable excuse or justification.

Restrictions on the private life of a Constable

Unlike ordinary employees the unique status of Office of Constable does place some restrictions on the private life of police officers and their families. These include:

- Abstaining from any activity which is likely to interfere with the impartial discharge of duty, or to give the impression to the public that it may interfere. This can be applicable to immediate family also.

- Getting permission from the appropriate disciplinary authority for place of residence

- Not wilfully refusing or neglecting to discharge any lawful debt.

- Not being able to have a business interest without the consent of the appropriate disciplinary authority.

- Abstaining from an 'active' role in any party politics.

> The office of constable is the bedrock which underpins the delivery of justice in this country. It reminds us that those charged with enforcing law and order are office holders who are ultimately accountable to the law, not to any employer, politician or anyone else with a vested interest, for their actions. Its value and worth to the public has been demonstrated time and time again and it is the office which provides chief constables with their operational independence – from which legitimacy and consent flows.
>
> **Ken Jones, President, Association of Chief Police Officers**

How are those who hold the Office of Constable different to employees?

- Employment law requires all employees to be 'protected' by a contract of employment. Constables are not employees.

- Police officers' conditions of service are provided by Police Regulations, Police Conduct Regulations and Police Performance Regulations; many reflect similar provisions to employment law but from a police perspective. The Police (Health & Safety) Act 1997 requires chief officers to provide safe working environments for police officers.

- Some employment law specifically applies to police officers, some does not; i.e. Sex Discrimination Act, Race Relations Act.

- Once employed, a police officer (out of probation) cannot lose their job unless there is accompanied misconduct, poor attendance or poor performance and even then only after prescribed procedures. Police officers therefore cannot complain of constructive dismissal.

Can police officers strike?

It is illegal for police officers to take any form of industrial action. As Officers of the Crown, they are bound by the Police Act. Section 91 of the Police Act provides that a criminal offence will be committed by:
- those who cause, or attempt to cause, amongst members of the police service disaffection, and
- those that induce them to 'withhold their services'.

There would be a breach of Section 91 if anybody were to encourage or promote any of the following:
- strike action
- an overtime ban (including bans on both compulsory and voluntary overtime
- a 'work to rule' – in effect a withdrawal of goodwill; the incitement to do so by the Federation or by a member of other members might well be viewed as causing disaffection contrary to Section 91.

Can police officers withhold services?

It's been suggested that if officers could withdraw consent to certain activities (such as holding back their Firearms Certificate or Driving Permit), this is something they could be encouraged to do. However:

- Any incitement to members to do so would probably breach the terms of Section 91 ('causing disaffection', if not inciting members to 'withhold services').

- There is a (albeit limited) risk that such a move (industrial action being unlawful) might leave a member open to claims of misfeasance in public office if their action was to lead to, say, injury to a third party.

- Depending on the circumstances the officer and any person encouraging them might incur criminal liability for misconduct in a public office.

What are the Principles of Policing?

Since the modern policing began in 1829 there have been fundamental principles that defined the function and purpose of policing. These principles have evolved over the years but the basics and core objectives have stood the passage of time.

The first principles were introduced by Sir Robert Peel. As Home Secretary, he introduced a number of important reforms of British criminal law, most memorably establishing the Metropolitan Police Force (Metropolitan Police Act 1829). Robert Peel developed the 'Peelian Principles' which defined the ethical requirements police officers must follow in order to be effective. His most memorable principle was: "The police are the public, and the public are the police."

It is interesting to note that the fundamentals of policing have not changed over the centuries, as the following versions of Nine Points of the Law demonstrate.

Sir Robert Peel's Nine Principles of Policing

1. The basic mission for which the police exist is to prevent crime and disorder.

2. The ability of the police to perform their duties is dependent upon public approval of police actions.

3. Police must secure the willing co-operation of the public in voluntary observance of the law to be able to secure and maintain the respect of the public.

4. The degree of co-operation of the public that can be secured diminishes proportionately to the necessity of the use of physical force.

5. Police seek and preserve public favour not by catering to public opinion but by constantly demonstrating absolute impartial service to the law.

6. Police use physical force to the extent necessary to secure observance of the law or to restore order only when the exercise of persuasion, advice and warning is found to be insufficient.

7. Police, at all times, should maintain a relationship with the public that gives reality to the historic tradition that the police are the public and the public are the police; the police being only members of the public who are paid to give full-time attention to duties which are incumbent on every citizen in the interests of community welfare and existence

8. Police should always direct their action strictly towards their functions and never appear to usurp the powers of the judiciary.

9. The test of police efficiency is the absence of crime and disorder, not the visible evidence of police action in dealing with it.

Sir Richard Mayne's Nine Principles of Policing, 1829

1. To prevent crime and disorder, as an alternative to their repression by military force and severity of legal punishment.

2. To recognise always that the power of the police to fulfil their functions and duties is dependent on public approval of their existence, actions and behaviour and on their ability to secure and maintain public respect.

3. To recognise always that to secure and maintain the respect and approval of the public means also the securing of the willing co-operation of the public in the task of securing observance of laws.

4. To recognise always that the extent to which the co-operation of the public can be secured diminishes proportionately the necessity of the use of physical force and compulsion for achieving police objectives.

5. To seek and preserve public favour, not by pandering to public opinion; but by constantly demonstrating absolutely impartial service to law, in complete independence of policy, and without regard to the justice or injustice of the substance of individual laws, by ready offering of individual service and friendship to all members of the public without regard to their wealth or social standing, by ready exercise of courtesy and friendly good humour; and by ready offering of individual sacrifice in protecting and preserving life.

6. To use physical force only when the exercise of persuasion, advice and warning is found to be insufficient to obtain public co-operation to an extent necessary to secure observance of law or to restore order, and to use only the minimum degree of physical force which is necessary on any particular occasion for achieving a police objective.

> Constables provide a service to the public by exercising their powers **with** honesty, fairness and understanding but **without** fear or favour for the benefit of and the protection of the communities they serve.
>
> **Steve Edwards, Chairman, Lancashire Police Federation**

7. To maintain at all times a relationship with the public that gives reality to the historic tradition that the police are the public and that the public are the police, the police being only members of the public who are paid to give full time attention to duties which are incumbent on every citizen in the interests of community welfare and existence.

8. To recognise always the need for strict adherence to police-executive functions, and to refrain from even seeming to usurp the powers of the judiciary of avenging individuals or the State, and of authoritatively judging guilt and punishing the guilty.

9. To recognise always that the test of police efficiency is the absence of crime and disorder, and not the visible evidence of police action in dealing with them.

Looking forward: Nine Points of the Law, 2008

This year the Police Federation of England and Wales has developed a new Nine Points of the Law. This captures the core principles which will continue to ensure that policing is delivered professionally, independent, impartially and remain fully accountable. If government and chief officers take note it will inject some healthy common sense back into policing, restore discretion, see more police officers back on the beat and value and protect the Office of Constable.

Police Federation's Nine Points of the Law, 1991

1. Law and order must be a first priority of government and a first claim on resources.
2. The police must have the means and the power to protect life and property.
3. Punishment must fit the crime, not just the criminal.
4. Victims must be compensated and helped to recover from their ordeals.
5. Priority must be given to cutting crime among the young.
6. More emphasis must be placed on crime prevention and partnership between the public and the police.
7. Criminal trials must become a search for the truth.
8. The bail scandal must end.
9. There must be a Royal Commission on policing.

> The Office of Constable is fundamental to our system of politically independent policing by consent. It's enabled the holders to discharge their duties with impartiality and discretion. Communities are policed by members of the community. You can't have greater accountability than that.
>
> Ian Pointon, Chairman, Kent Police Federation

Define and specify the role of the police
To re-define and clarify the role of the police in the face of increasing demands and reduced resources, restoring the independence of police forces from central control and recognising the responsibility of others in order to establish the necessary integrated structure, governance arrangements, accountability, performance framework and workforce and rewards systems.

Recognise Office of Constable
To ensure the Office of Constable remains the foundation of the police service, enabling officers to assume the personal responsibility to act impartially, with discretion and free from political control, recognising the restrictions on their personal lives which this entails; to also ensure that entry for all officers remains at the rank of constable, enabling a thorough grounding in the experiential skills which is imperative for all ranks.

Restore discretion
To ensure officers, and each police force, have the support and confidence they need to use their integrity, common sense, experience and discretion when enforcing the law and providing reassurance to the public.

Reduce bureaucracy
To ease the burden of unnecessary

bureaucracy, utilising new technology where appropriate to maximise useful and productive contact with the public.

Improve operational resilience through best use of resources

To provide continuous professional development that remains focused on operational improvements to balance the competing demands on the 24/7 police service: that of a crime-fighting organisation, an emergency response force and reassuring the public.

Establish fair and equitable pay agreements with binding arbitration on all parties

To establish fair, transparent and equitable pay agreements for all police officers in the UK, and, in the absence of industrial rights, an independent arbitration process that is binding on all parties without exception.

Establish meaningful targets that reflect public priorities and take account of quality of policing delivered

To ensure meaningful targets are set locally and address local priorities within the wider cross-border context, rather than a national political agenda.

Establish shared accountability for re-offending rates throughout the criminal justice process

To recognise the impact of re-offending on police resources and society in general, understanding that it is a small number of offenders who commit a significant proportion of the volume crime, and that the bodies that share responsibility for tackling re-offending must be held fully accountable.

Establish a fully-integrated, cohesive criminal justice system

To ensure a more cohesive, consistent and collaborative criminal justice system, with complementary targets and an IT structure that is secure, fully-integrated and fit for purpose.

> When the public see a uniformed police officer attend an incident, they are confident that that person has the power to deal with it.
>
> **PC 852 Edwards, Lancashire Constabulary**

The Police Federation of England and Wales will fight to protect the independent, impartial and accountable Office of Constable, and to ensure that it is supported and valued in modern day policing structures and processes.

© Rudi Tapper / iStockphoto

POLICE *Federation*

www.polfed.org

May 2008. Published by the Police Federation of England and Wales, Federation House, Highbury Drive, Leatherhead, Surrey, KT22 7UY

What restrictions are there, if any, on police officers relying on the European Convention on Human Rights in relation to employment matters such as disciplinary proceedings?

A As government servants, police officers cannot rely on the Convention rights in any circumstances.

B A police officer has the same rights as any citizen to rely on the Convention rights in any circumstances.

C All citizens have the right to implement the Convention rights in relation to employment, including police officers.

D As government servants, police officers cannot rely on the Convention rights in relation to employment matters, but they may be able to do so in other matters.

Question 3.7

Article 2 of the European Convention on Human Rights relates to the protection of a person's right to life.

In relation to the level of force that may legitimately be used when a life is taken in breach of this Article, which of the following statements is correct?

A No more force than is necessary in the circumstances may be used.

B No more force than is reasonable in the circumstances may be used.

C No more force than is absolutely necessary may be used.

D No more force than would appear necessary to a reasonable person may be used.

Question 3.8

LAWTON was the father of an 8-year-old boy who was murdered by his neighbour, PEARSON, a convicted sex offender. Prior to the murder, LAWTON had made several complaints to the police that PEARSON had been seen pestering his child. Following PEARSON's conviction, LAWTON brought an action against the police under Art. 2 of the European Convention on Human Rights, alleging that the police had failed to prevent his son's death.

What must LAWTON prove to the court in order to convince it that the police failed to prevent the death of his son?

A Nothing — the police have an absolute obligation to protect life under Art. 2.

B That the police actually foresaw the risk to life, and that they failed to act upon it.

C That the police failed to see a risk to life which would have been obvious to a reasonable person.

D That the police did not do all that was expected of them to avoid a real and immediate risk to life.

Question 3.9

ANDERSON was found guilty of raping and murdering a 5-year-old girl after confessing during an interview. ANDERSON is now appealing against his conviction by using Art. 3 of the European Convention on Human Rights (right to freedom from torture). ANDERSON claims that police officers showed him several pictures of the mutilated body of the young girl prior to the interview and that this caused him severe mental anguish. ANDERSON claims that he was not guilty of the offence and his conviction was unsafe on the grounds that he was psychologically affected by the photographs, because his own daughter was murdered two years previously, and he would not have admitted the offence had he not been shown them.

Which of the following statements is correct, in respect of whether ANDERSON's confession should be admitted in evidence?

A The evidence should not be admitted if the court finds, on the balance of probabilities, it was obtained by torture.

B The evidence should be admitted because mental anguish does not constitute torture.

C The evidence should not be admitted if the court finds beyond reasonable doubt that the evidence was obtained by torture.

D All evidence should be admitted and heard by the court and there should be no exceptions.

Question 3.10

ZILICH is suspected of entering the country illegally and is wanted for murder in Kosovo. ZILICH has been held in a detention centre for over 3 years while the immigration authorities attempt to organise extradition procedures. ZILICH is fighting the extradition procedure by using Art. 5 of the European Convention on Human Rights (right to liberty and security), citing that his detention is unjust and oppressive because of the 3-year delay.

What obligation, if any, do the authorities have to demonstrate that ZILICH's detention is not unjust and oppressive?

A They need only show that the detention was necessary — there is no requirement to justify the delay in ZILICH's extradition.

B There is no requirement to show either that the detention was necessary, or to justify the delay in ZILICH's extradition.

C They must show that the detention was necessary and that the delay in ZILICH's extradition was justified, otherwise the detention may be unlawful.

D ZILICH has been 'detained' for deportation, this does not constitute an 'arrest' and therefore Art. 5 does not apply.

Question 3.11

Constable WILSON was called to an incident in a local supermarket. The manager was complaining about SHEPPARD, who was homeless. SHEPPARD had entered the store and told the manager that he had scabies and a severe lice infection, both of which were highly contagious and needed treatment. The manager feared that customers and staff would be infected by disease and requested that the officer remove SHEPPARD from the store.

What power does Art. 5 of the European Convention on Human Rights (the right to liberty and security) provide in relation to an arrest in these circumstances?

A SHEPPARD can be arrested, provided he is taken to a medical centre.

B SHEPPARD can be arrested and taken to a place of safety.

C SHEPPARD cannot be arrested under the Convention; the officer would need to seek powers from elsewhere.

D SHEPPARD can be arrested and brought before a competent legal authority.

Question 3.12

Constable OSBORN has been charged with an internal discipline offence arising from the performance of his duties. He was interviewed by a senior police officer, but was not allowed to have a legal representative present. He is due to appear before a Police Conduct hearing and is seeking advice as to how the Human Rights Act 1998 affects his treatment and those proceedings.

In relation to Art. 6 of the European Convention on Human Rights (the right to a fair trial), which of the following statements is correct?

A Article 6 applies to court cases only; therefore the disciplinary proceedings are not affected.

B Article 6 applies to all disciplinary hearings and OSBORN's rights appear to have been infringed by the failure to allow him access to a solicitor.

C Article 6 applies to purely criminal cases only; therefore OSBORN's rights have not been infringed and the proceedings are not affected.

D Article 6 applies to some disciplinary hearings; however, OSBORN's rights have not been infringed by denying him access to a solicitor.

Question 3.13

BRACE owns 15 private children's nurseries, each of which is managed separately by his employees. BRACE has computerised records dating back several years of applicants for posts in his nurseries. Amongst these records are details of people whom he considers are unsuitable for work with children.

Would the people on the list be able to bring proceedings against BRACE under Art. 8 of the European Convention on Human Rights (right to a private life) in these circumstances?

A Yes, he is in breach of the human rights of the people on the list.

B No, he could claim a pressing social need to maintain the list.

C No, because the list is not being maintained by a public authority.

D Yes, because he could not point to a lawful authority enabling him to maintain the list.

Question 3.14

CLAYTON is appearing in the Crown Court, having been charged with an offence of stirring up racial hatred under s. 18 of the Public Order Act 1986. He had displayed a picture in his shop window, indicating that he would not serve refugees. He is pleading not guilty, claiming that his human rights have been interfered with, as he is entitled to express his opinions freely.

Would CLAYTON be able to use Art. 10 of the European Convention on Human Rights (freedom of expression) as a defence in these circumstances?

A No, as his actions are probably not proportionate to the crime committed.

B Yes, every person has a right to express themselves freely.

C No, but he could use Art. 9 (freedom of thought) as a defence.

D Yes, provided he held a genuine belief that his rights had been interfered with.

Question 3.15

The Westford anti-hunt lobby arranged a demonstration outside a farm where a fox hunt was being organised. The organisers of the hunt arranged for marshals to be present and the local police were also in attendance. Demonstrators protested peacefully in the road nearby but, on the instructions of the hunt organisers, the marshals attempted to move the protestors away from the scene. The demonstrators felt intimidated by the marshals, but the police did nothing.

In these circumstances, do the police officers at the scene appear to have infringed Art. 11 of the European Convention on Human Rights (freedom of assembly and association)?

A No, as they have not interfered with the rights of the protestors or the members of the hunt.

B Yes, they should have stopped the protest; it breached the rights of the hunters and the farm owner.

C Yes, they had a duty to prevent the unlawful interference with the rights of the protestors by the marshals.

D No, they would have a duty to act only if public order offences were imminent.

ANSWERS

Answer 3.1

Answer **D** — Under s. 2 of the Human Rights Act 1998, the courts of England and Wales have a duty to take into account any decision made in the European Court of Human Rights, and therefore answers B and C are incorrect. However, there is no stipulation that the courts of England and Wales must follow the decisions, merely that they take decisions into account, and therefore answer A is incorrect.

General Police Duties, para. 4.3.2.2

Answer 3.2

Answer **B** — Where the European Convention on Human Rights gives individuals a particular right, any qualification or limitation on that right will be carefully defined and cautiously applied. Very generally, any limitations on a Convention right must be:

- prescribed by law;
- intended to achieve a legitimate objective;
- proportionate to the end that is to be achieved.

Known as the 'three tests', what this effectively means is that if a person's human rights are infringed the public body would have to show that all three tests had been met. As such one or two tests being met would not be enough; answers C and D are therefore incorrect.

Any intrusion into someone's rights has to have a clear legal source. However, it is not enough that such a source of legal authority exists; it must also be readily accessible to the people of the relevant State (see *The Sunday Times* v *United Kingdom* (1979) 2 EHRR 245). This means that the law must be clearly and precisely defined and publicised so that people can make themselves aware of it and regulate their conduct accordingly. Acts of Parliament (primary legislation) and statutory instruments (secondary legislation) would invariably meet this requirement; answer A is therefore incorrect.

General Police Duties, para. 4.3.3.2

Answer 3.3

Answer **B** — Under Art. 3 of the European Convention on Human Rights, a person must not be subjected to torture, inhuman or degrading treatment or punishment. Therefore, the actions of the guard would amount to a breach.

Under s. 6 of the Human Rights Act 1998, it is unlawful for a public authority to act in a way that is incompatible with a Convention right. An individual working for an authority is included in the definition.

'Public authorities' are divided into 'pure public authorities' (such as the police and courts, etc.) and 'quasi-public authorities'. There has been no test as yet as to who might fall into the second category, but they do include authorities who have a duty to discharge some public duties (such as security companies running private prisons and government contractors). Therefore, answer A is incorrect.

Answer C is incorrect because 'government authorities' are not mentioned; and answer D is incorrect as regard must be given to the type of authority a person works for.

General Police Duties, para. 4.3.4.3

Answer 3.4

Answer **A** — Under s. 7(1) of the Human Rights Act 1998, a person who claims that a public authority has acted (or proposed to act) in a way that is incompatible with his or her human rights (s. 6(1)) may bring proceedings against the authority in the appropriate court or tribunal.

In order to rely on s. 7, however, a person must first be a 'victim', and must show that he or she is either directly affected or at risk of being directly affected. Section 7 will not enable public interest groups to institute proceedings, only individuals. Therefore, answers B and C are incorrect.

Answer A is correct because DANE is an individual who is at risk of being directly affected. The circumstances are similar to the case of *Dudgeon* v *United Kingdom* (1983) 5 EHRR 573, where the petitioner was able to challenge the law proscribing consensual homosexual activity even though he had not been prosecuted under the legislation himself. A person may institute proceedings under s. 7 regardless of whether or not he or she has been convicted of an offence. This is known as using the European Convention on Human Rights as a 'sword' against a public authority.

Of course, whether the police should have been engaged in such surveillance, bearing in mind the Regulation of Investigatory Powers Act 2000, is another issue!

General Police Duties, para. 4.3.4.6

Answer 3.5

Answer **A** — Section 7(5)(a) of the Human Rights Act 1998 states that proceedings under s. 7(1)(a) must be brought before the end of 1 year beginning with the date on which the act complained of took place, or such longer period as the court or tribunal considers equitable having regard to all the circumstances. Answers B, C and D are therefore incorrect.

General Police Duties, para. 4.3.4.6

Answer 3.6

Answer **D** — There are restrictions on police officers relying on the Convention rights in the context of recruitment and disciplinary procedures. The European Court of Justice regards police officers in Member States as being government servants and as such they cannot generally rely on their Convention rights against the employer (see *Pellegrin* v *France* (2001) 31 EHRR 26). Answers B and C are therefore incorrect.

However, there are certain circumstances where police officers *may* be able to rely on their Convention rights, for example in *R (on the application of A and B)* v *HM Coroner for Inner South London* [2004] EWCA Civ 1439, where the coroner refused to allow police officers to give evidence anonymously in a fatal shooting case. The Divisional Court held the risk of serious harm to the officers and their families was sufficient to engage Article 2 and the coroner ought to have protected their anonymity. Answer A is therefore incorrect.

General Police Duties, paras 4.3.4.6, 4.3.6

Answer 3.7

Answer **C** — The term 'reasonable force' does not apply to the application of lethal force under the Human Rights Act 1998, making answers B and D incorrect.

Answer A is close; however, the Act states that when life is taken, any force used must be shown to have been no more than absolutely necessary (which is why answer C is correct).

General Police Duties, para. 4.3.6.1

Answer 3.8

Answer **D** — The circumstances are similar to those in the case of *Osman* v *United Kingdom* (2000) 29 EHRR 245, where a man had been killed by a person who had become fixated with him. Although there the European Court of Human Rights dismissed the case, it examined the positive obligation of the State to protect life under Art. 2.

First, the positive obligation on the State to protect life is not an absolute one (and answer A is incorrect). Other factors should be taken into consideration, such as the source and degree of danger and the means available to combat it. The court said in *Osman* that it will be enough for the applicant to show that the authorities did not do all that could reasonably be expected of them to avoid a real and immediate risk to life of which they have or ought to have knowledge. Answer B is incorrect, as there is no need to show that the State actually saw the risk and failed to act upon it. Answer C is incorrect, as the 'reasonable person' test is not mentioned in this ruling.

General Police Duties, para. 4.3.6.2

Answer 3.9

Answer **A** — Under Art. 3 of the European Convention on Human Rights (right to freedom from torture), no person shall be subjected to torture or to inhuman or degrading treatment or punishment. The prohibition contained in Art. 3 of the European Convention on Human Rights is absolute and the treatment goes far beyond the traditional image of 'torture'. Included in this treatment are the following broad categories:

- torture — deliberate treatment leading to serious or cruel suffering;
- inhuman treatment — treatment resulting in intense suffering, both physical and mental;
- degrading treatment — treatment giving rise to fear and anguish in the victim, causing feelings of inferiority and humiliation.

It has been held by the European Commission of Human Rights that causing mental anguish without any physical assault could be a violation of Art. 3 (see *Denmark* v *Greece* [1969] 12 YB Eur Conv HR special vol.). Answer B is incorrect.

In *A & Others* v *Secretary of State for Home Department* [2005] 3 WLR 1249, it was held that, if on the balance of probabilities, it was concluded that any evidence had been obtained by torture then it should not be admitted. Answers C and D are therefore incorrect.

General Police Duties, para. 4.3.7

Answer 3.10

Answer **B** — Under Art. 5 of the European Convention on Human Rights, every person has the right to liberty and security of person. When it comes to unauthorised entry into the country and deportation/extradition matters, a detainee is *still* afforded protection by virtue of Art. 5(1)(f). Answer D is therefore incorrect.

However, the House of Lords has ruled that unlike Art. 5(1)(c), Art. 5(1)(f) does not require the detention to be necessary to be justified (*R (On the application of Shayan Barom)* v *Secretary of State for the Home Department* [2002] LTL 31 October). In that case it was held that the temporary detention of asylum seekers pending their application to remain in the United Kingdom was not unlawful simply by reason of it not being necessary. Answers A and C are therefore incorrect.

In *Owalabi* v *Court Number Four at the High Court of Justice in Spain* [2005] EWHC 2849 (Admin), it was held that where a person was being extradited to Spain, the hearing was entitled to conclude that the delay of over 5 years between the individual's arrest and their extradition did not render the extradition unjust or oppressive. Answer C is also incorrect for this reason.

General Police Duties, paras 4.3.9.7, 4.3.9.8

Answer 3.11

Answer **C** — Under Art. 5 of the European Convention on Human Rights, every person has the right to liberty and security of person. This is a qualified right, and exceptions are provided in Art. 5(1), allowing the lawful arrest in certain cases, where the procedure is prescribed by law.

Article 5(1)(e) provides that a person may be detained without his or her human rights being infringed where his or her detention is necessary 'for the prevention of the spreading of infectious diseases, of persons of unsound mind, alcoholics or drug addicts or vagrants'. However, the Convention itself does not provide a specific power of arrest for the above offences, and arresting officers would have to rely on existing legislation to detain a person (which is why answer C is correct and answers A, B and D are incorrect).

Article 5(1) merely sets out the conditions under which the State may remove a person's liberty. (In real terms, it is hard to imagine that the legislators intended to provide a power to arrest all people with infectious diseases, drug addicts, alcoholics and vagrants!)

General Police Duties, para. 4.3.9.6

Answer 3.12

Answer **D** — Article 6 of the European Convention on Human Rights has been held to apply to some professional and disciplinary hearings, and it is possible that it will affect police disciplinary hearings (answers A and C are incorrect for this reason).

However, it was held in the case of *Lee* v *United Kingdom* (2000) LTL 22 September, that where an officer was interviewed for a purely disciplinary matter, there was no standing right of access to a lawyer, even if he or she were being interviewed under caution. This decision can be interpreted as meaning that the officer was not being interviewed for an 'offence', and would therefore not enjoy the usual right to legal representation under the Police and Criminal Evidence Act 1984 that he or she would otherwise have had. Since the matter was an internal police investigation, the officer would not be entitled to legal representation, even if he or she were authorised before the interview (making answer B incorrect).

General Police Duties, para. 4.3.10

Answer 3.13

Answer **C** — Article 8 of the European Convention on Human Rights states that everyone has the right to respect for his private life, his home and his correspondence. However, the Human Rights Act 1998 aims to protect people from arbitrary interference by 'public authorities'. Therefore, even though it might seem that BRACE is acting contrary to the Convention, the list of names is not maintained by a public authority (which is why answer C is correct).

Had BRACE been acting on behalf of a public authority, he would probably still be protected, because of the case of *R* v *Worcester County Council, ex parte W* [2000] 3 FCR 174. Here, it was decided that the Consultancy Services Index maintained by the Secretary of State, which provided access to employers' records on people considered unsuitable for work with children, was not an infringement of the human rights of those included on it. It has also been held that maintaining such a list is proportionate to the lawful objective sought (*R* v *Secretary of State for Health, ex parte L (M)* [2001] 1 FLR 406). Answers A, B and D are incorrect for this reason.

General Police Duties, para. 4.3.12

Answer 3.14

Answer **A** — Under Art. 10 of the European Convention on Human Rights, everyone has a right to freedom of expression. However, as with all aspects of human rights, this has to be balanced against other social needs. In the case of *Hutchinson* v *DPP*, The Independent, 20 November 2000, a conviction for criminal damage was upheld when it was decided that there were other ways in which the defendant could have expressed her opinions without committing a crime. Answer B is incorrect for this reason.

Because his actions were probably not proportionate, CLAYTON would not be able to use Art. 9 as a 'shield' for the same reasons as above (making answer C incorrect).

A person's belief, no matter how genuine, that his or her rights had been interfered with, will not provide an automatic defence to a criminal offence if that belief is not proportionate to the crime committed. Answer D is therefore incorrect.

General Police Duties, para. 4.3.14

Answer 3.15

Answer **C** — Under Art. 11 of the European Convention on Human Rights, everyone has the right to freedom of peaceful assembly. Therefore, the protestors had the right to protest, provided they were going about it peacefully. They do not appear to have interfered with the rights of the members of the hunt or the farm owner on these facts. Answer B is incorrect for this reason.

The State (or public authority) has two main obligations in these circumstances. In the first instance, it must not interfere with the protestors' rights to peaceful assembly. However, equally as important, it has a positive duty to prevent others from interfering with that right (which is why answer C is correct).

Therefore, even though the officers at the scene did not actively prevent the protest, arguably they should have acted to stop the marshals from doing so (which is why answers A and D are incorrect).

General Police Duties, para. 4.3.15

4 | Policing Powers

STUDY PREPARATION

The areas covered in this chapter could hardly be more important. In practical terms, this chapter contains the police officer's tool kit — and if it is relevant in practice, it is highly relevant in preparing for an examination or course of study.

In deciding what to do in any given situation, it is vital that you know what you are *empowered* to do. Following on from the previous chapter, it is also important to realise that each police power equals a reduction of, or interference with, someone's human rights. As holders of such powers, police officers are under a duty to exercise them properly — lawfully, proportionately and fairly.

The main tools in the bag are powers of entry, arrest, search and seizure. Some are very broadly based (such as indictable offences), while others are contextual, requiring very specific circumstances to exist first before they are available. Knowing and understanding all of these leads to confidence, not just as a student or exam candidate but as a police officer generally.

The Serious Organised Crime and Police Act 2005 introduced extensive changes to policing powers, in respect of arrest and detention, with particular emphasis on the 'necessity' test to be applied before arrests are made, and the abolition of 'arrestable offences'. Further changes have been made in respect of the application and execution of warrants.

QUESTIONS

Question 4.1

Section 107 of the Police and Criminal Evidence Act 1984 refers to officers performing duties in acting ranks.

In which circumstances would a constable be able to perform the functions of a custody officer at a designated police station?

A When he or she has been authorised to do so by an inspector.
B When he or she has been authorised to do so by a superintendent.
C When no other custody officer is readily available.
D When he or she has been temporarily promoted to sergeant.

Question 4.2

BRIDGE is aged 16 and has been issued with a disorder penalty notice under s. 2 of the Criminal Justice and Police Act 2001 for depositing litter.

What would be the value of the fine attached to such a notice?

A £30.
B £40.
C £50.
D £80.

Question 4.3

SPEARS is aged 14 and has been issued with a disorder penalty notice under s. 2 of the Criminal Justice and Police Act 2001 for throwing fireworks on a main road.

Who would be liable for paying the fine attached to such a notice, should SPEARS accept liability for this offence?

A SPEARS only, as the person responsible for the offence.
B SPEARS' parent or guardian, because of her age.
C Either SPEARS or her parent or guardian.
D Neither SPEARS nor her parent or guardian; she should not have been issued with a notice because of her age.

Question 4.4

Following the setting up of the Stop and Search Action Team (SSAT) and recommendation 61 of the Lawrence Report, police officers must now record all 'stop' encounters, as well as those where a person was actually searched.

In which of the following circumstances would an officer *not* be required to submit a 'stop' form following an encounter with a member of the public?

A The officer encountered a person and asked them to account for their presence in an area late at night, where a burglary had recently occurred. The person was not searched.

B The officer had reasonable grounds to stop a person and search them. However, after speaking to the person, the officer decided that the search was no longer necessary and the person was allowed to leave without a search taking place.

C The officer spoke to a group of 8 people outside a public house where an assault had taken place. The people were regarded as witnesses and not suspects and provided information in relation to the offence.

D The officer stopped a vehicle using powers under the Road Traffic Act 1988 in a remote location which had recently suffered a number of crimes. The officer asked the occupants to account for their presence there.

Question 4.5

Constable MULLER was on patrol one evening when he saw KELLS, aged 15. Constable MULLER was aware that KELLS was a divisional target suspected of committing several burglaries, none of which could be proved. Constable MULLER intended stopping and searching KELLS; however, he had no particular reason to suspect that he might be in possession of stolen or prohibited articles. Constable MULLER stopped KELLS and spoke to him, eventually obtaining his consent to submit to a search. The search proved negative.

Were the officer's actions legal in these circumstances?
A No, because of KELLS's age.
B Yes, provided Constable MULLER submits a search from.
C No, regardless of KELLS's age.
D Yes, and a search form need not be submitted.

Question 4.6

Constable TALLAC was on patrol when he heard a message on his radio describing a male person who had broken into a car. The description had been given by an anonymous caller to the control room. Constable TALLAC saw PEARSON walking along the street and realised that his clothing was similar to that of the person described in the radio message. Constable TALLAC intended stopping PEARSON in order to search him for prohibited articles.

Would Constable TALLAC be entitled to search PEARSON, based on the information from the radio message alone?

A No, anonymous information would not provide reasonable grounds for suspicion to conduct the search.

B Yes, provided a reasonable person would think that there were reasonable grounds for suspicion to conduct the search.

C No, the anonymous information would amount to hearsay, which would not provide reasonable grounds for suspicion to conduct the search.

D Yes, regardless of whether a reasonable person would think that there were reasonable grounds for suspicion to conduct the search.

Question 4.7

Constable AMIR was on patrol looking for a person who had committed theft from a vehicle. Witnesses had given a description of the person responsible, who they said was carrying a screwdriver. Constable AMIR discovered JACKSON, who matched the description, in the front garden of a house. JACKSON lived some 3 miles away from the house.

Would Constable AMIR have the power to search JACKSON for the screwdriver in these circumstances?

A No, as JACKSON was in the garden of a dwelling.

B Yes, as JACKSON was not inside a dwelling.

C No, as JACKSON was not in a public place.

D Yes, as JACKSON was not in his own garden.

Question 4.8

Code A, para. 3 of the Codes of Practice outlines the circumstances in which a constable need not make a written record, when a person has been searched under s. 1 of the Police and Criminal Evidence Act 1984.

In what circumstances, if any, may a constable delay making a written record of such a search?

A When it is not practicable to make a written record.

B The written record must be made at the time; there are no exceptions.

C When it is wholly impracticable to make a written record.

D When it is not possible to make a written record.

Question 4.9

Constables GREATHEAD and LIPINSKI are conducting a stop in the street, having proper grounds. Constable LIPINSKI carries out a search whilst Constable GREAT-HEAD completes the stop/search record.

Which of the officers' details *must* go on the stop/search record?

A Those of Constable GREATHEAD as she completed the record.

B Those of Constable LIPINSKI as he conducted the search.

C Both officers' details must be recorded.

D Either of the officers' details should be recorded, as long as one of them is.

Question 4.10

Constable BAIRD attended a suspicious incident reported by POOLE, a closed circuit television (CCTV) operator. POOLE saw two men acting suspiciously near a four-wheel-drive vehicle, and saw one of the men hand the other a bag of white powder. He believed the bag was placed inside the cover of the spare wheel, attached to the rear door of the vehicle. As a result of this information, Constable BAIRD searched the spare wheel, but found nothing inside.

Is Constable BAIRD required to supply a notice of this search, under s. 2 of the Police and Criminal Evidence Act 1984?

A Yes, it should be placed on the vehicle, and a copy sent to the registered owner.

B No, a notice is not required as the inside of the vehicle was not searched.

C Yes, it should be placed inside the vehicle, which may be entered by force to do so.

D Yes, a notice must be placed somewhere on the vehicle.

Question 4.11

Constable ROBERTS attended a large retail store, where the occupants of a green 4 × 4 vehicle had been captured on closed circuit television (CCTV) as they entered the store and stole two bottles of wine from within. The vehicle was seen to make off immediately prior to Constable ROBERTS' arrival. Constable ROBERTS contacted the control room and asked the duty sergeant to authorise an urgent road check, under s. 4 of the Police and Criminal Evidence Act 1984, for the vehicle and its occupants.

Can the officer's request be granted in these circumstances?
A Yes, but Constable ROBERTS could have authorised the road check himself.
B Yes, provided the sergeant authorises it.
C No, only an inspector may authorise a road check in urgent circumstances.
D No, only a superintendent may authorise a road check in any circumstances.

Question 4.12

Superintendent HAYES has provided written authorisation for a road check to take place. Officers in Superintendent HAYES' area are investigating a case of causing death by dangerous driving and the suspect was believed to have driven away from the scene without stopping in a red Nissan motor vehicle. The superintendent has authorised that all red vehicles of a similar size and colour are to be stopped at the location of the incident, at the approximate time of day, for the next 7 days. No useful information was gleaned during the initial period of 7 days and the officer in the case has asked Superintendent HAYES to extend the period.

If Superintendent HAYES agrees to extend this period, what would be the maximum period that may be granter beyond the initial 7 days?
A One further period of 7 days.
B Two further periods of 7 days.
C Three further periods of 7 days, to a maximum period of 28 days.
D Unlimited period, provided the authorisations are for 7 days at a time.

Question 4.13

Section 4(15) of the Police and Criminal Evidence Act 1984 requires the police to provide a written statement when a motor vehicle has been stopped during a road check.

Who would be entitled to apply for such a statement?
A The person in charge of the vehicle at the time it was stopped.
B The owner of the vehicle at the time it was stopped.
C The driver of the vehicle at the time it was stopped.
D Any person who was in the vehicle at the time it was stopped.

Question 4.14

A football match is due to take place in Inspector CARTER's area, and she is the officer in charge of a support unit positioned outside the train station. Intelligence has suggested that approximately 200 away supporters will be arriving, and staff on the train have reported seeing several weapons being carried by fans. Inspector CARTER is considering searching all supporters before they leave the train station.

In relation to the powers to authorise searches under s. 60 of the Criminal Justice and Public Order Act 1994, which statement is correct?

A The inspector may authorise the searches, but only if she suspects there will be incidents involving serious violence.

B The inspector may authorise the searches, but only of those suspected of carrying weapons.

C The inspector may authorise the search of any of the fans, in these circumstances alone.

D The inspector may not authorise the searches; this power is restricted to super-intendents.

Question 4.15

Constable WILLIS was on patrol in uniform in the early hours of the morning in an area where there had recently been outbreaks of serious public order between two gangs, who were known to carry weapons. An order was in force, under s. 60 of the Criminal Justice and Public Order Act 1994, to stop and search persons in the locality. Constable WILLIS saw MOORE walking in the street wearing a ski mask, which was concealing his face.

In what circumstances could Constable WILLIS ask MOORE to remove his mask?

A If he reasonably believed that MOORE was likely to be involved in violence.

B No further circumstances are required, as an order is in force under s. 60.

C If he reasonably believed that MOORE was attempting to conceal his identity.

D If he reasonably believed that MOORE was carrying a dangerous instrument or an offensive weapon.

Question 4.16

Section 44 of the Terrorism Act 2000 provides a power for the police to author-ise stop and search operations, in order to prevent acts of terrorism. In certain circumstances, police community support officers (PCSOs) may be utilised to assist in such operations.

What restrictions, if any, are placed on PCSOs, when exercising their powers un-der s. 44?

A They must be accompanied by a police officer; they have the power to stop and search pedestrians or vehicles.

B They may stop and search both pedestrians and vehicles, while on their own, or while accompanied by a police officer.

C They must be accompanied by a police officer; they have no power to stop persons or vehicles, but may assist officers to conduct searches.

D They must be accompanied and supervised by a police officer; they have the power to stop and search pedestrians or vehicles.

Question 4.17

Constable DEVEREAUX attended a report of a dwelling burglary in progress, and on arrival saw CHRISTIE climbing out of a ground floor window and running away from the scene. Constable DEVEREAUX chased and caught CHRISTIE nearby and had to struggle to detain the suspect, while other officers arrived at the scene. While they were struggling, Constable DEVEREAUX told CHRISTIE, 'You're nicked'.

Does Constable DEVEREAUX have any further duty to provide CHRISTIE with information, for example, the reason and grounds for the arrest and why the arrest was necessary?

A No, the facts of the arrest were obvious and CHRISTIE has been provided with sufficient information.

B Yes, CHRISTIE should be told the grounds for the arrest and why the arrest was necessary as soon as practicable.

C Yes, CHRISTIE should be told why the arrest was necessary as soon as practicable; the reason and grounds for the arrest were obvious.

D Yes, 'You're nicked' would not satisfy the criteria of informing someone they are under arrest; CHRISTIE must be informed of all three of the above.

Question 4.18

PERRY entered a large retail clothing shop and whilst being watched by IQBAL, a store detective, PERRY hid a pair of jeans in her carrier bag. PERRY left the store without paying and was stopped outside by IQBAL. IQBAL decided that it was necessary to arrest PERRY for theft.

Does IQBAL have to inform PERRY of the grounds for the arrest, under s. 28 of the Police and Criminal Evidence Act 1984?

A Yes, unless it is made impracticable by her escaping arrest before the information could be given.

B No, IQBAL would only have to inform PERRY of the fact that she was under arrest.

C No, s. 28 applies to police officers only.

D Yes, unless it is impracticable due to her condition or behaviour.

Question 4.19

POINTER entered an off-licence with another man and they stood near the wine display. The two left without buying anything. However, the owner, STROUD, noticed that three bottles of wine were missing. STROUD checked the closed circuit television (CCTV), which showed POINTER and the other man removing the bottles of wine, but they had their backs to the camera and it was unclear which of the two had actually taken the wine. STROUD had placed the bottles on display before the men had entered the shop and no other customers had been in since that time, and the bottles were now missing. STROUD saw POINTER alone in the street the next day, he was just around the corner from the local police station at the time he saw him.

Does STROUD have a power to arrest POINTER for theft in these circumstances?

A No, POINTER was not actually in the act of committing an indictable offence.

B No, as it is reasonably practical for a police officer to make the arrest if necessary.

C Yes, as an indictable offence had been committed and STROUD has reasonable grounds for suspecting that POINTER is guilty.

D Yes, as an indictable offence had been committed and STROUD has reasonable grounds to believe that POINTER is guilty.

Question 4.20

Section 24 of the Police and Criminal Evidence Act 1984 (as inserted by s. 110 of the Serious Organised Crime and Police Act 2005) describes circumstances in which a constable may arrest a person where it is necessary to do so.

In which of the following circumstances might it be necessary for a constable to arrest a person who has provided his or her name?

A Where the constable has reasonable grounds for suspecting that the person has not given his or her real name.

B Where the constable knows that the person has not given his or her real name.

C Where the constable has reasonable grounds for believing that the person has not given his or her real name.

D Where the constable has reasonable grounds for doubting that the person has given his or her real name.

Question 4.21

Section 16(2A) of the Police and Criminal Evidence Act 1984 grants certain powers to an 'authorised person' in respect of warrants to enter and search premises.

Which of the following statements is correct in relation to the powers granted to an authorised person under s. 16(2A) above, when executing a search warrant?

A An authorised person may enter premises and seize property, but only when accompanied and supervised by a constable.

B An authorised person may enter premises and seize property under their own authorisation, without being accompanied by a constable.

C An authorised person must enter premises with a constable, but may seize property under their own authorisation.

D An authorised person must enter premises with a constable and may only assist with identifying property; they have no authority to seize it.

Question 4.22

Detective Constables COPE and FRIEDEL received information from NEWMAN, a security guard at a private flying club based in a small airport, who suspected the importation of drugs was taking place. NEWMAN stated that every Saturday morning, a vehicle attended the club and met a light aircraft and people loaded packages into the car. They tasked NEWMAN to keep an eye out and one Saturday, NEWMAN called them, reporting the car was at the airport. On their arrival, they saw WILLARD standing near the suspected car.

What powers, if any, did the officers have to search WILLARD or the car, in these circumstances, utilising powers under s. 24B of the Aviation Security Act 1982?

A None, they were not in uniform.

B None, the power relates to searching aircraft only.

C They may search WILLARD and the vehicle.

D None, this Act relates to commercial airports, not private ones.

Question 4.23

Constable AHMED has arrested GRANT for an offence of burglary. Constable AHMED has been advised to seek permission from the duty inspector to search GRANT's home address, under s. 18 of the Police and Criminal Evidence Act 1984.

In relation to where Constable AHMED may search, and what he may search for, which of the following statements is correct?

A Premises occupied or controlled by GRANT, for evidence related to the offence for which he is in custody, or another similar indictable offence.
B Premises suspected to be occupied or controlled by GRANT, for evidence related to the offence he is in custody for, or other similar indictable offences.
C Premises occupied or controlled by GRANT, for evidence related to the offence for which he is in custody only.
D Premises occupied or controlled by GRANT, for evidence related to the offence for which he is in custody, or any other indictable offence.

Question 4.24

Constable WILSON attended a burglary in the early hours of the morning. A witness, COLE, had seen a man breaking into a shop and removing two video recorders. COLE saw the man enter a house next to the shop. A short while later COLE saw the same man emerge empty handed and walk up the street. Constable WILSON made a search of the area and arrested GREEN, who matched the description given, nearby within minutes.

Constable WILSON considered searching the house GREEN had been seen entering. What authority would she have to do so in these circumstances?
A She has no authority to search immediately and would have to seek permission under s. 18 of the Police and Criminal Evidence Act 1984.
B She would have authority to search any premises which GREEN was in at any time prior to his arrest under s. 32 of the Police and Criminal Evidence Act 1984.
C She would have authority to search any premises which GREEN was in immediately prior to his arrest under s. 32 of the Police and Criminal Evidence Act 1984.
D She would have authority to search any premises occupied or controlled by GREEN and which he was in immediately prior to his arrest under s. 32 of the Police and Criminal Evidence Act 1984.

Question 4.25

Detective Constable ULHAQ has been called to a house fire and is the first officer on scene; he is not in uniform. He is unsure if there are persons present in the building or not and is considering whether he has power to force entry, using s. 17 of the Police and Criminal Evidence Act 1984.

Which of the following is correct?

A The officer may enter immediately to save life and limb, whether he believes there are persons in there or not.

B The officer may enter immediately to save life and limb if he has reasonable cause to *suspect* there are persons in there.

C The officer may enter immediately to save life and limb if he has reasonable cause to *believe* there are persons in there.

D The officer may not enter using s. 17 as he is not in uniform.

Question 4.26

HUDSON was arrested by Constable BALL from the Stolen Vehicle Squad, following the execution of a warrant at HUDSON's garage, where several stolen vehicles were found. Constable BALL received intelligence that HUDSON had another vehicle, which was parked outside his house. Constable BALL suspected that this vehicle might also be stolen.

In relation to searching and seizing the vehicle or its contents under ss. 18 and 19 of the Police and Criminal Evidence Act 1984, what powers would be available to Constable BALL?

A The vehicle is 'premises', which cannot be seized; the officer may search it and seize any contents obtained as a consequence of the commission of an offence.

B The vehicle is not 'premises' and may not be searched under s. 18; the officer would have to use powers available under s. 1 of the Act.

C The vehicle may be searched and seized if it is suspected it was obtained as a consequence of the commission of an offence, or for intelligence purposes.

D The vehicle and its contents may be searched and seized if it is suspected they were obtained as a consequence of the commission of an offence.

Question 4.27

Officers from the Fraud Squad were investigating an insurance company owned by MELROSE. The officers attended the company offices to execute a search warrant, to recover documentary evidence relating to offences. MELROSE was arrested at the premises and taken to the police station. Officers searching the premises recovered a substantial amount of paperwork, but could not be certain at that time whether all the documents related to offences. Because of the amount of time it would take to go through the documents at the premises, the officers conveyed as much paperwork as possible to their police station, where they began sifting through it. During this process, it became apparent that some of the documents were of no evidential value, and that other documents consisted of letters from the company solicitor.

Have the officers acted unlawfully, in relation to the recovery of the documents?

A Yes, in relation to the material which was the subject of legal privilege only.

B Yes, in relation to all material which was not evidence of an offence.

C No, provided the material not needed is returned as soon as reasonably practical.

D No, provided the material not needed is returned immediately.

ANSWERS

Answer 4.1

Answer **C** — Under s. 107(4), an officer of any rank may perform the functions of a custody officer at a designated police station if a custody officer is not readily available to perform them. However, the case of *Vince* v *Chief Constable of Dorset Police* [1993] 1 WLR 415, made it clear that this should only be an exception.

Custody officers should be appointed, and, according to s. 107(3), will be of at least the rank of sergeant.

There is nothing in s. 107(4) stating that a person performing the function in these circumstances must be authorised. There is also no requirement for the person to be temporarily promoted (which is why answers A, B and D are incorrect).

General Police Duties, para. 4.4.2

Answer 4.2

Answer **C** — Under s. 2 of the Act, a disorder penalty notice may be issued to a person who is 10 years or over, where there is reason to believe the person has committed a s. 1 offence (previously the age limit was 16 years).

The offences and penalties are listed in Parts I and II of the Penalties for Disorderly Behaviour (Amount of Penalty) Order 2002 (SI 2002/1837) (as amended). Under Part I, the list of offences includes behaviour likely to cause harassment, alarm or distress contrary to s. 5 of the Public Order Act 1986 and some licensing offences. The penalty for these offences is £80 for people aged 16 and over and £40 for people under 16.

Part II includes offences such as being drunk in a highway contrary to s. 12 of the Licensing Act 1872 and depositing litter. The penalty for offences covered by Part II is £50 for people aged 16 years and over and £30 for people under 16. Since BRIDGE is 16 years of age and has committed an offence listed in Part II, the fine would amount to £50. Answers A, B and D are therefore incorrect.

General Police Duties, para. 4.4.3

Answer 4.3

Answer **B** — Under s. 2 of the Act, a disorder penalty notice may be issued to a person who is 10 years or over, where there is reason to believe the person has committed a s. 1 offence (previously the age limit was 16 years). Answer D is therefore incorrect.

Where the recipient of a notice is under 16, the relevant chief officer of police must notify such parent or guardian as he/she sees fit (see Penalties for Disorderly Behaviour (Amendment of Minimum Age) Order 2004 (SI 2004/3166)). Where a parent or guardian of a young penalty recipient is notified in this way, then they are liable to pay the penalty under the original notice (see art. 5). Answers A and C are therefore incorrect.

General Police Duties, paras 4.4.3, 4.4.3.2

Answer 4.4

Answer **C** — All of the scenarios in the questions are listed in the table of guidance issued by the Home Office. The essential difference between answer C and the others is that the officer did not at any time suspect the people of offences, nor were they being asked to account for their presence in the area. In scenarios A, B and D, the officer would have to record the fact that the people had been 'stopped' and a form submitted. A form would not be required for answer C. Since the question required you to identify when a form would not be required, answers A, B and D are incorrect.

General Police Duties, para. 4.4.4

Answer 4.5

Answer **C** — Clearly the officer did not have the grounds to conduct a search in these circumstances; however, such a search would have been lawful prior to the changes in the Codes of Practice. Code A, para. 1.5 now specifically provides that where an officer has no power to search a person under s. 1 of the Police and Criminal Evidence Act 1984, he or she must not do so, even where the person being searched consents. Answers B and D are incorrect, regardless of whether the officer submits a search form. Section 1 makes no mention of an age limit in relation to searches. The search was unlawful because of the above reasons, and not the person's age, making answer A incorrect.

General Police Duties, para. 4.4.4.1

Answer 4.6

Answer **B** — In order to conduct a search under s. 1 of the Police and Criminal Evidence Act 1984, a constable must have 'reasonable grounds for suspecting' that he or she will find the required articles as a result of the search. Suspicion has been described as 'a state of conjecture or surmise when proof is lacking' (*Shaabin Bin Hussein* v *Chong Fook Kam* [1970] AC 492). That suspicion can be based on any evidence, even if the evidence would be inadmissible in a trial (e.g. because of hearsay). Also, the courts have accepted that reasonable grounds for suspicion can arise from anonymous information, (see *O'Hara* v *Chief Constable of the Royal Ulster Constabulary* [1997] 1 All ER 129). Answers A and C are therefore incorrect.

It must be shown that the grounds on which the officer acted would be enough to give rise to that suspicion in a 'reasonable person' (*Nakkuda Ali* v *Jayaratne* [1951] AC 66). This means that answer B is correct, and answer D is incorrect.

General Police Duties, para. 4.4.4.3

Answer 4.7

Answer **D** — Powers to stop, search and seize are essentially intended for use in public places, meaning places to which the public, or any section of the public, has access, on payment or otherwise, as of right or by virtue of express or implied permission, or any other place to which people have ready access at the time when it is proposed to exercise the powers but which is not a dwelling (s. 1(1)(a) and (b) of the Police and Criminal Evidence Act 1984).

However, although powers to stop and search may not be exercised in a dwelling house, they may be exercised in a garden or yard of a house (s. 1(4) and (5)), provided it is not the person's own garden, and the officer has reasonable grounds for believing that he or she does not have permission (express or implied) to be there.

Therefore, although the search could not take place under s. 1(1)(b), the officer may use powers available under s. 1(4) and (5) as JACKSON was not in his own garden. For these reasons answers A, B and C are incorrect.

General Police Duties, para. 4.4.4.5

Answer 4.8

Answer **C** — Section 3(1) of the Police and Criminal Evidence Act 1984 states that a written record of a search under s. 1 need not be made at the time, when it is not practicable to do so. However, Code A, para. 3 of the Codes of Practice narrows this exception to those occasions where it is wholly impracticable to make the record. Answer C reflects the wording of Code A; therefore answers A and D are incorrect.

This exception will be met only if there is virtually no chance of the officer being able to make the written record (for example, the officer has been called to an emergency immediately after the search). Since an exception does exist, answer B is incorrect.

General Police Duties, para. 4.4.4.8

Answer 4.9

Answer **C** — Section 3 of the Police and Criminal Evidence Act 1984 states:

(6) The record of a search of a person or a vehicle —
  (a) shall state —
    (i)   the object of the search;
    (ii) the grounds for making it;
    (iii) the date and time when it was made;
    (iv) the place where it was made;
    (v)   whether anything, and if so what, was found;
    (vi) whether any, and if so what, injury to a person or damage to property appears to the constable to have resulted from the search; and
  (b) shall identify the constable making it.

This is further explained in The Police and Criminal Evidence Act 1984 Codes of Practice Code A at Note 15:

Where a stop and search is conducted by more than one officer the identity of all the officers engaged in the search must be recorded on the record. Nothing prevents an officer who is present but not directly involved in searching from completing the record during the course of the encounter.

Both officers must be identified on the record; answer A, B and D are therefore incorrect.

General Police Duties, para. 4.4.4.8

Answer 4.10

Answer **D** — Section 2(6) of the Police and Criminal Evidence Act 1984 states that 'on completing the search of an unattended vehicle, or anything in or on such a vehicle, a constable shall leave a notice'. Therefore, even though the spare tyre was not actually in the vehicle, a notice must be left and answer B is incorrect.

There may be occasions when officers have to force entry into a vehicle in order to search it. On such an occasion, the officer must, if practicable, leave the vehicle secure (Code A, para. 4.10). However, where the vehicle has not been damaged during the search, s. 2(7) states that 'the constable shall leave the notice inside the vehicle unless it is not reasonably practicable to do so without damaging the vehicle'. Answer C is therefore incorrect.

There is no obligation on the officer to send a notice to the registered owner's address, and answer A is incorrect.

General Police Duties, para. 4.4.4.9

Answer 4.11

Answer **A** — Section 4 of the Police and Criminal Evidence Act 1984 states that a road check may be authorised only where the officer has reasonable grounds for believing that the offence committed is an indictable offence. Therefore, as the offence is one of shoplifting, which is indictable, a road check can be authorised. Generally speaking an officer of at least the rank of superintendent must authorise a road check.

In urgent cases the authorising officer may be any rank below the rank of superintendent, and in this case Constable ROBERTS could have authorised the check provided a written record is made and a superintendent informed as soon as possible; answers B, C and D are therefore incorrect as the officer could have authorised the road check himself.

General Police Duties, para. 4.4.4.10

Answer 4.12

Answer **D** — Section 4 of the Police and Criminal Evidence Act 1984 states that a road check may be authorised only where the officer has reasonable grounds for believing that the offence committed is an indictable offence. Generally the authorisation will be given by a superintendent, however, an officer of any rank may authorise the road check in urgent circumstances.

Section 4(11)(a) states that the authorising officer must specify a period, not exceeding 7 days, during which the road check may continue. This period may be either continuous, or conducted at specified times during that period. If it appears to a superintendent that the road check ought to continue beyond the initial seven days, he/she may authorise a further period of 7 days during which it may continue. There is no limit as to how many road checks may be authorised, provided each period does not exceed 7 days. Answers A, B and C are therefore incorrect.

General Police Duties, para. 4.4.4.11

Answer 4.13

Answer **A** — Under s. 4(15) of the Police and Criminal Evidence Act 1984, where a vehicle has been stopped during a road check, the person in charge of the vehicle is entitled to a written statement of the purpose of the check, if he or she applies no later than 12 months from the time the vehicle was stopped. Consequently, answers B, C and D are incorrect.

General Police Duties, para. 4.4.4.11

Answer 4.14

Answer **C** — Under s. 60 of the Criminal Justice and Public Order Act 1994, if an inspector reasonably believes that incidents of serious violence may take place in his or her area, or that people are carrying dangerous instruments or offensive weapons, he or she may give an authorisation to stop any pedestrian and search him or her for offensive weapons or dangerous instruments.

The power used to be restricted to superintendents, but may now be exercised by an inspector (which is why answer D is incorrect). The authorisation may be given either for incidents of serious violence *or* to search for weapons (making answer A incorrect). The power is to search any pedestrian, and is not restricted to those who may be carrying weapons (which is why answer B is incorrect).

General Police Duties, para. 4.4.4.12

Answer 4.15

Answer **C** — Under s. 60AA(1) of the Criminal Justice and Public Order Act 1994, where an authorisation under s. 60 is in force, a constable in uniform may require any person to remove any item which the constable reasonably believes that person is wearing wholly or mainly for the purpose of concealing his or her identity. The power is not absolute, as the constable has reasonably to believe that the person is wearing the item to conceal his or her identity (therefore answer B is incorrect). There is no need, however, for the constable reasonably to believe that the person is carrying a dangerous instrument or an offensive weapon, or that the person is likely to be involved in violence, in order to exercise the power under s. 60AA(1). Those matters would have been considered before the authorisation was granted under s. 60. Answers A and D are therefore incorrect.

General Police Duties, para. 4.4.4.14

Answer 4.16

Answer **D** — Under s. 44 of the Terrorism Act 2000, an assistant chief constable/ commander may authorise stop and search operations within his or her area, in or- der to prevent acts of terrorism. When an authorisation has been given, a police constable in uniform may stop and search vehicles and their passengers, or pedes- trians, for articles in connection with terrorism. These same powers are also given to police community support officers (PCSOs) by virtue of sch. 4, para. 15(2) to the Police Reform Act 2002 (answer C is incorrect). However, in order to exercise these powers, PCSOs must be in the company and under the supervision of a constable. Answers A and B are incorrect for this reason.

General Police Duties, para. 4.4.5.3

Answer 4.17

Answer **B** — Under s. 28(1) of the Police and Criminal Evidence Act 1984, an arrest is not lawful unless the person arrested is informed that he or she is under arrest as soon as is practicable after his or her arrest. Under s. 28(3), an arrest will not be lawful unless the person arrested is informed of the ground for the arrest at the time of, or as soon as is practicable after, the arrest. As a result of the changes made by the Serious Organised Crime and Police Act 2005, the Codes of Practice have been amended to require an arrested person to be informed of the detail of why the officer believes the arrest is necessary. This information need not be given in its entirety at the time of arrest, but must be given (and recorded) as soon as practicable afterwards. Therefore, an arrested person must be informed of all three of the above things.

Section 28(2) and (4) provide that the person must be told that they are under arrest and informed of the grounds regardless of whether the facts of the arrest or the grounds are obvious. Answers A and C are therefore incorrect.

In *Christie* v *Leachinsky* [1947] AC 573, it was held that the arresting officer must clearly indicate to the person the fact that he/she is being arrested. This requirement might be met by using a colloquialism, provided that the person is familiar with it and understands the meaning, (e.g. 'you're locked up' or 'you're nicked'). Answer D is therefore incorrect.

Summing up this particular question, because of *Christie* v *Leachinsky* above, the suspect has been informed of the reason for the arrest. However, the officer will still need to inform them of the grounds for the arrest, and why the arrest was necessary, as soon as reasonably practicable.

General Police Duties, para. 4.4.6.1

Answer 4.18

Answer **A** — Section 28(1) of the Police and Criminal Evidence Act 1984 states that subject to subs. (5) below, where a person is arrested, otherwise than by being informed that he or she is under arrest, the arrest is not lawful unless the person arrested is informed that he or she is under arrest as soon as is practicable after his or her arrest.

Under s. 28(3), subject to subs. (5) below, no arrest is lawful unless the person arrested is informed of the ground for the arrest at the time of, or as soon as is practicable after, the arrest. This subsection applies to arrests made by members of the public as well as police officers; therefore, answers B and C are incorrect.

Section 28(5) states that nothing in this section is to be taken to require a person to be informed —

(a) that he or she is under arrest; or

(b) of the ground for the arrest,

if it was not reasonably practicable for him or her to be so informed by reason of his or her having escaped from arrest before the information could be given.

Answer D is therefore incorrect.

General Police Duties, para. 4.4.6.1

Answer 4.19

Answer **B** — Under s. 24A of the Police and Criminal Evidence Act 1984 (as inserted by s. 110 of the Serious Organised Crime and Police Act 2005), certain powers of arrest are provided for any person. Section 24A states:

(1) A person other than a constable may arrest without a warrant —
   (a) anyone who is in the act of committing an indictable offence;
   (b) anyone whom he has reasonable grounds for suspecting to be committing an indictable offence.

(2) Where an indictable offence has been committed, a person other than a constable may arrest without a warrant —
   (a) anyone who is guilty of the offence;
   (b) anyone whom he has reasonable grounds for suspecting to be guilty of it.

(3) But the power of summary arrest conferred by subsection (1) or (2) is exercisable only if —
   (a) the person making the arrest has reasonable grounds for believing that for any of the reasons mentioned in subsection (4) it is necessary to arrest the person in question; and

(b) it appears to the person making the arrest that it is not reasonably practicable for a constable to make it instead.
(4) The reasons are to prevent the person in question —
(a) causing physical injury to himself or any other person;
(b) suffering physical injury;
(c) causing loss of or damage to property; or
(d) making off before a constable can assume responsibility for him.

The power is not limited to the time an indictable offence is actually being committed; answer A is therefore incorrect, but extends to where an indictable offence has been committed and there are reasonable grounds to 'suspect' (not the higher test of 'believe') a person of that offence; answer D is therefore incorrect.

However note the element in s. 24A(3)(b) on the practicality of a constable making the arrest; being just round the corner from the police station it is unlikely that STROUD could say it was not reasonably practical, this means it would be wrong for him to use his powers under s. 24A; answer C is therefore incorrect.

However were an officer to be called to arrest, they would have to ensure that the 'necessity test' was passed (as outlined in s. 24(5) of the 1988 Act) prior to them making such an arrest.

General Police Duties, paras 4.4.7.1, 4.4.7.5

Answer 4.20

Answer **D** — Under s. 24(5) of the Police and Criminal Evidence Act 1984 (as inserted by s. 110 of the Serious Organised Crime and Police Act 2005), the officer must have 'reasonable grounds for doubting' that the name furnished by the relevant person is his or her real name. This would appear to be a very wide expression, and is not limited to suspecting that the name given is false, and therefore answers A, B and C are incorrect. However the officer is required to show that he/she has reasonable grounds for believing that the details given are in doubt. These must be objective grounds and not just simple opinion on the part of the officer.

General Police Duties, para. 4.4.7.4

Answer 4.21

Answer **A** — Section 16(2A) of the Police and Criminal Evidence Act 1984 states that an authorised person has the same powers as a constable in respect of:

(a) executing a search warrant, and

(b) the seizure of anything to which the warrant relates.

Answer D is therefore incorrect.

However, s. 16(2B) states that an authorised person may only exercise the above powers when in the company, and under the supervision, of a constable. Answers B and C are therefore incorrect.

General Police Duties, para. 4.4.12.2

Answer 4.22

Answer **C** — Section 12 of the Police and Justice Act 2006 inserts a new s. 24B into Part 3 of the Aviation Security Act 1982 (policing of airports or aerodromes). The power enables a police constable to stop and search, without warrant, any person, vehicle or aircraft in any area of an airport (excluding a dwelling house). Answer B is therefore incorrect.

The search may be conducted if the constable has reasonable grounds to suspect that he or she will find stolen or prohibited articles. There is no mention of the constable having to be in uniform; therefore, answer A is incorrect.

The term aerodrome, as defined by s. 38(1) of the 1982 Act, is used rather than airport, as it has wider meaning and covers major airports as well as airfields used only by private flying clubs. Answer D is incorrect.

General Police Duties, para. 4.4.4.13

Answer 4.23

Answer **A** — Under s. 18 of the Police and Criminal Evidence Act 1984, a constable may enter and search any premises occupied or controlled by a person who is under arrest for an indictable offence, if there are reasonable grounds to suspect that there are items on the premises that relate to that offence, *or* to some other indictable offence which is connected with or similar to that offence.

Answer B is incorrect because the premises must be controlled or occupied by the person; it is not enough that the officer suspects or believes that they are.

Answers C and D are incorrect as the officer may search for evidence relating to either the offence for which the suspect has been arrested, or those which are similar.

General Police Duties, para. 4.4.13.1

Answer 4.24

Answer **C** — Authority is provided under s. 32(2)(b) of the Police and Criminal Evidence Act 1984 for a constable to enter and search any premises in which the person was when arrested or immediately before being arrested, if the constable has reasonable grounds for believing that there is evidence on the premises in consequence of the commission of an offence. As COLE had been in the premises immediately before his arrest, the officer could use s. 32; answer A is therefore incorrect. The search may be conducted for the purpose of finding evidence relating to the offence for which the person was arrested. As the defendant in the scenario was arrested within minutes of leaving the premises, this would be classed as 'immediately' (although the term 'immediately' is open to interpretation).

Answer B is incorrect as the search relates to premises the person was in immediately prior to arrest.

The Divisional Court has held that where a person had not been in the relevant premises (where he did not live) for over 2 hours preceding his arrest, the power under s. 32 may not be used (see *Hewitson* v *Chief Constable of Dorset Police* [2003] EWHC 3296).

Answer D is incorrect, as s. 32 does not state that the premises must be one which is occupied or controlled by the person arrested. (This requirement may be found in s. 18 of the Act.)

General Police Duties, para. 4.4.13.2

Answer 4.25

Answer **A** — Section 17 of the Police and Criminal Evidence Act 1984 provides authority for a constable to enter premises to arrest a person in several circumstances.

Under s. 17(1)(e), a constable may enter premises for the purposes of saving life or limb, or preventing serious damage to property. When entering premises, including dwellings, to search for a person, the constable must have reasonable grounds for believing that the person he is seeking is on the premises (s. 17(2)(a)). This expression is narrower than 'reasonable cause to suspect' and you must be able to justify that belief before using this power (although see *Kynaston* v *DPP* (1988) 87 Cr App R 200, where the court accepted reasonable cause to suspect). Note however that 'having reasonable cause to believe' does not extend to the power to enter to save life and limb; answers B and C are therefore incorrect.

Some parts of s. 17 require the officer to be in uniform; these relate to arresting a person for offences specified in s. 17, but again do not extend to entry to save life and limb; answer D is therefore incorrect.

No doubt persons trapped in buildings that are on fire will thank the legislator for such a common sense approach to powers of entry.

General Police Duties, para. 4.4.13.5

Answer 4.26

Answer **D** — Under s. 18 of the Police and Criminal Evidence Act 1984, a constable may enter and search any premises occupied or controlled by a person who is under arrest for an indictable offence if there are reasonable grounds to suspect that there are items on the premises that relate to that offence, or to some other indictable offence which is connected with or similar to that offence. For the purposes of the section, a vehicle is 'premises'. (Therefore, answer B is incorrect.)

Under s. 19 of the 1984 Act, an officer may seize anything which is on premises, if he or she has reasonable grounds for believing that it has been obtained in consequence of the commission of an offence and that it is necessary to do so in order to prevent it from being concealed, lost, damaged, altered or destroyed. Section 19 does not allow the seizure of property for intelligence purposes, and answer C is incorrect for this reason.

Where the 'premises' searched is a vehicle (see s. 23), the vehicle can itself be seized (*Cowan* v *Commissioner of Police for the Metropolis* [2000] 1 WLR 254) (making answer A incorrect).

This power has now also been added to the PACE Codes of Practice, Code B, Note 7B.

General Police Duties, para. 4.4.15.1

Answer 4.27

Answer **C** — Part 2 of the Criminal Justice and Police Act 2001 has provided a power allowing officers searching premises to seize documents which would fall outside the scope of the warrant, and sift through them at a different location.

One of the purposes of the legislation is to balance the competing needs of the criminal justice system with the owner's rights, but officers would have to show it was essential to seize documents. Other factors may be taken into consideration, such as whether or not it would be reasonably practical to sift through the evidence on the premises, which could include the length of time it would take to do so. Answer B is therefore incorrect.

The 2001 Act does not provide a power actually to seize material subject of legal privilege; however, it does allow for such material to be taken, provided the conditions above apply (answer A is incorrect). Where documents have been seized, which are subject of legal privilege or are outside the scope of the warrant, they must be returned as soon as is practical (answer D is incorrect).

General Police Duties, para. 4.4.17.1

Harassment, Hostility and Anti-social Behaviour

STUDY PREPARATION

The focus on community safety within the whole criminal justice process has been sharply defined since the Crime and Disorder Act 1998 and looks set to continue.

As a result, a range of statutory measures has been brought in, giving the police (and other agencies) duties in relation to community safety and powers to help them discharge those duties. Other measures to protect the community from fear, intimidation and anti-social behaviour already existed before the Crime and Disorder Act 1998. The Anti-social Behaviour Act 2003 placed further pressure on the police and statutory partners to take positive action and work together to deal with harassment and intimidation.

Taken together, these measures feature highly in regional and local policing strategies to tackle crime and the fear of crime. This makes them important, not only to police officers but also, as a result, to those training and examining police law.

QUESTIONS

Question 5.1

GULLICK has been found guilty of an offence, which was racially aggravated. The court will shortly impose sentence upon him.

 With regard to the sentence the court can pass, which of the following statements is correct in relation to taking the aggravating feature into account?

A It must be taken into account, and the court must openly state it did so.

B It can be taken into account, and the court must openly state if it did so.
C It must be taken into account, but the court does not have to state it did so.
D It can be taken into account, but the court does not have to state if it did so.

Question 5.2

Section 28 of the Crime and Disorder Act 1998 defines racial aggravation and the time during which the hostility must be shown towards the victim.

At what time during the commission of the offence should the racial hostility be shown?
A It must be shown during the offence.
B It can be shown during the offence, immediately before or sometime after.
C It can be shown during the offence or immediately before.
D It can be shown during the offence, immediately before or immediately after.

Question 5.3

HANSEN is white and comes from a strong Catholic family; however HANSEN has become a Muslim. He was assaulted by his brother, receiving injuries amounting to actual bodily harm, because of the upset caused to his parents. HANSEN's brother was charged with the offence and in court, the prosecution alleged that the assault was motivated by hostility towards HANSEN on religious grounds. He denied this, stating that he had assaulted HANSEN because he had turned away from Catholicism, not because he had become a Muslim.

Would HANSEN's brother's claim amount to a defence in these circumstances?
A No, the assault was based on HANSEN's lack of a religious belief.
B Yes, the assault was not based on HANSEN's religious belief, but his lack of belief in Catholicism.
C Yes, Muslims have been held not to be a religious group.
D Yes, the assault was not based on HANSEN's race or colour.

Question 5.4

MEREDITH is a racist. One day he was at home with several friends who share his beliefs, when COWANS, who is black, knocked on his door collecting money on behalf of charity. MEREDITH invited COWANS into his house on the pretext of looking for money. When they were in the living room of the house, MEREDITH began racially abusing COWANS in front of his friends. His intention all along was to stir up racial hatred. When COWANS eventually left the house, he contacted the police to report the incident.

Considering offences under s. 18 of the Public Order Act 1986 (using words or behaviour or displaying written material stirring up racial hatred), does the fact that the incident took place in a dwelling affect whether or not the police can take any action?

A No, the offence may be committed anywhere.

B Yes, the offence may only be committed in a public place.

C No, the offence may be committed in a public or private place.

D Yes, the offence may not be committed when both persons are in a dwelling.

Question 5.5

HAWKINS was walking through a city centre after a lunchtime drink one afternoon. At the time, a religious Hindu festival was taking place, involving people in traditional dress, who were walking to a place of worship nearby. HAWKINS began shouting, 'If these people want to live in our country, they should adopt a proper religion' and 'Look at those stupid costumes they've got on, they're ridiculous'. HAWKINS' words were heard by pedestrians standing nearby, but not by the people in the procession. HAWKINS' intention was to insult the people taking part in the procession, because of their religious beliefs, and to stir up hatred amongst passers-by who did not share the same beliefs.

Would HAWKINS' behaviour amount to an offence under s. 29B of the Public Order Act 1986, (use of words or behaviour intending to stir up religious hatred)?

A Yes, as HAWKINS' intention was to stir up religious hatred.

B Yes, whether or not HAWKINS intended stirring up religious hatred.

C No, as HAWKINS' words were not threatening.

D No, as the people in the procession did not hear the comments.

Question 5.6

KNIGHT has been charged with an offence under the Protection from Harassment Act 1997 and is due to appear in court.

What must the prosecution show in relation to KNIGHT's state of mind (*mens rea*) in order to prove the offence of harassment?

A That KNIGHT knew the behaviour amounted to harassment.

B That KNIGHT ought to have known the behaviour amounted to harassment.

C That KNIGHT suspected or believed the behaviour amounted to harassment.

D That KNIGHT knew or ought to have known the behaviour amounted to harassment.

Question 5.7

BARON has sent two threatening letters to his probation officer. However, the second letter was not received until 4.5 months after the first.

Could BARON be guilty of harassment contrary to ss. 1 and 2 of the Protection from Harassment Act 1997?

A No, as probation officers are unlikely to be distressed.

B No, owing to the length of time between the letters.

C Yes, but only if the probation officer is likely to be alarmed and distressed.

D Yes, but only if actual distress is caused to the probation officer.

Question 5.8

CRUTCHER and BOYCE are members of an animal rights extremist group and were targeting two companies, which CRUTCHER and BOYCE believed were suppliers to a third company, which tested its products on animals. Following a discussion between the two, CRUTCHER sent a threatening letter to the chief executive of one company and BOYCE sent a threatening email to the chief executive of the other. Their intention was to persuade both companies to stop supplying the third company with their products.

Given that the recipients are likely to be caused alarm and distress by the communications, would CRUTCHER and BOYCE's actions amount to a 'course of conduct' in respect of an offence under s. 1(1A) of the Protection from Harassment Act 1997?

A Yes, their conduct would be sufficient to amount to a 'course of conduct' in these circumstances.

B No, each person would have to send communications to at least two people.

C No, each person would have to send communications to at least two people from each company.

D No, because the communication they sent to each person was in a different form.

Question 5.9

STOCKWIN is infatuated with a female colleague from work; however, she has rejected his attempts to go out with her. STOCKWIN was upset and telephoned his colleague, threatening to burn her house down, but she was not concerned by his threats. A week later, STOCKWIN again telephoned his colleague and threatened to do the same thing and on this occasion, she *was* put in fear that he would carry out the threat and contacted the police.

Would STOCKWIN be guilty of an offence under s. 4 of the Protection from Harassment Act 1997 in these circumstances?

A Yes, as the work colleague was put in fear of violence on at least two occasions.

B No, as the work colleague was not put in fear of violence on at least two occasions.

C Yes, provided that it can be shown that violence was intended by STOCKWIN.

D Yes, provided that it can be shown that STOCKWIN actually knew that the work colleague was in fear of violence.

Question 5.10

HEDLEY is in police detention, waiting to attend the magistrates' court, after being charged with harassing a former partner, contrary to s. 2 of the Protection from Harassment Act 1997. The officer in the case has asked the Crown Prosecution Service to apply for a restraining order, because of HEDLEY's history of domestic violence against the partner.

In relation to this request, which of the following statements is correct?

A The request cannot be granted; HEDLEY has not been convicted of an offence contrary to s. 4 of the Act.

B The request cannot be granted; an application for a restraining order may only be made in the crown court or a civil court.

C The request may be granted; an application for a restraining order may be heard in the magistrates' court following conviction for this offence.

D The request cannot be granted; an application for a restraining order may only be made in the High Court or a civil court.

Question 5.11

Members of a gang were responsible for serious anti-social behaviour on an estate. The behaviour included throwing stones and rubbish and spitting from balconies, causing damage to windows, doors and motor vehicles, starting fires, defacing walls with graffiti, shouting and screaming, playing loud music, obstructing, abusing and threatening residents, and smoking drugs. The police and the council obtained anti-social behaviour orders (ASBOs) against 7 members of the gang aged 15, 16 and 18. Following the magistrates' court hearing, the police and the council wish to publish a leaflet entitled 'Keeping Crime off the Streets' in which they hope to identify (by name, age and photograph) the gang members who are subject to the ASBOs and summarise what they have done and the restrictions that they are subject to.

Which of the following is correct?

A They can name the gang members, their ages and can publish their photographs.

B They can name the gang members and their ages but they can only publish the photographs of those aged at least 18 years.

C They can name the gang members, their ages but cannot publish photographs.

D They cannot advertise this way at all as this is a direct violation of the youths' rights under Art. 8 of the European Convention on Human Rights.

Question 5.12

STEPHENS, aged 19, was convicted by the magistrates' court for using threatening behaviour contrary to s. 5 of the Public Order Act 1986, towards an elderly resident living on an estate near his own home. He received a conditional discharge for the offence. Prior to issuing his sentence, the court heard that he had previously received both a reprimand and a final warning for the same offence, towards other residents in the area, while he was a youth. Although no application was made by the CPS, the magistrates took the decision to issue an anti-social behaviour order (ASBO) against STEPHENS, utilising the evidence provided during his hearing, preventing him from entering the housing estate where the offences took place.

In relation to the ASBO issued, has the court acted within its powers in these circumstances?

A No, the court should not have issued an ASBO of its own volition; it may only respond to an application by a relevant authority.

B No, but the actions of the court would have been permissible if STEPHENS had not been given a conditional discharge for the offence.

C No, the evidence heard during the prosecution's case should not have been re-used to support an ASBO.

D Yes, the court has acted properly in the circumstances, and the ASBO against STEPHENS will be lawful.

Question 5.13

BRYAN is about to be the subject of an anti-social behaviour order (ASBO), and the court is considering whether he should be subject to a curfew between 11.00 pm and 7.00 am as part of his ASBO.

Can a prohibition such as a curfew be placed as part of an ASBO?

A Yes, and the prohibition within the order has to endure for the life of the order.

B Yes, and the prohibition within the order can be set at less than the full life of the order in light of behavioural progress.

C No, ASBOs are prohibitory in their nature, they order people not to do certain things rather than to do certain things.

D No, curfews relate only to the release of short term prisoners.

Question 5.14

BRIGGS has been charged with 10 offences of theft (shoplifting), having been arrested following a series of separate complaints from various shops in a high street. BRIGGS was identified on CCTV for each offence. If BRIGGS is convicted of the offences, the Crown Prosecution Service is considering applying to the magistrates' court for an anti-social behaviour order (ASBO), to prevent BRIGGS from entering the shopping area again.

Could the magistrates' court issue an ASBO if BRIGGS is convicted of these offences?

A No, a person would need to be caused harassment, alarm or distress, which would not occur during shoplifting offences.

B Yes, shoplifting would automatically amount to anti-social behaviour.

C Yes, in some circumstances, shoplifting would amount to anti-social behaviour.

D No, ASBOs are intended to focus on a person's *behaviour*, which does not include instances of theft.

Question 5.15

An anti-social behaviour order (ASBO) can be passed in respect of a person who has acted in an anti-social manner.

Against whom can that 'anti-social manner' be directed for an ASBO to be relevant?

A Any person likely to suffer harassment, alarm or distress from that person.

B At least 2 people likely to suffer harassment, alarm or distress from that person.

C Any person, not of the same household, likely to suffer harassment, alarm or distress from that person.

D At least 2 people, not of the same household, likely to suffer harassment, alarm or distress from that person.

Question 5.16

The crown court has made an exclusion order against HENDERSON for anti-social behaviour. The order excludes him from the city centre after 10 pm.

What is the maximum period this exclusion order can run for?

A 6 months.

B 1 year.

C 18 months.

D 2 years.

Question 5.17

REGAN is the subject of an exclusion order under s. 205 of the Criminal Justice Act 2003, preventing her from entering a shopping centre on weekends, due to previous anti-social behaviour. Constable MALIK has been called to the centre by security staff who are aware of the order and have spotted REGAN in the centre on CCTV.

What potential powers are available to Constable MALIK, to deal with REGAN in these circumstances?

A He may take REGAN's details and serve a written notice on her that she was in breach of the order. They may send a copy of the notice to the court.

B He may direct REGAN to leave the premises verbally; if she fails, she may be prosecuted.

C He may arrest her for breach of the exclusion order.

D He may summons her for breach of the exclusion order, unless an arrest is necessary.

Question 5.18

Section 1(7) of the Crime and Disorder Act 1998 gives guidance as to the duration of an anti-social behaviour order (ASBO).

Which of the following statements is correct, in relation to the duration of an ASBO?

A An ASBO has a minimum period of 2 years' duration.

B An ASBO has a minimum period of 3 years' duration.

C An ASBO has a maximum period of 2 years' duration.

D An ASBO has a maximum period of 3 years' duration.

Question 5.19

WATTS was responsible for a house, which was in an extremely poor state and likely to fall down. The house was on a highway that was used by several people, including those going to a nearby school. Its ruinous state was endangering people using the highway, and a few have to cross the road every day to avoid it. WATTS has continually refused to do anything about the house.

Could WATTS be guilty of public nuisance?

A No, as the offence does not include omissions, only actions by the accused.

B No, as not everyone is affected, only a few had to cross the road.

C Yes, provided WATTS intended to cause a public nuisance.

D Yes, as people's material rights have been interfered with.

Question 5.20

MULLER owns a company which organises large firework displays, for which he is authorised. He has several employees working for him, who help in his warehouse, accepting delivery of fireworks from the manufacturer and loading them into his van prior to displays. One such person is PLATT, who is 17 years of age. PLATT does not accompany MULLER to the displays; however, on a daily basis in the warehouse he handles large fireworks, which are specified as category 4 fireworks under the Fireworks Regulations 2003.

Does PLATT commit an offence under reg. 5(1) of the Fireworks Regulations 2004, by being in possession of fireworks that fall under category 4?

A Yes, as he is under the age of 18.

B No, as he is handling the fireworks as part of his work.

C Yes, regardless of his age.

D No, as he is not in a public place.

Question 5.21

Regulation 7 of the Fireworks Regulations 2004 (SI 2004/1836) prohibits the use of certain fireworks at night.

What are 'night hours' in relation to this prohibition?

A The period beginning at 11 pm and ending at 7 am the following day.

B The period beginning at 11 pm and ending at 7.30 am the following day.

C The period beginning at 11.30 pm and ending at 7 am the following day.

D The period beginning at 11.30 pm and ending at 7.30 am the following day.

Question 5.22

Regulation 7(2) of the Fireworks Regulations 2004 provides certain exemptions to the prohibition of the use of fireworks at night.

In which of the following cases will the person be exempt from using adult fireworks during night hours?

A WU who began using fireworks at 11.00 pm on the first day of the Chinese New Year and carried on until 12.30 am the following day.

B ANDREWS who is a professional firework company employee setting off fireworks at midnight at a local authority display.

C REELEY who is using fireworks at 12.15 am on 6 November.

D COYNE who is using fireworks at 1.30 am on 1 January.

Question 5.23

The Noise Act 1996 allows for the serving of warning notices in relation to 'excessive noise' emanating from one house which can be heard in another at night.

During what time is 'night'?

A 10.30 pm–6.30 am.

B 10.00 pm–6.00 am.

C 11.00 pm–7.00 am.

D 11.30 pm–7.30 am.

Question 5.24

Section 87(1) of the Environmental Protection Act 1990 creates an offence of depositing litter.

Which of the sentences below best describes where such an offence may take place?

A Any public place.

B Any place in the area of a local authority, in the open air.

C Any place in the open air.
D Any public place in the area of a local authority, in the open air.

Question 5.25

FISHER phones up the local radio station and says 'There's a bomb going off in 10 minutes'; however, no actual location is given. FISHER is doing this as a joke and did not mean the station to take the matter seriously.

Has FISHER committed an offence contrary to s. 51(2) of the Criminal Law Act 1977 (communicating false information)?
A Yes, as the words spoken are sufficient.
B Yes, even though a specific location was not given.
C No, because it was only a practical joke.
D No, as there was no specific location given.

Question 5.26

Section 85 of the Postal Services Act 2000 deals with sending obscene articles through the post. MARSHALL has sent some indecent pictures, which have accidentally been delivered to a 65-year-old woman, who is a devout Christian.

In deciding if the pictures are 'obscene', what factors will the court take into account?
A The fact that they were sent to an old lady.
B The fact that she found them obscene.
C The fact that a reasonable person may find them obscene.
D The fact that the old lady has Christian views.

Question 5.27

HEALD is infatuated with his female neighbour, and continually asks her out on dates. She is flattered and not at all threatened by this, but refuses to go out with him. HEALD then starts making indecent phone calls to her in an effort to 'turn her on'. He does not, however, intend his neighbour to be distressed by these calls. She is not threatened and finds it all mildly amusing.

Consider the offence outlined in s. 127 of the Communications Act 2003 of improper use of a public electronic communications network. Has HEALD committed this offence?

5. Harassment, Hostility and Anti-social Behaviour

A Yes, even though there is no intention to cause distress and distress is not caused to the person.

B Yes, even though there is no intention to cause distress and distress is not caused to the person and the officer could issue a Disorder Penalty Notice.

C No, there has to be an intention to cause alarm, harassment or distress.

D No, the receiver of the calls has to be alarmed, harassed or distressed by the calls.

ANSWERS

Answer 5.1

Answer **A** — Case law generally dictated that racially aggravated offences should attract a higher penalty. Section 153 of the Powers of Criminal Courts (Sentencing) Act 2000 places this principle on a statutory footing by stating that if an offence was racially aggravated the court must treat that as a factor which increases the seriousness of the offence (answers B and D are therefore incorrect). Section 153 further requires that the court shall state in open court that the offence was so aggravated (answer C is therefore incorrect).

General Police Duties, para. 4.5.2

Answer 5.2

Answer **D** — Under s. 28(1)(a) of the Crime and Disorder Act 1998, an offence is racially aggravated if:

- at the time of the offence;
- immediately before committing the offence; *or*
- immediately after committing the offence,

the offender demonstrates, towards the victim of the offence, hostility based on the victim's membership (or presumed membership) of a racial or religious group.

   The time is not limited to hostility shown during the offence (therefore answer A is incorrect) and is not exclusive to 'at the time' or 'before' the offence, but does include hostility shown after the offence (therefore answer C is incorrect). However, the hostility must take place immediately afterwards, and not sometime after (therefore, answer B is incorrect).

General Police Duties, para. 4.5.2.2

Answer 5.3

Answer **A** — Religious groups were added to s. 28 of the Crime and Disorder Act 1998 by the Anti-terrorism, Crime and Security Act 2001. An offence is racially or religiously aggravated for the purposes of ss. 29 to 32, if:

(a) at the time of committing the offence, or immediately before or after doing so, the offender demonstrates towards the victim of the offence hostility based on the victim's membership (or presumed membership) of a racial or religious group; or

(b) the offence is motivated (wholly or partly) by hostility towards members of a racial or religious group based on their membership of that group.

Since s. 28 covers both racial and religious matters, answer D is incorrect.

Section 28(5) goes on to state —

'In this section "religious group" means a group of persons defined by reference to religious belief or lack of religious belief.'

Therefore, HANSEN's brother's claim that the assault was based on his brother's lack of belief in Catholicism would not amount to a defence. Answer B is incorrect.

Finally, Muslims have also been held not to be a racial group (*J.H. Walker* v *Hussain* [1996] ICR 291) but they are clearly members of a religious group and, as such, are covered by the Act. Answer C is therefore incorrect.

General Police Duties, paras 4.5.2.2, 4.5.2.5

Answer 5.4

Answer **D** — An offence is committed contrary to s. 18(1) of the Public Order Act 1986, where a person uses threatening, abusive or insulting words or behaviour, intending to stir up racial hatred (or where it is likely to be stirred up). Certainly, the behaviour of the person in the question would meet these criteria. However, s. 18(2) states that the offence may be committed in a public or private place, but not when the words or behaviour used are not heard by persons other than those in that or another dwelling. The requirement is similar to those under ss. 4 and 5 of the same Act, and since both persons were in the same dwelling, no offence is committed, whatever MEREDITH's intentions! Answers A, B and C are incorrect for this reason.

General Police Duties, para. 4.5.3.2

Answer 5.5

Answer **C** — When in force, the Racial and Religious Hatred Act 2006 will insert s. 29B into the Public Order Act 1986. Section 29(B)(1) states that:

A person who uses threatening words or behaviour, or displays any written material which is threatening, is guilty of an offence if he/she intends thereby to stir up religious hatred.

This offence is similar to the one contained in s. 18 of the Act, where a person may be guilty of stirring up racial hatred by using threatening, abusive or insulting words or behaviour (or displays any written material) with intent to stir up racial hatred or it is likely to be stirred up. One of the key differences between these offences is that under s. 29B, the words or behaviour must amount to some sort of threat. To reinforce this, s. 29J of the Act provides that the offences of stirring up religious hatred are not intended to limit or restrict discussion, criticism or expressions of antipathy, dislike, ridicule or insult or abuse of a particular religion or belief.

Therefore, even though HAWKINS' words were insulting and intended to stir up religious hatred, this particular offence would not be made out. (There may of course be a case to prosecute HAWKINS for an offence under s. 18 or even s. 4A of the Public Order Act 1986). Answers A and B are incorrect.

Since it is the defendant's intent that is relevant under this section, it is immaterial whether or not religious hatred was actually stirred up, or whether the people who were subject of the behaviour were actually concerned by it. Answer D is therefore incorrect.

General Police Duties, para. 4.5.3.6

Answer 5.6

Answer **D** — Section 1(1) of the Protection from Harassment Act 1997 states:

A person must not pursue a course of conduct —
(a) which amounts to harassment of another, and
(b) which he knows or ought to know amounts to harassment of the other.

Answers A, B and C are therefore incorrect.

General Police Duties, para. 4.5.4.1

Answer 5.7

Answer **D** — If an accused intends to cause alarm or distress and actually does so, that is likely to meet the requirements of s. 1 (*Baron* v *Crown Prosecution Service*, 13 June 2000, unreported), provided he follows a course of conduct. Course of conduct has been considered by the courts. In *Lau* v *DPP* [2000] Crim LR 580, the Divisional

Court held that although only two incidents are necessary, the fewer the number of incidents and the further apart they are, the less likely it is that there will be a finding of harassment. In *Baron*, the court accepted that the more spread out and limited in number the incidents and the more indirect their means of delivery (in this case by letter), the less likely it is that a course of conduct amounting to harassment will be found. However, there is no rule and it will depend upon the facts of each individual case. In *Baron*, two letters sent some 4.5 months apart could be a course of conduct amounting to harassment, and therefore answer B is incorrect. Note it is alarm *or* distress; the court need only be satisfied that the behaviour involved one or the other (*DPP* v *Ramsdale* [2001] ILR 19 March), and therefore answer C is incorrect. Finally, the court in *Baron* refused to endorse the view that public service employees are less likely to be caused distress by threatening letters, and therefore answer A is incorrect.

General Police Duties, para. 4.5.4.1

Answer 5.8

Answer **A** — Under s. 1(1A) of the Protection from Harassment Act 1997, a person commits an offence if he/she pursues a course of conduct which involves harassment of two or more persons and which he/she knows or ought to know involves harassment of those persons and by which he/she intends to persuade any person not to do something which he or she is entitled or required to do, or to do something that he or she is not under any obligation to do.

Under s. 7(3)(b) of the Act, a course of conduct for this offence must involve, in the case of conduct in relation to two or more people, conduct on at least one occasion to each of those people. The fact that the letters were sent by two different people is irrelevant, because under s. 7(3A), a person's conduct may be aided and abetted by another, and both would commit this offence provided it can be shown they were acting together. Answer B is therefore incorrect.

Home Office Circular 34/2005 provides examples of offences, which might be committed under s. 1(1A). In this guidance, it cites the example of an animal rights extremist sending a threatening email to an individual on one occasion working for one company and another similar letter to a different individual working for another company, with the intention of persuading them to stop supplying a third company with their products (similar to the circumstances in this question). Since the offence may be committed by sending different forms of communication to only one person from each company, answers C and D are incorrect (this is true even though the communications were sent by two different people).

General Police Duties, para. 4.5.4.1

Answer 5.9

Answer **A** — For an offence of putting people in fear of violence contrary to s. 4 of the Protection from Harassment Act 1997, it has to be shown that a course of conduct caused a person to fear, on at least two occasions, that violence would be used against them. The Divisional Court examined this issue in the case of *R (on the application of A)* v *DPP* [2004] EWHC 2454. In a case similar to the one in this question, the defendant argued that the victim had only been put in fear of violence by his threats to burn her house down on the second occasion; therefore the offence had not been made out. The Divisional Court disagreed and held that the magistrates were entitled to find that the two incidents had put the victim in fear of violence, notwithstanding her admission that, on the first occasion, she had not been too concerned. Answer B is therefore incorrect.

It must then be shown that the defendant knew or ought to have known that the victim would fear that violence would be used against them. Therefore answer D is incorrect. This is not an offence of 'intent' but is subject to a test of reasonableness against the standard of an ordinary person in possession of the same facts as the defendant, and therefore answer C is incorrect.

General Police Duties, para. 4.5.4.7

Answer 5.10

Answer **C** — Section 5(2) of the Protection from Harassment Act 1997 states:

> The order may, for the purpose of protecting the victim or victims of the offence, or any other person mentioned in the order, from conduct which —
> (a) amounts to harassment, or
> (b) will cause a fear of violence,
> prohibit the defendant from doing anything described in the order.

The power to make a restraining order is available where a defendant who had been convicted of an offence under s. 2 or s. 4 of the Act; therefore, answer A is incorrect.

Restraining orders may be granted by criminal courts, as they are granted following a person's *conviction* for an offence. Injunctions (under s. 3) are only issued by the High Court or a Civil Court. Answers B and D are therefore incorrect.

General Police Duties, para. 4.5.4.11

Answer 5.11

Answer **A** — The extent to which the police (and local authorities) can use such publicity and include a photograph of the person made the subject of an anti-social behaviour order (ASBO) was clarified by the Divisional Court in *R (on the application of Stanley)* v *The Metropolitan Police Commissioner, Brent London Borough and the Secretary of State for the Home Department* [2005] EMLR 3. Following that decision the Home Office has produced guidance in relation to using such publicity. This guidance reflects the judgment of Lord Justice Kennedy, presiding judge in the case. The principles of this publicity are:

- Publicity is essential if local communities are to support agencies tackling antisocial behaviour. There is an implied power in the Crime and Disorder Act 1998 and the Local Government Act 2000 to publicise an order so that the order can be effectively enforced.
- ASBOs protect local communities. Obtaining the order is only part of the process; its effectiveness will normally depend on people knowing about the order.
- Information about ASBOs obtained should be publicised to let the community know that action has been taken in their area.
- A case-by-case approach should be adopted and each individual case should be judged on its merits as to whether or not to publicise the details of an individual subject to an ASBO — publicity should be expected in most cases.
- It is necessary to balance the human rights of individuals subject to an ASBO against those of the community as a whole when considering publicising ASBOs.
- Publicising should be the norm not the exception. An individual who is subject to an ASBO should understand that the community is likely to learn about it.

These principles do not relate to the age of the persons subject to the ASBO and clearly outline that publicity, including photographs, will be used. Therefore answers B, C and D are incorrect.

General Police Duties, para. 4.5.5

Answer 5.12

Answer **D** — Under s. 1C of the Crime and Disorder Act 1998, criminal courts may make an anti-social behaviour order (ASBO) in respect of a defendant where he or she has been convicted of a criminal offence. The court can make an order of its own volition, irrespective of whether any specific application has been made by the relevant authority (which makes answer A incorrect). The order can only be made in addition to any sentence or conditional discharge (which makes answer B incorrect) (s. 1C(4)).

The issue of whether the same material should be used from a criminal trial to support the application of an ASBO was examined in the case of *S* v *Poole Borough Council* [2002] EWHC 244. In this case, the defendant had been convicted of several offences under the Education Act 1996, and objected to the same material being used from his criminal trial to support the application of an ASBO. He argued that the use of the ASBO had been intended as an alternative to prosecution. The Divisional Court did not find in favour of the appellant, and it held that it was 'perfectly proper' to use the same material in this way and that an ASBO is akin to an injunction in a civil court. Answer C is therefore incorrect.

General Police Duties, paras 4.5.5, 4.5.5.1

Answer 5.13

Answer **B** — Although anti-social behaviour orders (ASBOs) are prohibitory in their nature (in that they order people not to do certain things rather than to do certain things) the purpose of the prohibition is not to punish but to prevent anti-social behaviour and to protect members of the public from further instances of it. Therefore, there is nothing legally wrong with including a curfew provision in an ASBO if it is necessary for such protection (*Lonergan* v *Lewes Crown Court & Others* [2005] EWHC 457). Answers C and D are therefore incorrect.

Although an ASBO has to run for a minimum of two years, it does not follow that every prohibition within the order has to endure for the life of the order. In many cases it is possible that a period of curfew could properly be set at less than the full life of the order or, in light of behavioural progress, an application to vary the curfew could be made under s. 1(8) of the 1998 Act (*Lonergan*). Answer A is therefore incorrect.

General Police Duties, paras 4.5.5.1, 4.5.5.6

Answer 5.14

Answer **C** — Criminal courts can make an ASBO in respect of a defendant who has been convicted of an offence (see s. 1C). In *R (on the application of Mills)* v *Birmingham Magistrates' Court* [2005] EWHC 2732, it was held that cases of theft, including shoplifting, would not automatically fall within the criteria laid down for issuing ASBOs. Answer B is therefore incorrect.

However, the court stated that there may be circumstances where some thefts or acts of shoplifting could cause harassment, alarm or distress and amount to anti-social behaviour. Answers A and D are therefore incorrect.

General Police Duties, para. 4.5.5.1

Answer 5.15

Answer **C** — For an anti-social behaviour order to be relevant, a person must act in an anti-social manner that caused or was likely to cause harassment, alarm or distress to one or more people not of the same household as himself or herself. Thus, it applies even where only one other person is affected by the 'anti-social manner'; therefore answers B and D are incorrect. The other person should not be from the same household as the person acting in an anti-social manner; answer A is therefore incorrect.

General Police Duties, para. 4.5.5.1

Answer 5.16

Answer **D** — Where a person of any age is convicted of an offence, the youth court, adult magistrates' court or crown court by or before which he is convicted may make an order prohibiting him from entering 'a place' (which includes 'an area') by virtue of s. 40A of the Powers of Criminal Courts (Sentencing) Act 2000.

An order prohibiting a person from entering a place specified in the order can last for a period so specified of not more than 2 years; consequently answers A, B and C are incorrect.

General Police Duties, para. 4.5.5.2

Answer 5.17

Answer **B** — Exclusion orders may be granted under s. 205 of the Criminal Justice Act 2003 prohibiting a person from entering a place specified in the order, for a period specified but for a period of no more than 2 years. The order may specify different places for different periods or days.

Under s. 112(1) of the Serious Organised Crime and Police Act 2005, a constable may direct a person to leave a place if he or she believes, on reasonable grounds, that the person is in breach of an order.

A person who knowingly contravenes a direction given to him under this section is guilty of a summary offence (see s.112(5)). Since the offence is committed when the person fails to comply with the direction (not when they simply breach the order), answers C and D are incorrect.

A direction under this section may be given orally (see s.112(4)). Answer A is incorrect — there is no requirement to send a notice in writing.

General Police Duties, paras 4.5.5.4, 4.5.5.5

Answer 5.18

Answer **A** — Under s. 1(7) of the Crime and Disorder Act 1998, an anti-social behaviour order (ASBO) has a minimum period of 2 years' duration. Answer B is therefore incorrect. There appears to be no maximum period and it will be for the court to decide, taking into account the circumstances of the case, how long to issue the order for (provided it keeps to the minimum period). Answers C and D are therefore incorrect. Note that under s. 1(8) of the Act, either the applicant or the defendant may apply to have the order varied or discharged, but under s. 1(9), no ASBO shall be discharged before the end of 2 years except with the consent of both parties.

General Police Duties, para. 4.5.5.6

Answer 5.19

Answer **D** — The Court of Appeal has expressed approval of the following definition of public nuisance:

> A common nuisance is an act not warranted by law or an omission to discharge a legal duty, which act or omission obstructs or causes inconvenience or damage to the public in the exercise of rights common to all of Her Majesty's subjects. (*Attorney General* v *PYA Quarries Ltd (No. 1)* [1957] 2 QB 169)

This means that public nuisance can be committed by omissions, and therefore answer A is incorrect. It is not necessary to prove that every member within a class of people in the community has been affected by the defendant's behaviour, simply that a representative cross-section has been so affected (*PYA Quarries*). Therefore answer B is incorrect. There is no need to prove intent; the *mens rea*, therefore, is that the defendant is guilty of the offence charged 'if either he knew or he ought to have known' that the conduct would bring about a public nuisance (*R* v *Shorrock* [1994] QB 279). The fact that WATTS has refused to do anything about the house would be sufficient; answer C is therefore incorrect. The circumstances of this question have been held, in a fairly ancient case, to amount to a public nuisance (*R* v *Watts* (1757) 1 Salk 357).

General Police Duties, para. 4.5.6.1

Answer 5.20

Answer **B** — There are two offences covering *possession* of fireworks under the Fireworks Regulations 2004. First, an offence is committed by a person under the age of 18, who is in possession of an adult firework in a public place (reg. 4(1)). Adult fireworks are ordinary fireworks, which may be purchased by people over the age of 18, and will usually be used for families in their own homes on Bonfire Night. The second offence is committed where any person is in possession of a category 4 firework anywhere (reg. 5(1)). Fireworks listed under category 4 are those which are more powerful than the ordinary ones referred to above, and are used in large displays.

However, both of the above offences are subject to the exception listed in reg. 6, which states that possession will not be unlawful if a person is in possession of fireworks in the course of his or her work or business, or where he or she has been properly authorised to conduct displays. Therefore, even though PLATT may not be authorised to conduct displays, he will be in possession of the fireworks as part of his work and does not commit the offence. Answer C is therefore incorrect. Also, because of this exception, it is irrelevant that he is under 18 (and answer A is incorrect). Answer D is incorrect, as PLATT has a defence not because he is not in a public place, but because of the above exception.

General Police Duties, para. 4.5.6.7

Answer 5.21

Answer **A** — Regulation 7 of the Fireworks Regulations 2004 (SI 2004/1836) states:

(1) Subject to paragraph (2) below, no person shall use an adult firework during night hours...

'Night hours' are the period beginning at 11 pm and ending at 7 am the following day (reg. 7(3)). Consequently answers B, C and D are incorrect.

General Police Duties, para. 4.5.6.8

Answer 5.22

Answer **A** — The exception referred to in reg 7(2) of the Fireworks Regulations 2004 deals with three main types of firework display, namely:

- a 'permitted fireworks night';
- a firework display by a local authority; and
- a national public celebration or a national commemorative event.

Taking the first exception, the above restriction on using adult fireworks will not apply to use during permitted fireworks nights — an exception that has been built into the legislation to take account of the various festivals and celebrations that traditionally involve fireworks. The expression 'permitted fireworks night' means a period:

- beginning at 11 pm on the first day of the Chinese New Year and ending at 1 am the following day;
- beginning at 11 pm on 5 November and ending at 12 am the following day;
- beginning at 11 pm on the day of Diwali and ending at 1 am the following day; or
- beginning at 11 pm on 31 December and ending at 1 am the following day.

(See reg. 7(3).)

Applying these times means therefore that answers C and D are incorrect. The exception to a display by a local authority only applies to a person who is employed by a local authority, not a private firework company; answer B is therefore incorrect.

General Police Duties, para. 4.5.6.8

Answer 5.23

Answer **C** — The time as outlined in the Noise Act 1996 is 11 pm to 7 am. Therefore answers A, B and D are incorrect.

General Police Duties, para. 4.5.6.12

Answer 5.24

Answer **D** — Under s. 87(1) of the Environmental Protection Act 1990, a person is guilty of an offence if he or she throws down, drops or otherwise deposits any litter in any place to which this section applies and leaves it.

Section 87(1) applies to any place in the area of a principal litter authority (i.e. local council) other than a place to which the public does not have access (with or without payment) (see s. 87(3)). Although this section could be worded better, it means that the offence may only take place in an area covered by a local authority, to which the public has access (a public place) and which is in the open air. Answer A is incorrect as the public place must be 'in the open air'.

The offence may not be committed in any place in the open air (answer C is therefore incorrect), or in any place in the area of a local authority (this could take in private places also). Therefore answer B is incorrect.

It should be noted that the Clean Neighbourhoods and Environment Act 2005 clarifies that 'litter', for the purposes of Part 4 of the Environmental Protection Act 1990, specifically includes cigarettes, cigars and like products and discarded chewing gum (including bubble gum).

General Police Duties, para. 4.5.6.13

Answer 5.25

Answer **C** — A call stating 'there is a bomb' is sufficient to comprise an offence contrary to s. 51(2) of the Criminal Law Act 1977, even though there is no reference to a place or location (*R* v *Webb* [1995] 92(27) LS Gaz 31), and answer D is therefore incorrect. Thus, answers A and B could both be correct. However, as this is an offence of 'specific intent', the defendant's intention is a factor. Although it is not necessary for FISHER to have any particular person in mind, this subsection states that the defendant has to have 'the intention of inducing in him or any other person a false belief that a bomb or other thing liable to explode or ignite is present in any place'. It is clear then that FISHER would have to intend that someone believed him, and a practical joke would not be covered by this section (answers A and B are therefore incorrect).

General Police Duties, para. 4.5.7.2

Answer 5.26

Answer **C** — Whether an article is obscene is a question of fact for the court to determine in each case. That test will not involve looking at the particular views or frailties of the recipient (answers A, B and D are therefore incorrect) but will be an objective test based on a reasonable bystander (*Kosmos Publications Ltd* v *DPP* [1975] Crim LR 345).

General Police Duties, para. 4.5.7.4

Answer 5.27

Answer **A** — This offence is designed to deal with nuisance calls, and the offence is complete when the defendant sends the relevant message or other matter that is, as a matter of fact, indecent, obscene or menacing (Communications Act 2003, s.127(1)). There is no need to show intention on the part of the defendant (answer C is therefore incorrect), nor any resultant distress caused (answer D is therefore incorrect). The offence is complete by simply making an indecent phone call.

Section 127 is divided into two subsections, and it is only s. 127(2) that is a 'penalty' offence for the purposes of s. 1 of the Criminal Justice and Police Act 2001; answer B is therefore incorrect.

You should note that this offence only applies to a public electronic communications network and would not include internal, private or workplace telephones.

General Police Duties, para. 4.5.7.8

6 | Public Disorder and Terrorism

QUESTIONS

Question 6.1

ANDREWS is out in town one day with his wife, who is wearing a fur coat, when BROWN, an animal rights protestor, approaches them and says, 'You murderer, how

6. Public Disorder and Terrorism

many animals have died to clothe you?'. BROWN is calm and makes no threat. ANDREWS is infuriated and starts a heated argument. Constable WILLIAMSON is nearby and hears the commotion and goes to investigate. On arrival, ANDREWS tells the officer what had happened and says, 'If this clown isn't taken out of my sight I will not be responsible for my actions'. The officer fears that a breach of the peace will take place and that there will be violence.

Which of the following actions is appropriate or available to the officer?

A Arrest ANDREWS for breach of the peace.

B Arrest BROWN for breach of the peace.

C Arrest neither, as breach of the peace is not taking place currently.

D Arrest both for breach of the peace.

Question 6.2

DENNIS owns an off-licence and had just closed the premises late at night, locking the door. HUDSON arrived at the premises in a drunken state demanding to be let in to buy a bottle of wine. DENNIS refused to allow HUDSON in and HUDSON began shouting, 'If you don't let me in, I'll smash all these windows'. HUDSON then sat on the wall waiting for DENNIS to open the shop door.

Assuming that an arrest may be necessary in these circumstances, does DENNIS have the power to arrest BATES for a breach of the peace, contrary to common law?

A No, the threats were made towards DENNIS' property, not DENNIS.

B Yes, provided DENNIS reasonably believed HUDSON would carry out the threat.

C Yes, provided DENNIS reasonably believed HUDSON was capable of carrying out the threat.

D No, only a police officer has the power of arrest to prevent a breach of the peace that has not yet occurred.

Question 6.3

A lawful assembly was due to take place by prior arrangement with the local police and the demonstrators. The police received reliable intelligence that some hard-line protesters were also going to attend and that violence was likely to occur. An order was made under s. 60 of the Criminal Justice and Public Order Act 1994 and, on the day of the demonstration, police stopped several coaches about a mile from the intended location. The occupants were searched and, fearing that there would be a breach of the peace if the coaches were allowed to continue, the police turned the coaches away without allowing them to proceed to the demonstration. Several people brought an action against the police, citing that they had intended to demonstrate peacefully and that the police should have allowed them to continue.

Were the actions of the police lawful in these circumstances?

A Yes, the officers' actions were justified as the threat of a breach of the peace was imminent.

B No, turning the coaches away was a disproportionate reaction to the threat of a breach of the peace.

C No, the officers' actions were not justified as there was no imminent threat to the peace.

D Yes, in relation to the protesters who were suspected of planning a non-peaceful demonstration, but not in relation to the peaceful demonstrators.

Question 6.4

A group of 20 people have been charged with the offence of riot, following a serious incident of disorder on a housing estate. The Crown Prosecution Service intends introducing evidence that at least 15 of the defendants were threatening violence towards people from a minority ethnic group, while 5 defendants actually used violence towards them. Other evidence shows that at least 10 other people were gathered near those charged. These people did not take part in the threats or violence, but their presence added to the intimidation.

According to s. 1 of the Public Order Act 1986, who can be found guilty of riot in these circumstances?

A Any of the people present, who were not victims of the incident.

B Any of the defendants who used or threatened to use unlawful violence.

C The 5 defendants who actually used unlawful violence.

D None of the people present, as only 5 defendants actually used violence.

Question 6.5

A large group of people are appearing in crown court to answer a charge of riot, contrary to s. 1(1) of the Public Order Act 1986. The court has heard objections from the defence relating to the evidence provided by the Crown Prosecution Service regarding the defendants' 'common purpose'.

What evidence would the court require, relating to the issue of a 'common purpose'?

A That the defendants used simultaneous violence for a common purpose.

B That the defendants had an agreed common purpose.

C That the defendants had an unlawful common purpose.

D Only that the defendants had a common purpose.

Question 6.6

HOWLEY has been charged along with a number of other people, with an offence of violent disorder, under s. 2 of the Public Order Act 1986. HOWLEY intends to use the defence that he was intoxicated at the time of the incident, and that he was not aware of his actions.

What does s. 6 of the Public Order Act 1986 state in relation to the defence of intoxication?

A It cannot be used as a defence in relation to this offence, or an offence under s. 1.

B HOWLEY *may* use this defence if he can show either that his intoxication was not self induced, or it was caused solely by taking a substance in the course of medical treatment.

C HOWLEY *may* use this defence, but only if he can show that his intoxication was not self induced.

D HOWLEY *may* use this defence, but only if he can show that his intoxication was caused solely by taking a substance in the course of medical treatment.

Question 6.7

WORTON and CAMERON appeared in crown court for violent disorder, following a fight in a pub. The court heard that two other people had been involved in the fight, but the police were unable to trace them. After hearing the evidence, the jury acquitted WORTON, but believed the conduct of the other people and CAMERON together was such as would cause a person of reasonable firmness present at the scene to fear for their personal safety. However, they were undecided whether or not they could convict CAMERON of violent disorder because of WORTON's acquittal.

Could CAMERON be convicted of the offence in these circumstances?

A Yes, if the jury found that the untraced people also used or threatened unlawful violence.

B Yes, but only if the police could trace the other two people and secure a conviction against them also.

C No, when one defendant is acquitted of this offence, all other defendants must also be acquitted.

D Yes, the acquittal of one defendant for this offence has no relevance as to whether other defendants may be convicted or not.

Question 6.8

Section 3 of the Public Order Act 1986 outlines the definition of 'affray'.

In relation to this definition and the presence of 'a person of reasonable firmness', which of the following statements is correct?

A There has to be an actual person present who was threatened with violence.

B There has to be an actual person present who was in fear for his or her safety.

C There does not have to be anyone present, merely a 'hypothetical person' who may feel threatened with violence.

D There does *not* have to be anyone present, as violence conducted towards property is enough.

Question 6.9

LOADER had recently split up from his wife, GAIL, and one day he saw her in a car in the street, accompanied by her new partner, ANWAR. GAIL got out of the car and LOADER approached her, angry that she was with another man. He shouted at her, 'That's the man you left me for; I'm going over there to smash his face in'. During the conversation, ANWAR remained in the car.

Has LOADER committed an offence contrary to s. 4 of the Public Order Act 1986 in these circumstances?

A Yes, if he intended that GAIL would believe violence would be used against ANWAR.

B Yes, but only if GAIL believed violence would be used against ANWAR.

C Yes, regardless of his intent, the offence is complete.

D No, because the threat was to use violence against ANWAR, who was not present.

Question 6.10

SADIQUE, who is Asian but from Uganda, has bought a product, which has failed to work. He returns it to the shop and is dealt with by AKANJI, a shop assistant who is Nigerian by birth. Less than happy with the service, SADIQUE calls AKANJI 'an

African twat' and 'an African bitch'. AKANJI is very distressed by this and contacts the police.

Has SADIQUE committed an offence contrary to s. 31(1)(b) of the Crime and Disorder Act 1998 (racially aggravated intentional harassment, alarm or distress)?

A No, as 'African' does not describe a racial group.

B No, as SADIQUE is from the same racial group as AKANJI.

C Yes, provided SADIQUE intended to distress AKANJI.

D Yes, there is no need to prove intent, provided distress is caused.

Question 6.11

RICHARDS was caught using a video camera near a school and the evidence obtained indicated that he had been committing an offence contrary to s. 5 of the Public Order Act 1986. When viewed, the video showed that he was dancing naked in front of the school whilst children played in the background. The children were unaware that they were being filmed and no one had seen or heard the behaviour.

Has an offence contrary to s. 5 of the Public Order Act 1986 been committed?

A Yes, a person of reasonable firmness would have been distressed had they been present.

B Yes, a person of reasonable firmness would have been distressed had they seen the video.

C No, as the defendant's behaviour was not seen or heard by anyone.

D Yes, but only if the prosecution could produce a witness who saw or heard the behaviour.

Question 6.12

Constable ROBINSON was on patrol in a shopping centre, when she saw INCE walking along, shouting and swearing in a loud voice. There were a number of shoppers in the area and Constable ROBINSON approached INCE and advised him to stop swearing and annoying people. INCE ignored Constable ROBINSON and walked away, continuing to swear loudly at passers-by. Constable ROBINSON decided that it was necessary to issue INCE with a Disorder Penalty Notice for an offence contrary to s. 5 of the Public Order Act 1986.

What would have to be proved in relation to INCE's state of mind, for the offence under s. 5 to be made out?

A That he ought to have been aware that his behaviour was insulting.

B That he intended his behaviour to be insulting, or was aware that it was.

C That someone was actually insulted by his behaviour.

D That he intended his behaviour to be insulting and was aware that it was.

Question 6.13

Inspector LOTT has been called to a residential property because a group of animal rights protesters have gathered outside. The group have followed PRICE to the house, believing that he lives there; however, he does not. The group is protesting against PRICE, who works at a local laboratory where they believe experiments take place involving animals. The group's intention is to intimidate PRICE into giving up his job at the laboratory. Also in the house is PRICE's friend, BLUNT, the house owner. BLUNT and PRICE have asked Inspector LOTT to move the protesters away from the premises.

What would Inspector LOTT reasonably have to believe in order to utilise his powers under s. 42 of the Criminal Justice and Police Act 2001, to direct the group to leave the area?

A That their presence amounts to, or is likely to amount to, the harassment of PRICE.

B That their presence amounts to, or is likely to amount to, the harassment of PRICE or BLUNT.

C That their presence amounts to, or is likely to amount to, the harassment of any person in the dwelling.

D That their presence amounts to, or is likely to amount to, the harassment of BLUNT.

Question 6.14

Constable JEFFERS, who is in full uniform, has been deployed to deal with a trespassory assembly, in respect of which an order under s. 14A of the Public Order Act 1986 has been obtained prohibiting it taking place. The officer is 4.5 miles from the monument where the assembly was due to take place, and is carrying out powers granted by s. 14C of the 1986 Act, preventing access to the site. The officer has stopped a vehicle, and has directed the occupants not to proceed in the direction of the assembly.

Are the officer's actions lawful?

A Yes, as the officer was in uniform the actions are lawful.

B Yes, the actions are lawful; it is immaterial that the officer was in uniform.

C No, the officer is outside the radius set by the Act at 4 miles.

D No, the officer has no power to stop vehicles under this section.

Question 6.15

FLEMMING is part of a student protest group intending to demonstrate against university fees. FLEMMING delivered a notice to the Commissioner of Police 48 hours before the demonstration was due to start, stating the group's intention to demonstrate in the vicinity of Parliament Square in London. The notice contained the relevant details as to the location of the demonstration and the people taking part.

Has FLEMMING provided the police with sufficient notice of the intention to hold the demonstration?

A Yes, provided it was not reasonably practicable to deliver the notice sooner.

B No, a notice *must* be delivered at least 7 clear days before the demonstration.

C Yes, a notice is only required at least 24 hours before the demonstration.

D No, a notice *must* be delivered at least 6 clear days before the demonstration.

Question 6.16

Constable DONAHUE is the community beat officer on a housing estate, which has been suffering an ongoing youth annoyance problem outside a small shopping centre. One Bank Holiday weekend, the police were called to the location to deal with intimidation and annoyance towards shopkeepers and customers, on average 20 times a day. Constable DONAHUE was on duty on the Bank Holiday Monday and visited the shopping centre during the afternoon. There were 2 youths present who the officer knew were the main instigators. After speaking to the shopkeepers, Constable DONAHUE formed the opinion that there would be further harassment that afternoon and evening. Constable DONAHUE asked the control room if they could contact the on-duty superintendent, to consider whether an order should be given under s. 30 of the Anti-social Behaviour Act 2003, to disperse the 2 youths before the problem escalated again.

Would the on-duty superintendent be able to authorise such a request in the circumstances?

A No, because there are only 2 people present.

B Yes, because there are 2 or more people present.

C No, this power may not be used at such short notice.

D Yes, this is a significant and persistent problem; it is irrelevant how many people are present.

Question 6.17

A dispersal order under s. 30 of the Anti-social Behaviour Act 2003 is in place in a shopping centre, because of anti-social behaviour that had been caused by youths drinking excessively, intimidating shoppers and committing a number of robberies. One Saturday, a group of 20 people attended the shopping centre to stage a protest against America's involvement in Iraq. The group had not notified the police of their intention to protest. Their target was a large food hall area, which contained several American-owned fast food outlets. They intended preventing people from entering the shops and persuading them not to buy food there. They began shouting at shoppers who were entering the food hall and many people felt harassed and intimidated by their actions. The police were called to deal with the incident.

Would the officers attending the scene be able to use powers under s. 30(4) of the Anti-social Behaviour Act 2003 to disperse the protesters, by virtue of the order already in place?

A No, this would be an abuse of power; the order was in place for unrelated incidents of anti-social behaviour.

B Yes, but they would need the superintendent who gave the original order to extend the criteria to include the protest.

C No, a fresh dispersal order will need to be applied for by any superintendent to take in the behaviour by the protesters.

D Yes, the protesters may be dispersed using the powers granted by the first dispersal order.

Question 6.18

Constable LONGMAN was working in an area in which an order had been given under s. 30 of the Anti-social Behaviour Act 2003, enabling officers to disperse people from the locality, because of persistent harassment and intimidation from young people. Constable LONGMAN was patrolling the relevant area in uniform one evening, when he saw a group of 10 young people. One member of the group appeared to be intimidating a person who was walking past them. Constable LONGMAN recognised the people as being local residents.

What powers does Constable LONGMAN have to deal with the people, under s. 30(3) of the Anti-social Behaviour Act 2003, in these circumstances?

A He may give a direction to the youth concerned not to come back to the locality for 24 hours.

B He may give a direction to the whole group to disperse from the area immediately.

C He may give a direction to the whole group not to come back to the locality for 24 hours.

D He may not give a direction, as only one person was involved in the intimidation.

Question 6.19

PCSO KELLY was on patrol at 11.00 pm one evening in a park where there had recently been incidents of significant and persistent anti-social behaviour, and a dispersal order was in place. On arrival, PCSO KELLY saw PARISH and WHEELER, both of whom appeared to be drunk. PCSO KELLY discovered that PARISH and WHEELER were 14 years of age and intended taking them home to their parents. PARISH appeared compliant and agreed to go home, however, WHEELER began to walk away from PCSO KELLY.

Did PCSO KELLY have the power to take WHEELER home by force in these circumstances, utilising powers under s. 30(6) of the Anti-social Behaviour Act 2003?

A No, the power to use force only applies to a police constable.

B Yes, but only to prevent PARISH and WHEELER from participating in anti-social behaviour.

C No, neither a constable nor a PCSO may use force to utilise this power.

D Yes, but only to prevent PARISH and WHEELER from participating in anti-social behaviour, or to protect them from such behaviour.

Question 6.20

Section 3 of the Football (Offences) Act 1991 (misbehaviour at designated football match) deals with 'chanting of indecent or racialist nature'. This chanting is defined by s. 3(2)(a).

Which of the following is defined as 'chanting' in relation to the words or sounds uttered?

A It must be repeated and in concert with others.

B It need not be repeated but must be in concert with others.

C It need not be repeated and can be committed acting alone.

D It must be repeated and can be committed acting alone.

Question 6.21

MILLER has organised a trip to a Premier League football match and will be using his 7-seat multi passenger vehicle for transport. At the last minute some of his party drop out and only MILLER and his friend go on the trip. His friend has taken 12 cans of lager on board.

In relation to this taking of intoxicating liquor on board, has there been an offence contrary to s. 1A of the Sporting Events (Control of Alcohol etc.) Act 1985?

A No, because of the number of seats on the vehicle.

B No, as there are only 2 people in the vehicle.

C Yes, provided MILLER knew alcohol had been taken on board.

D Yes, even though MILLER did not take the alcohol on board.

Question 6.22

DAWKINS is entering a designated sports ground and has been searched by a police officer. The officer finds a hip flask on DAWKINS, which contains malt whisky. When questioned, DAWKINS said he had it with him to drink from and did not intend using it to harm anyone.

Has DAWKINS committed an offence contrary to s. 2 of the Sporting Events (Control of Alcohol etc.) Act 1985 (alcohol at sports grounds)?

A No, as he has no intention of using the article to cause injury.

B No, because the article is not of the kind normally discarded.

C Yes, because the article contains alcohol.

D Yes, because the article is capable of causing injury to a person.

Question 6.23

WINGROVE supports a football team which is a member of the English Football League, which has qualified for the EUEFA Cup. WINGROVE has managed to buy 50 tickets for an away game in Germany and has advertised them for sale on a website. WINGROVE intends making a profit by selling the tickets at more than their market value.

Does WINGROVE commit an offence under s. 166 of the Criminal Justice and Public Order Act 1994, in these circumstances?

A No, the offence does not apply to football matches abroad.

B No, the offence will only be committed when WINGROVE actually sells a ticket.

C No, the offence only applies to international football matches abroad.

D Yes, provided WINGROVE is not authorised by the organisers of the match.

Question 6.24

GIRVAN is an employee of a well-known high street bank. Over the last few months she has been becoming increasingly suspicious of a customer's account and has started to collect information which she suspects demonstrates links between the customer's account and an animal rights group. She suspects, but has no evidence, that the customer is providing money that will be used for acts of terrorism. However, she has collected information relating to his personal bank account that she suspects to be important.

In relation to disclosing her suspicions to the police, which of the following statements is correct?

A She should disclose the information as soon as it amounts to admissible evidence.

B She must disclose the information now even if it does not amount to admissible evidence.

C She should disclose only her suspicions now, the information she collected is confidential.

D There is no obligation to disclose, it is a matter of choice.

Question 6.25

PORTER has long been suspected of being involved in money laundering for a proscribed terrorist organisation. He has no previous convictions, neither is there any evidence at all that he is now committing, or that he has in the past committed, any specific offence.

Considering only the power of arrest under s. 41 of the Terrorism Act 2000, could the police arrest PORTER now?

A No, as he has no convictions for terrorism offences.

B No, as he is not reasonably suspected of committing a specific offence.

C Yes, provided he is reasonably suspected of being a terrorist.

D Yes, provided he is reasonably suspected of having links to terrorists.

Question 6.26

OLIVER was a disaffected student who arranged to have some home-made bombs delivered to his house. He never got to use them, however, and stored them in the attic for future use. Three months later OLIVER moved out leaving his flatmate in the house. Two months after this new tenants moved in and found the items in the attic; not realising what they were they took them to the dump. An astute person at the dump found them and the police were called. An investigation led to locating OLIVER.

In relation to the offence of making or possessing explosive under suspicious circumstances contrary to s. 4 of the Explosive Substances Act 1883, which of the following is true?

A OLIVER was still in possession of the bombs when they were found at the dump and commits the offence.

B OLIVER loses possession when he leaves them with his flatmate and does not commit the offence.

C OLIVER loses possession when the new tenants move in and does not commit the offence.

D OLIVER loses possession when the bombs are discarded at the dump and does not commit the offence.

Question 6.27

Control orders are defined by s. 1 of the Prevention of Terrorism Act 2005.

What is the expiry date of a non-derogating control order, as defined by s. 1(1) of this Act?

A 6 months and it cannot be renewed.

B 6 months and can be renewed for a further 6 months.

C 12 months and it cannot be renewed.

D 12 months and it can be renewed for a further 12 months.

Question 6.28

MENDEZ is suspected of terrorist activity and the Secretary of State is going to apply to the court for a derogating control order against her. It is suspected that she will try to escape the country and will not be available to be given notice of the order if it is made.

In these circumstances what powers do the police have to ensure MENDEZ is available to be given notice of the order if it is made?

A The police can apply to the court to seize the passport of MENDEZ prior to the obtaining of an order.

B The police can arrest MENDEZ and detain her at a police station for 24 hours from time of arrest.

C The police can arrest MENDEZ and detain her at a designated place for 48 hours.

D The police have no powers prior to the obtaining of an order, and will have to await an order being obtained prior to arresting MENDEZ.

Question 6.29

HIGGINS is a campaigner opposed to the exploitation of animals. HIGGINS has managed to arrange a meeting with O'SULLIVAN, the CEO of Eastshire Holdings, a company which HIGGINS believes is about to supply products to Westshire Sciences Institute (WSI). WSI is known to conduct experimentation work with animals. At the meeting, HIGGINS intends to peacefully persuade O'SULLIVAN not to enter into a contract with WSI on moral grounds.

Would HIGGINS commit an offence under s. 145(1) of the Serious Organised Crime and Police Act 2005, in these circumstances?

A Yes, HIGGINS has tried to induce O'SULLIVAN into not entering a contract.

B No, this offence does not apply to contractual issues between companies.

C No, the offence would only be complete if HIGGINS had tried to persuade O'SULLIVAN to break a contract already in place.

D No, HIGGINS' peaceful behaviour would mean that no offence has been committed in these circumstances.

ANSWERS

Answer 6.1

Answer **A** — Police officers are expected to focus their attention on those who are likely to present the actual threat of violence or disorder, which was the approach taken by the Divisional Court in the case of *Redmond Bate* v *DPP* [1999] Crim LR 998. The court held that in this case, where preachers who were antagonising passers-by were unlawfully arrested for breach of the peace, the officers should have directed their attention to the passers-by from whom the threat of violence was emanating. The Court of Appeal, in *Bibby* v *Chief Constable of Essex Police* (2000) 164 JP 297, set out conditions that must be met before the power to arrest for breach of the peace should be used:

- The common law power to arrest for breach of the peace should be exercised only in the clearest circumstances.
- The threat must come from the person to be arrested.
- His or her conduct must clearly interfere with the rights of others.
- The person to be arrested must be acting unreasonably so as to give rise to a well-founded fear that a breach of the peace will be occasioned.

The second point in the above list makes B and D incorrect as BROWN is not making any threats. Also, as the power of arrest can be used to prevent a future breach of the peace, answer C is incorrect. Arresting ANDREWS would fit the test in *Bibby* and would be lawful. As BROWN has made no threat, arresting him would be unlawful, as it does not fit the test in *Bibby*.

General Police Duties, paras 4.6.2, 4.6.2.3

Answer 6.2

Answer **B** — A breach of the peace was defined specifically in *R* v *Howell* [1982] QB 416. A breach of the peace generally occurs when an act is done, or threatened to be done:

- which harms a person or, in his or her presence, his or her property; or
- which is likely to cause such harm; or
- which puts someone in fear of such harm.

Since DENNIS was in fear that harm would be done to the shop, answer A is incorrect.

A constable or any other person may arrest without warrant any person:

- who is committing a breach of the peace;
- whom he or she reasonably believes will commit a breach of the peace in the immediate future; or
- who has committed a breach of the peace, where it is reasonably believed that a recurrence of the breach of the peace is threatened.

The power of arrest is given to a constable or any other person (answer D is incorrect). There is no requirement for the person to reasonably believe that the person is capable of carrying out the threat, merely that the threat may be carried out. Answer C is incorrect.

General Police Duties, para. 4.6.2, 4.6.2.4

Answer 6.3

Answer **A** — It was held in the case of *Moss* v *McLachlan* [1985] IRLR 76 that the common law powers of the police allow them, where appropriate, to prevent people from travelling to certain locations (e.g. striking miners heading for a working coalfield where their presence would give reasonable grounds to apprehend a breach of the peace). Such an 'anticipatory' power is, however, exceptional (*Foulkes* v *Chief Constable of Merseyside Police* [1998] 3 All ER 705).

The issue of the police using such powers to impose anticipatory restrictions on the movement of individuals was further examined in the case of *R (on the application of Laporte)* v *Chief Constable of Gloucestershire and others* [2005] 1 All ER 473. This case was similar to the circumstances in the question, where protesters intended demonstrating against the war in Iraq at Fairford US Air Force base. The applicant argued that the police could not take 'containment' action in this way and that it was unlawful to restrict the movement and liberty of a group of people in this way without considering their individual motivation and without arresting them. The Court of Appeal held that it was reasonable for the police to apprehend a breach of the peace and to prevent the protestors from reaching their destination. Because of the limits of time and resources under which the police were operating, it would not have been practical to distinguish between those who planned to protest peacefully and those who planned to cause trouble. Answer D is therefore incorrect.

The Court also examined what would amount to an 'imminent' threat and found that each case should be examined on its own merits, and that in this case, there had been an imminent threat. Answer C is therefore incorrect. Finally, the Court found that the actions of the police in turning the protestors away could be held as being disproportionate and could not be justified; however, this was because the police on that occasion escorted them all the way back to London! The Court held that the officers were justified in not allowing the coaches to proceed to the demonstration, but their subsequent actions were not (and answer B is incorrect).

General Police Duties, para. 4.6.2.2

Answer 6.4

Answer **C** — Under s. 1(1) of the Public Order Act 1986:

> Where 12 or more persons who are present together use or threaten unlawful violence for a common purpose and the conduct of them (taken together) is such as would cause a person of reasonable firmness present at the scene to fear for his personal safety, each of the persons using unlawful violence for the common purpose is guilty of riot.

The offence of riot may be made out in these circumstances against the 5 defendants who actually used violence (answer D is therefore incorrect). However, only those defendants who actually used violence will be guilty and answers A and B are incorrect. Of course, other defendants present may also be guilty of other serious Public Order Act offences.

General Police Duties, para. 4.6.4

Answer 6.5

Answer **D** — Under s. 1(1) of the Public Order Act 1986:

> Where 12 or more persons who are present together use or threaten unlawful violence for a common purpose and the conduct of them (taken together) is such as would cause a person of reasonable firmness present at the scene to fear for his personal safety, each of the persons using unlawful violence for the common purpose is guilty of riot.

There must be a common purpose, but this need not be part of a pre-determined plan, nor be unlawful in itself. Answers B and C are incorrect.

Section 1(2) states that it is immaterial whether or not the 12 or more use or threaten unlawful violence simultaneously. Therefore, answer A is incorrect.

General Police Duties, para. 4.6.4

Answer 6.6

Answer **B** — Section 6(5) of the Public Order Act 1986 states:

> For the purposes of this section a person whose awareness is impaired by intoxication shall be taken to be aware of that of which he would be aware if not intoxicated, unless he shows either that his intoxication was not self-induced or that it was caused solely by the taking or administration of a substance in the course of medical treatment.

The defence under s. 6(5) applies to all of the general Public Order Act offences; therefore, answer A is incorrect.

The defence may be raised either when the defendant claims intoxication was not self-induced or that it was caused solely by the taking or administration of a substance in the course of medical treatment. Answers C and D are therefore incorrect.

General Police Duties, para. 4.6.4.2

Answer 6.7

Answer **A** — Section 2(1) of the Public Order Act 1986 states:

> Where 3 or more persons who are present together use or threaten unlawful violence and the conduct of them (taken together) is such as would cause a person of reasonable firmness present at the scene to fear for his personal safety, each of the persons using or threatening unlawful violence is guilty of violent disorder.

In order to convict any defendant of this offence, you must show that there were 3 or more people using or threatening violence. If this is not proved then the court should acquit each defendant (*R* v *McGuigan and Cameron* [1991] Crim LR 719). Answer D is incorrect.

However, in this question, the jury has found that there were 3 or more people using or threatening violence (including CAMERON), but the issue is whether or not the failure to trace 2 of these would be fatal to the case. This matter was addressed in *R* v *Worton* ((1989) 154 JP 201). In this case, the court held that the acquittal of one defendant would mean the acquittal of all, unless it can be proved that there were others taking part in the disorder who were not charged, regardless of whether a conviction could be secured against the missing people. Answers B and C are therefore incorrect.

General Police Duties, para. 4.6.5

Answer 6.8

Answer **A** — The House of Lords has held that, in order to prove the offence of affray, the threat of unlawful violence has to be towards a person(s) present at the scene (*I v DPP* [2002] 1 AC 285). This is violence and not fear for their safety, and therefore answer B is incorrect. There does have to be someone present, and in that respect answer D is incorrect. Answer D also incorrect in that violence towards property is specifically not included in affray as it is in riot and violent disorder. The second element that needs to be proved relates to the 'hypothetical person present'. It is necessary to prove that the defendant's conduct would have caused a hypothetical person present at the scene to fear for his or her personal safety, which is more than simply threatened with violence (*R v Sanchez* (1996) 160 JP 321 and *R v Carey* [2006] EWCA Crim 17), and therefore answer C is incorrect.

General Police Duties, para. 4.6.6

Answer 6.9

Answer **A** — A person is guilty of an offence under s. 4(1) if he or she uses towards another person threatening, abusive or insulting words or behaviour, with intent to cause that person to believe that immediate and unlawful violence would be used against him or her, or another. Since LOADER has threatened to use immediate and unlawful violence towards ANWAR, and he is in a position to do so as ANWAR is nearby, the offence is complete (and answer D is incorrect). It is immaterial that ANWAR was not present when the threat was made, or that he was not even aware of the threat.

Under s. 4(3) of the Act, a person is guilty of an offence only if he or she *intends* his or her words or behaviour to be threatening, abusive or insulting, or is aware that it may be, therefore answer C is incorrect. It is LOADER's intent that counts, not whether GAIL actually believed that violence would be used. Answer B is therefore incorrect.

General Police Duties, para. 4.6.7

Answer 6.10

Answer **C** — This question loosely follows the circumstances of *R v White* (*Anthony Delroy*) [2001] 1 WLR 1352, where the Court of Appeal upheld White's conviction for this offence. The Court held that the words used are to be construed as they are generally used in England and Wales; and on that basis the word 'African' described a racial group defined by reference to race and therefore answer A is incorrect. The word 'Asians' has been similarly recognised (see *DPP* v *Rishan Kumar Pal* [2000] Crim LR 756). This offence can be committed towards people from the same racial group as the accused and answer B is therefore incorrect. This is a crime of 'specific intent' and as such does require the intent to be proven, and therefore answer D is incorrect.

General Police Duties, para. 4.6.8

Answer 6.11

Answer **C** — The Public Order Act 1986, s. 5 states:

(1) A person is guilty of an offence if he —
  (a) uses threatening, abusive or insulting words or behaviour, or disorderly behaviour, or
  (b) displays any writing, sign or other visible representation which is threatening, abusive or insulting,

within the hearing or sight of a person likely to be caused harassment, alarm or distress thereby.

This requirement was confirmed in *Taylor v DPP* [2006] EWHC 1202 (Admin) where it was held that there must be at least evidence that there was someone who could see, or could hear, at the material time, what the individual was doing; answers A and B are therefore incorrect.

However, there was no requirement for the prosecution to call evidence that someone did actually hear the words spoken or see the behaviour. Answer D is incorrect.

General Police Duties, para. 4.6.9

Answer 6.12

Answer **B** — Section 6 of the Public Order Act 1986 states that a person is guilty of an offence under s. 5 only if:

... he intends his words or behaviour, or the writing, sign or other visible representation, to be threatening, abusive or insulting, or is aware that it may be threatening, abusive or insulting, or (as the case may be) he intends his behaviour to be or is aware that it may be disorderly.

This is a case of either/or: INCE would either have to intend his behaviour to be insulting, or he would have to be aware that it was (answer D is incorrect). There is no requirement for some person actually to have been insulted by the behaviour (although in the fact pattern of this question, there were many shoppers in the area who could provide useful evidence of their feelings at the time of the offence), therefore answer C is incorrect.

The fact that a person ought to have known that his or her behaviour was insulting is immaterial, making answer A incorrect. The person's state of mind is often ignored when it comes to charging people with offences under s. 5 (and s. 4 above). Occasionally, defence solicitors make a point of insisting that their client be interviewed before charge. While it may be impractical to interview all offenders for these offences, it may be worth considering when the facts are unclear.

General Police Duties, para. 4.6.9.1

Answer 6.13

Answer **D** — Section 42 of the Criminal Justice and Police Act 2001 gives the police certain powers to give directions in order to prevent intimidation or harassment. The legislation is designed to prevent protesters causing harassment to people in their own homes, as happened in this question. The most senior police officer present at the scene has discretionary powers to give directions to people in the vicinity, including a direction to leave the area.

In order to give a direction under s. 42, the officer must believe, on reasonable grounds, that the persons present are there for the purposes of persuading the resident or anyone else that they should not do something they are entitled or required to do, or that they should do something they are not obliged to do. The officer must also believe, on reasonable grounds, that the person's presence amounts to or is likely to result in the harassment of the resident, or is likely to cause alarm or distress to the resident. Therefore, in this question, even though the group's hostility is directed at PRICE, the outcome must be the harassment of BLUNT, the resident. Answers A, B and C are incorrect for this reason.

General Police Duties, para. 4.6.9.3

Answer 6.14

Answer **D** — Under s. 14A of the Public Order Act 1986, the chief officer of police has the power, if he or she reasonably believes that it is intended to hold a trespassory assembly which may result in serious disruption to the life of the community or significant damage to the land, building or monument which is of historical, archaeological or scientific importance, to apply to the district council for an order prohibiting for a specified period the holding of all trespassory assemblies in the district or part of it. The order must not last for more than 4 days and must not apply to an area greater than that represented by a circle of 5 miles radius from a specified centre, and therefore answer C is incorrect. A constable, who must be in uniform, has power to stop someone he or she reasonably believes to be on his or her way to an assembly prohibited by an order under s. 14A and to direct him or her not to proceed in the direction of the assembly, and therefore answer B is incorrect. This power, however, does not apply to vehicles and is restricted to 'stop that person', and answer A is therefore incorrect. Other powers exist to stop the vehicle, however.

General Police Duties, paras 4.6.11.7, 4.6.11.9

Answer 6.15

Answer **A** — Section 133(1) of the Serious Organised Crime and Police Act 2005 states that a person seeking authorisation for a demonstration in the designated area must give written notice to that effect to the Commissioner of Police of the Metropolis. Under s. 133(2), the notice must be given:

(a) if reasonably practicable, not less than 6 clear days before the day on which the demonstration is to start, or

(b) if that is not reasonably practicable, then as soon as it is, and in any case not less than 24 hours before the demonstration is to start.

If FLEMMING is able to show that it was not reasonably practicable to deliver the notice sooner, s. 133(2) has been complied with and answer D is incorrect. Answer B is incorrect, as the period referred to above is 6 clear days and not 7. Answer C is incorrect, because 24 hours is the minimum period allowed under s. 133(2).

General Police Duties, para. 4.6.11.12

Answer 6.16

Answer **C** — A written order may be given under s. 30 of the Anti-social Behaviour Act 2003, authorising the dispersal of groups of people if the relevant officer (a superintendent) has reasonable grounds for believing that any members of the public have been intimidated, harassed, alarmed or distressed as a result of the presence or behaviour of groups of 2 or more persons in public places. Answer A is incorrect, as an order may be given even if only 2 people are present. Answer D is incorrect as there must be at least 2 people present. The relevant officer must also be satisfied that the anti-social behaviour is a significant and persistent problem in the relevant locality (which would be the case in the circumstances given).

However, because of the implications of such an authorisation on the human rights of members of the public, further conditions are attached to the order; for example, the order may not be given without the consent of the local authority (s. 31(2)). More significantly, the authorisation must be given publicly, for example by notifying the local newspaper or by placing posters in a conspicuous place (s. 31(3)). The publicity must be given before the specified date on which the powers of dispersal are due to begin (see s. 31(2)). This means that these powers may not be given in matters of urgency, as in the scenario, and that appropriate planning must take place beforehand. Answer B is therefore incorrect.

General Police Duties, para. 4.6.12.1

Answer 6.17

Answer **D** — A written order granted by a superintendent must be in place before the police can act under s. 30(4) of the Anti-social Behaviour Act 2003 and order the group to disperse. If the order is in place, a constable in uniform, who has reasonable grounds for believing that the presence or behaviour of two or more persons in a public place has resulted, or is likely to result, in any members of the public being intimidated, harassed, alarmed or distressed, may issue directions:

(a) requiring the people in the group to disperse (either immediately or by such time and in such a way as the officer may specify);

(b) requiring any of those people whose place of residence is not within the relevant locality to leave the relevant locality (or any part of it) either immediately or by such time and in such a way as the officer may specify; and

(c) prohibiting any of those people whose place of residence is not within the relevant locality from returning to the relevant locality (or any part of it) for such period (not exceeding 24 hours) from the giving of the direction as the officer may specify.

In *R (on the application of Singh)* v *Chief Constable of West Midlands* [2005] EWHC 2840, it was held that the use of s. 30(4) powers to disperse a group of protesters of two or more people who were causing harassment, alarm or distress to members of the public, was lawful even though the order which was already in force related to quite different anticipated anti-social behaviour. Therefore, the police in this question may use their powers to disperse the group, without applying to the superintendent who originally granted the order, or any other superintendent. Answers A, B and C are all incorrect for this reason.

In addition, because of the implications of such an authorisation on the human rights of members of the public, further conditions are attached to the order; for example, the order may not be given without the consent of the local authority (s. 31(2)). More significantly, the authorisation must be given publicly, for example by notifying the local newspaper or by placing posters in a conspicuous place (s. 31(3)). The publicity must be given before the specified date on which the powers of dispersal are due to begin (see s. 31(2)). This means that these powers may not be given in matters of urgency, as in the scenario, and that appropriate planning must take place beforehand. Answers B and C are also incorrect for this reason.

General Police Duties, paras 4.6.12.1, 4.6.12.2

Answer 6.18

Answer **B** — Under s. 30(3) of the Anti-social Behaviour Act 2003, a written order must first have been given by a superintendent, authorising the dispersal of groups of people from a locality. If the order is in place, a constable in uniform, who has reasonable grounds for believing that the presence or behaviour of 2 or more persons in a public place has resulted, or is likely to result, in any members of the public being intimidated, harassed, alarmed or distressed, may do the following:

(a) require the people in the group to disperse either immediately or by a time as the officer may specify; *or*
(b) require any person whose place of residence is not within the locality, to leave locality immediately (or within specified time); *and*
(c) prohibit any person whose place of residence is not within the locality from returning within a specified period of time (not exceeding 24 hours).

Since the people in the group were all local residents, the officer will only be able to deal with them under s. 30(3)(a) above, and will not be able to prohibit them from returning within 24 hours (but he will be able to require the people in the group to disperse immediately). Answers A and C are therefore incorrect.

Any reference to the presence or behaviour of a group of people will include any one or more of those people. Therefore, even though only one of the group was actually intimidating a member of the public, the officer has the power to disperse the whole group in these circumstances. Answers A and D are incorrect for this reason.

General Police Duties, para. 4.6.12.2

Answer 6.19

Answer **D** — Section 30(6) of the Anti-social Behaviour Act 2003, states that if, between the hours of 9 pm and 6 am, a constable in uniform finds a person in any public place in the relevant locality who he/she has reasonable grounds for believing:

(a) is under the age of 16; and

(b) is not under the effective control of a parent or a responsible person aged 18 or over, he/she may remove the person to the person's place of residence unless he has reasonable grounds for believing that the person would, if removed to that place, be likely to suffer significant harm.

In *R (W)* v *Metropolitan Police Commissioner* [2006] EWCA Civ 458 it was held that the word 'remove' in s. 30(6) naturally and compellingly means 'take away using reasonable force if necessary'. However, this is not an arbitrary power and, within a designated dispersal area, a constable must only use this power, (a) to protect children under 16 from the physical and social risks of anti-social behaviour by others, or (b) to prevent children from themselves participating in anti-social behaviour. Since force may be used for the above reasons, answers B and C are incorrect.

The above power may be conferred on a PCSO, under sch. 4 to the Police Reform Act 2002. Answer A is therefore incorrect.

General Police Duties, para. 4.6.12.3

Answer 6.20

Answer **D** — For the offence under s. 3 of the Football (Offences) Act 1991, the defendant must be shown to have repeated the words or sound before it can be classed as 'chanting', and therefore answers B and C are incorrect. The definition under s. 3(2) has been amended by the Football (Offences and Disorder) Act 1999 to cater for occasions where the offence is committed by one person acting alone, and therefore answer A is incorrect for this reason.

General Police Duties, para. 4.6.13.1

Answer 6.21

Answer **A** — This offence is carried out in relation to the type of vehicle, its use and the number of people on board. If it is being used for a journey to or from a designated sporting event, and it is not a public service vehicle but is adapted to carry more than 8 passengers, it fits the criteria laid down in s. 1A of the Sporting Events (Control of Alcohol etc.) Act 1985. The vehicle in question does not fit the criteria in relation to the number of seats and therefore the offence cannot be committed. As far as the other options are concerned, the number of passengers can be 2 or more, and therefore answer B is incorrect; and the offence of carrying alcohol can only be committed by the driver or owner and therefore answers C and D are incorrect. Having been carried on by the driver, any person in possession of the alcohol also commits an offence, as do those who are drunk on such a vehicle, provided the conditions laid down in the statute are met.

General Police Duties, para. 4.6.13.8

Answer 6.22

Answer **C** — An offence under s. 2 of the Sporting Events (Control of Alcohol etc.) Act 1985 is committed by 'a person who has alcohol or an article to which this section applies in his possession'.

The article to which s. 2 applies is defined as any article capable of causing injury and there is no need to prove intention, and therefore answer A is incorrect. However, this article is further defined as:

- bottles, cans or other portable containers (including ones that are crushed or broken); *which*
- are for holding any drink; *and*
- are of a kind which, when empty, are normally discarded or returned to, or left to be recovered by, the supplier.

As the hip flask does not fit this definition, answer D is incorrect. The fact that DAWKINS is in possession of alcohol makes him liable; it does not have to be an article to which this section applies. So he commits the offence even though the hip flask is not an article to which s. 2 applies, and therefore answer B is incorrect.

General Police Duties, para. 4.6.13.10

Answer 6.23

Answer **D** — It is an offence under s. 166(1) of the Criminal Justice and Public Order Act 1994 for an unauthorised person to sell a ticket for a designated football match, or otherwise to dispose of such a ticket to another person. A person is 'unauthorised' unless he or she is authorised in writing to sell or otherwise dispose of tickets for the match by the organisers of the match (s. 166(2)(a)).

Section 166(2)(aa) outlines the criteria for 'selling' a ticket, which includes offering to sell a ticket, exposing a ticket for sale and advertising that a ticket is available for purchase. Answer B is therefore incorrect.

For the purposes of s. 166(2)(c) a 'designated football match' is described in art. 2 of the Ticket Touting (Designation of Football Matches) Order 2007 (SI 2007/790) as an association football match in England and Wales; whereas art. 3 designates association football matches *outside* England and Wales involving a national team (of England or Wales), or a team representing a club which is a member of the Football League, the Football Association Premier League, the Football Conference or League of Wales, or matches in competitions or tournaments organised by or under the authority of FIFA or UEFA, in which any of such English or Welsh domestic or national teams is eligible to participate or has participated. Answers A and C are therefore incorrect.

General Police Duties, para. 4.6.13.13

Answer 6.24

Answer **B** — There are a number of offences contained in the Terrorism Act 2000, and some relate to money and its use for the purposes of terrorism. GIRVAN's suspicions about the customer's activities, if proved to be true, would amount to such an offence. Section 19 of the 2000 Act places a statutory duty on people who form a suspicion about activities they believe amount to the offences outlined here, if that belief/suspicion is based on information that comes to their attention in the course of their employment. The duty is to inform the police without delay of those suspicions, and answers A and D are therefore incorrect. They must also disclose the information on which it is based, and therefore answer C is also incorrect. Failure to comply with this duty is an offence, punishable with 5 years' imprisonment.

General Police Duties, para. 4.6.14.4

Answer 6.25

Answer **C** — The Terrorism Act 2000 provides officers with an additional power of arrest in relation to 'terrorists'. This complements the existing powers under s. 24 of the Police and Criminal Evidence Act 1984 that exist for most of the offences connected with terrorist activities. It is a wide-ranging power in that it does not require reasonable suspicion of involvement in a specific offence, and therefore answer B is incorrect. It does not require evidence that the person is now, or has been in the past, a terrorist, and therefore answer A is incorrect. It is sufficient that the officer reasonably suspects the person to be a 'terrorist'. So what is a terrorist? Section 40 of the 2000 Act defines this as a person who:

- has committed an offence under any of ss. 11, 12, 15 to 18, 54 and 56 to 63; or
- is or has been concerned in the commission, preparation or instigation of acts of terrorism.

As far as the first statement is concerned, PORTER does not fit the definition in the fact pattern. However, where the officer has reasonable grounds to suspect him of being involved in the preparation of acts of terrorism through his money laundering activities, he may be justifiably arrested. This is true even though he is not suspected of a specific terrorist offence. Although it is a broad power, it requires more than mere links to terrorists, and answer D is therefore incorrect.

General Police Duties, para. 4.6.14.7

Answer 6.26

Answer **A** — The wording of this offence requires the prosecution — in cases of 'possession' — to prove that a defendant had the relevant article in his or her possession and that he or she knew the nature of it (see *R v Hallam* [1957] 1 QB 569). Clearly OLIVER knows the nature of the bombs and has possession when they are delivered to his address. At what point, if ever, does he lose possession of them?

However, the interpretation of 'in your possession' or 'under your control' is a wide one as demonstrated in a case where the defendant had moved out of his property and left home-made bombs and other articles in some boxes with a friend. New tenants in the property had discovered the boxes which later turned up on a rubbish tip. The defendant went to the police station after learning that he was a suspect and he claimed that he had collected the articles many years previously when he was too young to appreciate how dangerous they were. Although he had left the boxes with his friend he was nevertheless convicted of this offence as he still had the explosives under his control when he left the property (*R v Campbell* [2004] EWCA Crim 2309). There is also no need to show any criminal intent or an unlawful purpose on the part of the defendant (see *Campbell*).

OLIVER never loses possession; answers B, C and D are therefore incorrect.

General Police Duties, para. 4.6.14.8

Answer 6.27

Answer **D** — Control orders are defined by s. 1 of the Prevention of Terrorism Act 2005 as:

(1) In this Act 'control order' means an order against an individual that imposes obligations on him for purposes connected with protecting members of the public from a risk of terrorism...

These orders have an expiry period of 12 months and must specify the period over which they are to remain in force; they may be renewed (with or without modification) for a further 12 months. Consequently answers A, B and C are incorrect.

It should be noted that while the above legislation is still in place, it was held that the judicial procedure in relation to such orders does not meet the needs of Art. 6 of the European Convention on Human Rights (right to a fair trial) (*Re MB* [2006] EWHC 1000 (Admin)), and are in breach of Art. 5 (right to liberty and security) (*Re JJ (control orders)* [2006] EWHC 1623 (Admin) and *Secretary of State for the Home Department v E* [2007] EWHC 233 (Admin)). It remains to be seen whether this case will actually involve a change in legislation.

General Police Duties, para. 4.6.15.1

Answer 6.28

Answer **C** — Section 5 of the Prevention of Terrorism Act 2005 deals with arrest and detention pending a derogating control order. It states:

(1) A constable may arrest and detain an individual if —
   (a) the Secretary of State has made an application to the court for a derogating control order to be made against that individual; and
   (b) the constable considers that the individual's arrest and detention is necessary to ensure that he is available to be given notice of the order if it is made.
(2) A constable who has arrested an individual under this section must take him to the designated place that the constable considers most appropriate as soon as practicable after the arrest.
(3) An individual taken to a designated place under this section may be detained there until the end of 48 hours from the time of his arrest.

There is a power of arrest, where the constable considers it necessary to ensure the person is available to be given notice of the order if it is made. Answers A and D are therefore incorrect.

The arrestee would have to be taken to a designated place, where they may be detained for 48 hours, this time commencing at the time of arrest. Answer B is therefore incorrect.

General Police Duties, para. 4.6.15.1

Answer 6.29

Answer **D** — A person commits an offence under s. 145(1) of the Serious Organised Crime and Police Act 2005 if, with the intention of harming an animal research organisation, he or she:

(a) does a relevant act, or
(b) threatens that he or she or somebody else will do a relevant act,

in circumstances in which that act or threat is intended or likely to cause a second person to take any of the steps in subs. (2).

A 'relevant act' is an act amounting to a criminal offence, or a tortious act causing the other party to suffer loss or damage of any description.

The steps referred to in subs. (2) above are:

(a) not to perform any contractual obligation owed to a third person (whether or not such non-performance amounts to a breach of contract); or
(b) to terminate any contract; or
(c) not to enter into a contract with a third person.

Since the circumstances in the question are covered by s. 145(2)(c) above, answers B and C are incorrect.

Under s. 145(3)(b), no offence is committed if the only relevant tortious act is an inducement to break a contract. This means that no offence is committed by people peacefully arguing, or representing, that one person should cease doing business with another on the basis of the other's involvement with an animal research organisation. Answer A is therefore incorrect.

General Police Duties, para. 4.6.17.1

7 Firearms and Gun Crime

STUDY PREPARATION

Definitions play a big role in this chapter, and the first few pages are devoted to this area. You must understand these definitions, particularly 'firearm', 'shotgun' and 'imitation firearm' before you move on to the offences. Also, the familiar definitions of 'possession' and 'has with him' appear frequently throughout the legislation and their elements must be known.

There are several offences involving the criminal use of firearms with which you should familiarise yourself. This can be a confusing area, as some offences appear to cross over. Pay particular attention to those offences that may or may not be committed with an imitation firearm.

Police powers under the Firearms Act 1968 are wide ranging, and some offences carry their own power of entry and search. Do not ignore the various powers under the Act.

Ages play a significant part in this legislation, and you should familiarise yourself with the table contained in *Blackstone's Police Manual Volume 4: General Police Duties*.

In tackling questions on firearms, establish exactly what type of weapon is involved. Is it real or imitation? Is it an air weapon? Then, you will need to know whether the relevant offences carry a power of arrest.

Significant changes will be made to this area of legislation when the full provisions of the Violent Crime Reduction Act 2006 are enacted.

QUESTIONS

Question 7.1

Section 5 of the Firearms Act 1968 contains a list of prohibited weapons.

Which of the below is capable of being a 'prohibited weapon', under this section?

A Any smooth-bore revolver gun other than one which is chambered for 38 mm rim-fire cartridges.

B Any self-loading or pump-action rifled gun other than one which is chambered for 0.19 rim-fire cartridges.

C Any weapon of whatever description designed or adapted for the discharge of any noxious liquid, gas or other thing.

D Any firearm which is so designed or adapted that one or more missiles can be successively discharged without repeated pressure on the trigger.

Question 7.2

BUSH has recently acquired a shotgun, the barrel of which has been shortened so that it measures only 25 inches.

What authorisation would BUSH require in relation to the weapon?

A A firearms certificate to cover his possession.

B The permission of the Secretary of State, as it is a prohibited weapon.

C A shotgun certificate to cover his possession.

D The weapon is now prohibited, and is therefore illegal.

Question 7.3

BENTHAM was stopped by Constable RUBY while driving a motor vehicle. Constable RUBY stood outside the vehicle and conducted a radio check which revealed that the vehicle had just been circulated for its involvement in an armed robbery at a petrol station less than an hour previously. BENTHAM overheard Constable RUBY calling for assistance and got out of the car. BENTHAM placed his hand in his pocket and with his fingers extended, pretended that he had a pistol in his pocket and told the officer to back away. Constable RUBY was not fooled by BENTHAM's attempt and told him so. BENTHAM then gave up without resisting the officer.

Would BENTHAM be guilty of an offence under s. 17(1) of the Firearms Act 1968 (using a firearm/imitation firearm to resist arrest) in these circumstances?

A No, holding his fingers like this will not amount to an imitation firearm.

B No, because he did not have with him something which had been adapted or altered so as to resemble a firearm.

C No, because the officer was not fooled by his attempt.

D Yes, because his fingers had the appearance of a firearm.

Question 7.4

OWEN owned a rifle, for which he had a firearms certificate. He bought another rifle from his friend, VOYLE, whose own certificate had expired. OWEN did not have enough room in his own cabinet and asked VOYLE if he could keep the rifle for him until OWEN bought a new cabinet. OWEN intended applying for an extension to his certificate when he had the rifle in his home.

Which person, if either, would commit an offence in these circumstances?

A Only OWEN, as he has taken possession of the weapon.

B Only VOYLE, as OWEN has not yet taken possession of the weapon.

C Both people, from the time OWEN bought the rifle.

D Only VOYLE, as only one person may be in possession at any one time.

Question 7.5

CONNOR owns a large estate and he holds a s. 1 firearms certificate for a rifle. His friend, REES, came to stay and asked to go shooting. CONNOR had to go out for the day. However, he gave REES permission to use his rifle on his land, provided he was accompanied by WALTERS, CONNOR's estate manager.

In these circumstances, would REES be exempt from requiring a firearms certificate?

A No, the holder of the certificate must always be present for the exemption to apply.

B Yes, either the holder of the certificate or his servant may be present for the exemption to apply.

C No, the holder of the certificate must be on the premises for the exemption to apply.

D No, this type of exemption only applies to the holder of a shotgun certificate.

Question 7.6

BROWN's marriage has broken up because his wife had an affair with MEADE. BROWN was very upset and went to MEADE's home, where his wife was staying, with a shotgun and ammunition. BROWN intended to threaten them both into ending the affair. BROWN left the shotgun in the car and was let into the house; however, his wife was upstairs, refusing to see him. BROWN said to MEADE, 'Tell her to come down, or I'll get my shotgun from the car and I'll take it upstairs to shoot her'. BROWN's intent was genuine if his wife did not speak to him.

In relation to proof required that a person has committed an offence under s. 16 of the Firearms Act 1968 (endangering life), which of the following statements is correct?

A This offence will be complete if MEADE believed that a life was endangered.

B This offence is incomplete, as BROWN's threat was conditional.

C This offence is incomplete, as BROWN did not have the shotgun with him at the time of making the threat.

D This offence is complete as BROWN's intent to carry out the threat was genuine.

Question 7.7

NEVILLE has recently acquired a plastic toy gun, which has the appearance of a real pistol. He approaches PARSONS, who owes him money, and uses the gun to threaten him into believing violence will be used unless he repays the debt.

Has NEVILLE committed an offence under s. 16A of the Firearms Act 1968 (possession with intent to cause fear of violence)?

A Yes, the offence is complete in these circumstances.

B No, this offence may not be committed with an imitation firearm.

C No, because the toy cannot be readily converted into a s. 1 firearm.

D Yes, provided PARSONS actually believed violence would be used against him.

Question 7.8

Constable CHAVEZ stopped PETERS in his car. When he conducted a Police National Computer (PNC) check Constable CHAVEZ found that PETERS was wanted for attempted robbery, having threatened a garage cashier with a knife. Constable CHAVEZ searched the car and discovered a firearm in the boot. There was no evidence to show that PETERS was in possession of a firearm at the time of the original offence.

Would PETERS be guilty of an offence contrary to s. 17(2) of the Firearms Act 1968 (possession at time of committing/being arrested for a sch. 1 offence)?

A No, he was not in possession of the firearm during the original offence.

B Yes, because he has attempted to commit an indictable offence.

C No, because he did not commit the full offence of robbery.

D Yes, because he has been arrested for attempting to commit a sch. 1 offence.

Question 7.9

VEGA was in the 'Rat and Carrot' pub one night, when he sneaked upstairs into the living quarters while the licensee was serving in the bar. He found a loaded air rifle in a bedroom, and carried it with him in case he was disturbed.

Has VEGA committed an offence under s. 20 of the Firearms Act 1968 (trespassing with a firearm)?

A No, he did not enter the building as a trespasser.

B Yes, he has committed the offence in these circumstances.

C No, he was only in possession of an air weapon.

D No, he took possession of the weapon after he became a trespasser.

Question 7.10

SAUNDERS, a drug dealer, keeps a handgun in his house for protection. One day he drove to a local shop, where he entered and stole goods. As he was leaving the shop, he was stopped by a store detective. SAUNDERS punched the store detective and ran to his car and escaped. The handgun remained in his house during the incident.

Has SAUNDERS committed an offence relating to the handgun, under s. 18 of the Firearms Act 1968, in these circumstances?

A No, he did not have the firearm with him at the time of committing the offence.

B Yes, he was in possession of a firearm at the time of committing the offence.

C Yes, he was in possession of a firearm, while resisting arrest for the offence.

D No, as it cannot be shown that he committed an indictable offence.

Question 7.11

Constable MADDOX was on patrol when she stopped COLE, aged 17, who was driving his car. She saw that there was an air rifle on the front passenger seat. The air rifle was not loaded, and COLE did not have any pellets for the weapon with him.

COLE stated that he was on his way to an area of waste ground, where he intended shooting at tin cans with the air rifle. He stated that he was meeting his friend who would have pellets with him.

Has COLE committed an offence in relation to the air rifle, under s. 19 of the Firearms Act 1968, in these circumstances?

A   No, because he is 17 years of age or over.

B   No, because he did not have suitable ammunition with him for the air rifle.

C   Yes, of having an air rifle with him in a public place.

D   No, because the air rifle was not loaded.

Question 7.12

Section 28(1) of the Violent Crime Reduction Act 2006 creates an offence when a person uses another to look after, hide or transport a dangerous weapon for him or her.

Which of the following would constitute a 'dangerous weapon', according to the definition under this Act?

A   A firearm only, excluding an air weapon.

B   A firearm only, including an air weapon.

C   A firearm, or a knuckleduster and razor blade.

D   A firearm or a sharply pointed instrument only.

Question 7.13

DE'SOUZA is 18 years of age and has recently been released from a young offenders' institution, having served 2 years of a 3 years and 6 months sentence of detention.

What restrictions, if any, are placed on DE'SOUZA being in possession of a firearm?

A   He may only possess a firearm after 5 years from the date of his release.

B   He may not possess a firearm at any time from the date of his release.

C   He may only possess a firearm after 3 years from the date of his release.

D   There are no restrictions, as he was not sentenced to a term of imprisonment.

Question 7.14

PAUL, aged 14, was given an air rifle for his birthday, but he was not allowed to use it unless he was with his brother, DAVID, aged 21. One day they were in the back garden, with PAUL shooting at tins set up on a wall. Several pellets strayed into their neighbour's garden, but no damage was caused.

> Has either PAUL or DAVID committed an offence under s. 22(4) of the Firearms Act 1968, in these circumstances?

A No, neither person has committed an offence, as PAUL is 14 years of age or over.

B Yes, DAVID only, as the person supervising PAUL's use of the weapon.

C Yes, PAUL only, as a person firing pellets beyond the boundary.

D Yes, both people have committed an offence in these circumstances.

Question 7.15

KEETLEY owns a shotgun, which he keeps at GRIFFITHS' farm. He has a current shotgun certificate for the weapon and only uses it to shoot clay pigeons with GRIFFITHS on the farm, which is not open to members of the public. KEETLEY attended the farm one Saturday afternoon to shoot clay pigeons with GRIFFITHS; however, he had been to the local pub before he arrived and was intoxicated. KEETLEY took his shotgun out of the cabinet, but before he was able to load it, GRIFFITHS realised the state he was in and refused to allow him to use any cartridges.

> Would KEETLEY commit an offence under s. 12 of the Licensing Act 1872 (possession of a firearm when drunk) in these circumstances?

A No, as he was not in a public place.

B No, as the shotgun was not loaded.

C Yes, regardless of whether or not he was in a public place.

D Yes, regardless of whether or not the shotgun was loaded.

Question 7.16

Constable PEARCE attended a noisy house party. As Constable PEARCE arrived, one of the party-goers, BELSHAW, was leaving the party. BELSHAW told Constable PEARCE that he had seen ERNEST, the house owner, with what appeared to be a real pistol. Also, BELSHAW had overheard ERNEST and another man discussing a robbery that was to take place in an all-night petrol station that night.

> What powers, if any, would be available to Constable PEARCE under the Firearms Act 1968?

A No power under the Act, as ERNEST was not in a public place.

B Power to enter the premises without warrant and arrest ERNEST for an offence under the Act.

C Power to enter and search the premises without warrant, but only if Constable PEARCE suspects an offence has been committed.

D Power to enter the premises without warrant and search for the weapon.

ANSWERS

Answer 7.1

Answer **C** — There are many 'prohibited weapons' listed in s. 5 of the Firearms Act 1968. Amongst these are:

- any smooth-bore revolver gun other than one which is chambered for 9 mm rim-fire cartridges (answer A is therefore incorrect);
- any self-loading or pump-action rifled gun other than one which is chambered for 0.22 rim-fire cartridges (answer B is therefore incorrect);
- any weapon of whatever description designed or adapted for the discharge of any noxious liquid, gas or other thing;
- any firearm which is so designed or adapted that two or more missiles can be successively discharged without repeated pressure on the trigger (answer D is therefore incorrect).

General Police Duties, para. 4.7.4.2

Answer 7.2

Answer **C** — A shotgun is a smooth-bore gun with a barrel not less than 24 inches in length. Therefore, even though the barrel has been shortened, it is still within the required limit for a shotgun.

A shotgun with a barrel length of less than 24 inches will be treated as a s. 1 firearm — requiring a firearm certificate (which is why answer A is incorrect).

There is a list of 'prohibited weapons' under the 1968 Act, and the permission of the Secretary of State is required to possess them. This weapon does not appear on the list, which is why answers B and D are incorrect.

General Police Duties, para. 4.7.4.3

Answer 7.3

Answer **A** — Section 17(1) of the Firearms Act 1968 states:

It is an offence for a person to make or attempt to make any use whatsoever of a firearm or imitation firearm with intent to resist or prevent the lawful arrest or detention of himself or another person.

The issue of whether a person's fingers could be an imitation firearm was examined in the case of *R v Bentham* [2005] 1 WLR 1057. The Court of Appeal held that holding your fingers inside a jacket and threatening to shoot someone could amount to an offence involving an imitation firearm. However, the House of Lords overturned this decision, finding that the definition of an imitation firearm under s. 57 of the Firearms Act 1968 requires the defendant to carry a 'thing' which is separate and distinct from him or herself and therefore being capable of being possessed. Holding your fingers under your coat will *not* amount to an imitation firearm for the relevant offences, because an unsevered hand or finger is part of oneself and therefore could not be 'possessed'. Answer D is therefore incorrect.

The 'imitation' must have the appearance of a firearm but it is not necessary for any object to have been constructed, adapted or altered so as to resemble a firearm (*R v Williams* [2006] EWCA Crim 1650). Answer B is therefore incorrect. (Further, in *K v DPP* [2006] EWHC 2183 (Admin) it was held that in some circumstances a realistic toy gun, in this case a plastic ball bearing gun, could become an imitation firearm).

The offence allows for a person to make or attempt to make use of a firearm or imitation firearm; therefore answer C is incorrect.

General Police Duties, paras 4.7.4.7, 4.7.8.3

Answer 7.4

Answer **C** — Under s. 1 of the Firearms Act 1968, it is an offence for a person to have in his or her possession, or to purchase or acquire a firearm, without holding a certificate in force at the time or otherwise than as authorised by such a certificate.

The Act allows for a person to possess more than one firearm, but he or she must apply for any new firearm to be included on his or her certificate.

As VOYLE has retained possession of the rifle after his certificate has expired, he clearly commits an offence (which is why answer A is incorrect).

It remains to be proved that OWEN is also in possession of the weapon. There is no requirement to prove that he had the weapon *physically* in his possession — possession has a wider meaning than 'has with him'.

It is possible for one person to be in possession, even though some other person has physical control. It is also possible for more than one person to be in possession of the same article, which is why answers B and D are incorrect.

General Police Duties, para. 4.7.5.1

Answer 7.5

Answer **B** — There are several exemptions from the requirement to have a firearms certificate. Under s. 16 of the Firearms (Amendment) Act 1988, a person is allowed to borrow a rifle from the occupier of private premises for use on those premises.

It is specified that the borrowing must take place in either the occupier's presence or his 'servant's'. There is no specific requirement for the occupier to be on the premises while the 'servant' is with the borrower (making both answers A and C incorrect).

The same exemption applies under s. 11(5) of the Firearms Act 1968 for the holder of a shotgun licence. This is in addition to the exemption provided under the amended Act (which is why answer D is incorrect).

General Police Duties, para. 4.7.5.4

Answer 7.6

Answer **D** — It is an offence under s. 16 of the Firearms Act 1968 for a person to have in his or her possession, a firearm or ammunition with intent by means thereof to endanger the life of another. There is no requirement to show that a person had the firearm/ammunition 'with him'. The offence refers to possession, which is a wider requirement (which is why answer C is incorrect).

This is a crime of 'specific intent' and the prosecution would have to show an intention by the defendant to behave in a way that he or she knows will in fact endanger the life of another (*R v Brown and Ciarla* [1995] Crim LR 327). Therefore, the important factor is the defendant's belief, not some other person's and answer A is incorrect.

That intent does not have to be an immediate one and it may be conditional (e.g. intent to shoot someone if they do not do as they are asked — see *R v Bentham* [1973] QB 537. Answer B is therefore incorrect.

General Police Duties, para. 4.7.8.1

Answer 7.7

Answer **A** — This question tests understanding of two areas: the definition of imitation firearms and s. 16A of the Firearms Act 1968.

There are two types of imitation firearms: 'general imitations' (those which have the appearance of a firearm); and 'imitations of s. 1 firearms' (those which have the appearance of a s. 1 firearm, and which can be readily converted into one).

The weapon in the scenario would fall within the first part of the definition, which is why answer C is incorrect.

Under s. 16A of the 1968 Act, a person commits an offence if he or she has in his or her possession a firearm or imitation firearm, with intent by means thereof to cause any person to believe that unlawful violence would be used against him or another.

Because the offence can be committed with an imitation firearm, answer B is incorrect. There is no requirement to prove that the victim actually believed that violence would be used against him, which is why answer D is incorrect.

General Police Duties, paras 4.7.8.2, 4.7.4.7

Answer 7.8

Answer **D** — Under s. 17(2) of the Firearms Act 1968, a person is guilty if he is in possession of a firearm (or imitation) at the time of committing or being arrested for either committing or attempting an offence listed in sch. 1.

There is a list of offences in sch. 1 and some of these are indictable offences. However, as not all the offences mentioned in sch. 1 are indictable, answer B is incorrect.

Answer A is incorrect because the offence may be committed by possessing the firearm while being arrested for a sch. 1 offence regardless of any timescales between the arrest and the original offence (or whether the offender even had the firearm with him when that offence was committed).

The offence includes attempting to commit a sch. 1 offence and therefore answer C is incorrect.

General Police Duties, para. 4.7.8.4

Answer 7.9

Answer **B** — The offence is committed under s. 20(1) of the Firearms Act 1968 when a person has a firearm or imitation firearm with him and he enters, or is in any building or part of a building as a trespasser without reasonable excuse.

The offence does not require a person to have entered a building with the weapon — it includes a person who is in a building with one, i.e. takes possession of it when inside (which makes answer D incorrect).

The offence applies in any building or part of a building and there is no need to have entered the building as a trespasser (making answer A incorrect).

The offence includes having a firearm or imitation firearm, and firearm includes an air weapon (though the offence is summary) and therefore answer C is incorrect.

General Police Duties, para. 4.7.8.5

Answer 7.10

Answer **A** — This offence is similar to s. 17(2) of the Firearms Act 1968 (possession while committing or being arrested for a sch. 1 offence), and the person would be guilty of an offence under that section. However, an offence under s. 18 requires a person to have with him a firearm either at the time of committing an indictable offence, or when resisting arrest or preventing the arrest of another for such an offence. 'Have with him' may include nearby in his car, but would not include in a house as it would not be readily available to him. In *R v Bradish* [2004] LTL 2 April, the Court of Appeal held that the defendant did not have a firearm 'with him' when it was in his house a few miles away from the scene. Answers B and C are incorrect because this offence does not include being in 'possession', which has a wider meaning than 'has with him'.

Answer D is incorrect, as 'indictable offence' will include offences which are triable either way.

General Police Duties, para. 4.7.8.6

Answer 7.11

Answer **C** — Under s. 19 of the Firearms Act 1968, a person commits an offence if without lawful authority, or reasonable excuse, he or she has with him or her in a public place a loaded shotgun (s. 19(a)), a firearm, whether loaded or not, together with suitable ammunition (s. 19(c)), or an imitation firearm (s. 19(d)). Note that this area of legislation has changed. Previously, s. 19 made no reference to imitation firearms, and the offence would only be committed in relation to an air weapon when it was loaded.

Section 19(b) now states that an offence is committed when a person has with him or her an air weapon in a public place, whether it is loaded or not (which means that answer D is incorrect). This offence is committed by any person, regardless of his or her age, therefore answer A is incorrect. Further, the person will still commit the offence even if he or she does not have suitable ammunition for the air weapon with him or her, (answer B is incorrect). It is unlikely that COLE would have either lawful authority, or a reasonable excuse for having the air rifle with him in these circumstances, and an offence is likely to have been committed.

General Police Duties, para. 4.7.8.7

Answer 7.12

Answer **C** — Under s. 28(1) of the Violent Crime Reduction Act 2006, a person is guilty of an offence if he or she uses another to look after, hide or transport a dangerous weapon for him or her, and he or she does so under arrangements or in circumstances that facilitate, or are intended to facilitate, the weapon's being available to him or her for an unlawful purpose.

A 'dangerous weapon' means a firearm other than an air weapon or a component part of, or accessory to, an air weapon. Answer B is incorrect.

Also included are weapons to which ss. 141 and 141A of the Criminal Justice Act 1988 apply. These include, specified offensive weapons, such as knuckledusters, stealth knives and a host of other weapons (s. 141). Answer D is therefore incorrect.

They also include knives, razor blades, axes and any other article which has a blade or which is sharply pointed and which is made or adapted for use for causing injury to the person (s. 141A). Answers A and B are therefore incorrect.

General Police Duties, para. 4.7.8.8

Answer 7.13

Answer **B** — Under s. 21 of the Act, a person who has been sentenced to life imprisonment or 3 years' imprisonment (which includes detention in a youth offender institution) must not at any time have a firearm in his or her possession.

Note that the restriction applies to a person sentenced, and therefore it is immaterial that DE'SOUZA did not serve his whole sentence.

Answer A would be correct if DE'SOUZA had been sentenced to less than 3 years' detention (also covered by s. 21 of the Act). Answer C is merely a false statement and therefore incorrect.

As detention in a young offender's institution is included, answer D is incorrect.

General Police Duties, para. 4.7.9

Answer 7.14

Answer **D** — Under s. 22(4) of the Firearms Act 1968, a person under the age of 17 commits an offence if he or she has with him or her an air weapon or ammunition for an air weapon. There is an exception to this rule when a person is under the supervision of a person aged over 21, provided they are on premises and the missiles are not fired beyond the boundary of the premises. Missiles were fired beyond the premises in the scenario, therefore an offence was committed. The offence is committed both by the person who is under the age of 17 (answer A is therefore incorrect) and by the person supervising him or her (s. 23(1)). Since both persons in the scenario are liable, answers B and C are incorrect.

When in force, the Violent Crime Reduction Act 2006 will amend s. 22(4) so that the offence will be committed by a person under the age of 18, not 17.

General Police Duties, para. 4.7.9.2

Answer 7.15

Answer **B** — Under s. 12 of the Licensing Act 1872, it is an offence to be in possession of any loaded firearm, while drunk. Therefore, since KEETLEY did not load a cartridge into the shotgun, he would not be liable for this offence (and answer D is incorrect). There is no requirement for the person to be in a public place for this offence to be made out. Therefore it may be committed on private premises (answer A is incorrect). Had KEETLEY loaded the shotgun, he would have committed an offence, and answer C would have been correct. Since he did not, answer C is incorrect.

General Police Duties, para. 4.7.9.2

Answer 7.16

Answer **D** — Two powers are provided under s. 47 of the Firearms Act 1968. First, a constable may require a person in a public place to hand over a firearm for examination (the purpose being to detect offences).

A further power is provided by s. 47 to examine a weapon from a person elsewhere than in a public place — provided the officer has reasonable cause to suspect the person is committing or is about to commit a relevant offence (offences in ss. 18 and 20 of the Act apply). Consequently, answers A and C are incorrect.

Answer B is incorrect because the power is provided to enter premises to search for or examine a firearm only — not to arrest (although an arrest may well be necessary if a firearm is found).

General Police Duties, para. 4.7.10

8 | Weapons

STUDY PREPARATION

While the definition contained in s. 1 of the Prevention of Crime Act 1953 appears quite simple, you need to know the component parts to fully understand the offence. Learn the meaning of 'lawful authority', 'reasonable excuse', 'has with him' and 'public place'; there are many decided cases to assist (or confuse) you. You must also, of course, learn the three categories of offensive weapons.

Commonly, people tend to confuse the offence under the 1953 Act with the offence of carrying a bladed or sharply-pointed article, especially in relation to folding pocket-knives and the length of blades. Remember also where the evidential burden lies in relation to proof for both offences, and the special defences under the Criminal Justice Act 1988.

One of the greatest problems in this very relevant area is separating the different statutory requirements. It is essential to be able to distinguish between the requirements relating to offensive weapons (in the Prevention of Crime Act 1953) and those relating to pointed or bladed instruments as regulated by the Criminal Justice Act 1988. Unless you are very clear about these differences, life will get very confusing.

Further offences contained in the chapter relate to the carrying of weapons on educational premises. These mirror the two offences above, with similar definitions. The Violent Crime Reduction Act 2006 further extends these provisions, giving specific powers to teachers and head teachers.

Also, you must be able to tell the difference between an 'offensive weapon' and a 'weapon of offence', as contained in the offence of trespassing with a weapon of offence, under the Criminal Law Act 1977. The manufacture and sale of weapons receive attention, with a long list of weapons that may not be manufactured or sold, etc. Further offences may be committed by selling and marketing knives and articles to children under 16. Do not forget to learn about crossbows and

> the three offences contained in the Crossbows Act 1987. Also, pay attention to the powers given to a constable to search people and vehicles.
>
> Apart from that, it is very straightforward!

QUESTIONS

Question 8.1

Constable RICHARDS stopped POWER and conducted a search under s. 1 of the Police and Criminal Evidence Act 1984. The officer discovered a flick knife in POWER's trouser pocket. POWER stated that he had a reasonable excuse for the weapon being there.

In relation to POWER's claim to have a reasonable excuse, where does the burden of proof lie?

A The prosecution must show on the balance of probabilities that POWER did not have a reasonable excuse.

B POWER must show beyond reasonable doubt that he did have a reasonable excuse.

C The prosecution must show beyond reasonable doubt that POWER did not have a reasonable excuse.

D POWER must show on the balance of probabilities that he had a reasonable excuse.

Question 8.2

FAWCETT was driving home from work when he caused another car, being driven by GRANT, to brake sharply. GRANT followed him, shouting obscenities and sounding his horn. When FAWCETT stopped at traffic lights, GRANT got out of his car and ran towards him. FAWCETT got out of his own car and picked up a steering wheel lock, and threw it at GRANT, intending to injure him.

Is the steering wheel lock an 'offensive weapon' in these circumstances?

A No, FAWCETT formed the intention to use the article after it came into his possession.

B Yes, as soon as FAWCETT formed the intention to use the article.

C Yes, because FAWCETT used the article, intending to injure GRANT.

D Yes, as soon as FAWCETT picked the article up with the intention to use it.

Question 8.3

Constable BAKER was on patrol when she stopped a vehicle owned and being driven by CLEMENT. HARVEY was in the front passenger seat. Constable BAKER made a search of the vehicle and discovered a flick knife in the glove compartment.

Could HARVEY and CLEMENT be guilty of an offence under the Prevention of Crime Act 1953?

A No, only CLEMENT may commit the offence, being the owner of the car.

B Yes, the offence is complete against both; no further proof is required.

C No, it is not possible for two people to have the same weapon with them.

D Yes, provided they both knew that the other person had it with him at the time.

Question 8.4

PENFOLD was stopped and searched on his way to a football match while he was walking in High Street. The searching officer, Constable MARRIOTT, discovered in PENFOLD's pocket a number of 50 pence pieces that had been sharpened around the edges. Believing that they were offensive weapons, the officer lawfully arrested PENFOLD.

In order to prove that PENFOLD was guilty of possessing an offensive weapon would Constable MARRIOTT need to prove intent by PENFOLD to use the coins to cause injury?

A No, provided it can be shown that the coins have been made to cause injury.

B Yes, because there is no apparent victim in these circumstances.

C Yes, because the coins are not offensive weapons *per se*.

D No, provided it can be shown the coins have been adapted to cause injury.

Question 8.5

BARRY was stopped and searched in the street by Constable ROCH. The officer found a pocket-knife in BARRY'S pocket, which had a 4-inch blade. BARRY admitted that he was on his way to a football match and intended to use the knife in a fight with rival fans.

Is this weapon an offensive weapon under the Prevention of Crime Act 1953?

A Yes, as the blade is more than 3 inches long.

B   Yes, a folding pocket-knife with a blade of more than 3 inches will always be an offensive weapon.

C   Yes, it is an offensive weapon regardless of the length of the blade.

D   No, a folding pocket-knife will not be an offensive weapon regardless of the length of the blade.

Question 8.6

BROOKER was stopped and searched by the police in a public place, whilst on the way to a football match. At the time, BROOKER was carrying a butter knife, which was not sharpened, and which had a blade of at least 3.5 inches in length.

Could BROOKER commit an offence under s. 139 of the Criminal Justice Act 1988 in these circumstances?

A   No, because the blade was not sharp.

B   Yes, because the knife was a bladed instrument.

C   Yes, because the knife was a bladed instrument more than 3 inches long.

D   No, because it is unlikely that the blade was capable of causing injury.

Question 8.7

Constable WARREN was on duty on a Sunday evening when he stopped MOHAM-MED, who was driving a car on the road. Constable WARREN conducted a search of the vehicle and found a meat cleaver under the seat. MOHAMMED stated that he worked as a chef in a restaurant and that he used the meat cleaver as part of his work. He further stated that he had put it in his car the previous night, intending to take it to be sharpened on Monday morning.

Would MOHAMMED have a defence to a charge under s. 139 of the Criminal Justice Act 1988 (having a bladed or sharply pointed article), in these circumstances?

A   Yes, the statutory defence of 'good reason'.

B   Yes, because he had it for use in his work.

C   No, the offence is complete in these circumstances.

D   Yes, the statutory defence of 'lawful authority'.

Question 8.8

HUTCHINGS visited his friend, CARTER, who lives with his parents in the caretaker's house of a primary school. When he arrived, both boys played in the garden of the caretaker's house. Both boys were playing with flick-knives.

Who would commit an offence of having with him an offensive weapon on school premises in these circumstances?

A Neither, because they are not on school premises.

B Both, because they are on school premises.

C HUTCHINGS only, because he does not reside on the premises.

D Both, because they are not in a dwelling on school premises.

Question 8.9

A report was received by the police of a disturbance in a high school. The first person to arrive was Constable SANCHEZ, who was in plain clothes. He was told that 2 pupils had threatened a teacher and that one of them had a knife. After a search, Constable SANCHEZ found the 2 youths in the street outside.

What powers would Constable SANCHEZ have under the Criminal Justice Act 1988 in these circumstances?

A He has no powers under the 1988 Act and must use his powers under the Police and Criminal Evidence Act 1984.

B He has a power under the 1988 Act to search the youths for an offensive weapon.

C He has no powers under the 1988 Act as the pupils were not trespassing.

D He has no powers under the 1988 Act as he is not in uniform.

Question 8.10

PIETERSEN, a head teacher of a high school, was contacted by a member of staff stating that SNACHEZ, a pupil at the school, had been seen carrying a knife on school premises. The teacher kept SNACHEZ under observation until PIETERSEN arrived. Utilising powers under s. 550AA of the Education Act 1996, PIETERSEN searched SNACHEZ but did not find the knife. SNACHEZ was carrying a bag and the member of staff suggested that SNACHEZ may have hidden the knife inside it.

What authority would PIETERSEN have to search SNACHEZ's possessions, under this legislation?

A None, possessions may not be searched under this legislation, only a pupil may be searched.

B A pupil's possessions may be searched, but only in the pupil's presence and in the presence of another member of staff.

C A pupil's possessions may be searched, but only in the presence of another member of staff and with the pupil's permission.

D A pupil's possessions may be searched, but only in the presence of another member of staff.

Question 8.11

MEARS was a high school pupil on a field trip. The teacher in charge, SMITH, was told by another pupil that MEARS had taken a flick-knife on the trip and had hidden it in a coat pocket. SMITH told MEARS to hand over the weapon, however, MEARS denied being in possession of a knife.

What powers, if any, would SMITH have to search for the weapon, under s. 550AA of the Education Act 1996?

A SMITH may have searched MEARS, using force if necessary.

B None, as they were not on school premises.

C None, only a head teacher may search a pupil under this legislation.

D SMITH may have searched MEARS, but not by the use of force.

Question 8.12

The Violent Crime Reduction Act 2006 has inserted a new s. 550AA into the Education Act 1996, allowing pupils from a school to be searched for bladed and sharply pointed instruments and offensive weapons.

How should a weapon be disposed of, when seized utilising powers under this section?

A It must be taken to a police station as soon as reasonably practicable.

B It must be retained and returned to the pupil's parent.

C It must be disposed of or destroyed by the person seizing it as soon as reasonably practicable.

D It must be handed to a police constable as soon as reasonably practicable.

Question 8.13

Constable SNELL attended a disturbance at a premises belonging to FRASER. FRASER stated that TAYLOR, who was a tenant renting the house, had refused to leave after having been served with an eviction notice. TAYLOR was in the detached garage and had armed himself with a baseball bat, and was threatening to use it on anyone who tried to make him leave.

Has TAYLOR committed an offence under the Criminal Law Act 1977 in these circumstances?

A Yes, he was trespassing with a weapon of offence.

B No, because he was not in a dwelling as a trespasser.

C No, because he was not in a building attached to a dwelling as a trespasser.

D No, because he did not enter the premises as a trespasser.

Question 8.14

ANDREWS owned a house which was being renovated. One day he visited it and found HARVEY squatting inside. ANDREWS asked HARVEY to leave. However, HARVEY was carrying a knife and threatened ANDREWS with it. The police were called and Constable RAMAN arrived, and was considering how to deal with HARVEY.

Which of the following is the definition of a weapon of offence under s. 8 of the Criminal Law Act 1977?

A Any article made or adapted for use for causing injury to or incapacitating a person, or intended by the person having it with him or her for that use.

B Any article made or adapted for use for causing injury to or intended by the person having it with him or her for that use.

C Any article intended by the person having it with him or her for the purpose of causing injury.

D Any article made or adapted for use for causing injury to or incapacitating a person.

Question 8.15

STONE owns a shop which sells second-hand goods and has a reputation for being able to supply unusual weapons. COLLINS entered the shop looking for some weapons for himself and his friends for a football match the following week. STONE indicated that he could get his hands on some knuckle dusters, which he could sell at a good price. COLLINS agreed to return 3 days later to buy them.

At what point, if any, would STONE commit an offence under the Criminal Justice Act 1988?

A Not until he actually sells the weapons to COLLINS.

B Not until he is in possession of the weapons with intent to sell them.

C When he offered to sell the weapon to COLLINS.

D Not until he has the weapons with him with intent to sell them.

Question 8.16

WENDY, aged 15, has a Saturday job working in a chemist's shop owned by HUS-SEIN. One day she served PETER, who bought a packet of cartridge razor blades. WENDY was aware that PETER was also 15 as she was in his class at school.

Would either WENDY or HUSSEIN commit an offence of selling a bladed instrument to a person under 16 under s. 141A of the Criminal Justice Act 1988?

A Neither, the articles are not covered by the Criminal Justice Act 1988.

B Both WENDY and HUSSEIN.

C Neither, as WENDY was also under 16.

D WENDY only as HUSSEIN would have a statutory defence.

Question 8.17

GUY, aged 15, was in the back garden of his parents' house, and had with him a crossbow. He was using it to fire at a target in the garden, and was accompanied at the time by PREECE, aged 18. At no time did any of the bolts fired from the crossbow leave the garden.

Has GUY committed an offence in these circumstances?

A No, because he was accompanied by a person over 18.

B No, because he was not in a public place.

C No, because none of the missiles was allowed to leave the property.

D Yes, because he was not accompanied by a person over 21.

Question 8.18

Section 4 of the Crossbows Act 1987 provides a power of search for a crossbow, or a part of a crossbow.

Which of the following statements is correct in relation to a police officer exercising a power of search under this section?

A The officer must be in uniform to exercise a power of search under the Act.

B The officer may enter any premises in order to conduct the search.

C The power to search is governed by the PACE Codes of Practice, Code B.

D There is power to search vehicles as well as persons.

ANSWERS

Answer 8.1

Answer **D** — The prosecution must first show, beyond reasonable doubt, that the defendant had an offensive weapon with him — which in these circumstances should cause no problem. The burden of proof then lies with the defendant to show that he had a reasonable excuse for having the weapon, and therefore answers A and C are incorrect. The burden of proof will be judged on the balance of probabilities, and not beyond reasonable doubt; therefore, answer B is incorrect.

General Police Duties, para. 4.8.2

Answer 8.2

Answer **A** — The expression 'has with him' will not in most cases include circumstances where a person has an 'innocent' article, which he or she uses offensively. The purpose of the Prevention of Crime Act 1953 is to prevent people from arming themselves for some future event, and the intention of the Act is to deal with preventative issues.

The case of *Ohlson* v *Hylton* [1975] 1 WLR 724 demonstrates this. The defendant had a bag of tools with him in the course of his trade. He produced a hammer from the bag and used it to hit someone. The court held that, as he had formed the intention to use the hammer *after* it came into his possession, the offence was not made out (answers B and C are therefore incorrect). This decision was followed by several other similar cases (*Bates* v *Bulman* [1979] 1 WLR 1190, *R* v *Dayle* [1974] 1 WLR 181 and *R* v *Humphreys* [1977] Crim LR 225).

This is not to say that 'innocent' articles may never become offensive weapons, such as people carrying screwdrivers to defend themselves; it depends on the immediacy of the conversion from one to another, and therefore answer D is incorrect.

General Police Duties, para. 4.8.2.1

Answer 8.3

Answer **D** — It is possible for more than one person to have the same weapon 'with them' (*R* v *Edmonds* [1963] 2 QB 142), and therefore answers A and C are incorrect. It would be necessary to prove that they knew of the existence of the weapon in the hands of the other.

In this case it was decided that both parties knew of the existence of the weapon and that they knew the other party had it 'with him' at the time of the offence. Answer B is incorrect as the offence is not complete until this is proved.

General Police Duties, para. 4.8.2.1

Answer 8.4

Answer **D** — The prosecution would have to show that the coins have been adapted to cause injury in order to show that they are offensive weapons. However, once the prosecution have proved this, there is no need to show an intention to use them to cause injury (*Davis* v *Alexander* (1970) 54 Cr App R 398).

Answer A is incorrect because the coins have not been 'made' to cause injury; they are not offensive weapons *per se*. However, the fact that they are not offensive weapons *per se* still does not place a burden upon the prosecution to prove intent to use them (*Davis* v *Alexander*), which is why answer C is incorrect.

Answer B is incorrect because it is the adaptation of the article that is relevant, not the intention of the person carrying it (*Bryan* v *Mott* (1976) 62 Cr App R 71).

If PENFOLD were charged under the third leg of the definition, where the weapon is intended to cause injury, the prosecution would have to prove an intention to cause injury by PENFOLD. This would obviously be a harder case to prove than adaptation in the above circumstances.

General Police Duties, para. 4.8.2.3

Answer 8.5

Answer **C** — Under the Prevention of Crime Act 1953, an offensive weapon is an article which is made, intended or adapted for causing injury. The weapon in question will be an offensive weapon because BARRY intends that it will be used to cause injury.

Under the 1953 Act, it is irrelevant what length the blade happens to be. However, under s. 139 of the Criminal Justice Act 1988, a person commits an offence if he or she has a bladed or sharply pointed instrument in a public place — unless the instrument is a folding pocket-knife with a blade of less than 3 inches. Do not mix the two Acts.

Answers A and B are incorrect as they refer to the length of the blade as being relevant. Answer D is incorrect because a folding pocket-knife may be an offensive weapon, depending on the circumstances.

General Police Duties, para. 4.8.2.3

Answer 8.6

Answer **B** — Under s. 139 of the Criminal Justice Act 1988, a person commits an offence if he or she has a bladed or sharply pointed instrument in a public place. The Act provides for a person either carrying a sharply pointed instrument or a bladed instrument. There is no requirement for a bladed instrument to be sharp and in *Brooker* v *DPP* (2005) 169 JP 368, it was held that a blunt butter knife fell within s. 139. Answer A is therefore incorrect.

Under the Act, a folding pocket-knife is excluded, provided the cutting edge of the blade is less than 3 inches long. This does not apply to all bladed instruments and the length of the blade of any other bladed instrument is irrelevant, which is why answer C is incorrect.

There is no requirement under the Act to prove that the instrument was capable of causing injury, and therefore answer D is incorrect.

General Police Duties, para. 4.8.3

Answer 8.7

Answer **C** — A defendant charged with an offence under s. 139(1) of the Act may claim either that he or she had a 'good reason' for having the weapon with him or her, or that he or she had 'lawful authority'. Further, the defendant may also claim that he or she had the weapon for use at work.

The circumstances in the question mirror those in the case of *Mohammed* v *Chief Constable of South Yorkshire* [2002] EWHC 406. The defendant appealed against his conviction for an offence under s. 139(1), claiming that he had the meat cleaver with him for a 'good reason' (per s. 139(4)), or alternatively that he had it with him for use in his work (per s. 139(5)). The appeal failed in the Administrative Court, which held that the defendant had not shown that he had a 'good reason' for having the weapon, as the 'ultimate lawful purpose' claimed was too far distant from the time when the defendant was caught with the article. Answer A is incorrect.

The Court also held that the defendant did not have the cleaver for use at work; he had it for the purposes of *rendering it possible* to use at work. The Court held that he could have taken the cleaver directly from work on the Monday morning to be sharpened. Answer B is therefore incorrect.

'Lawful authority' means those occasions where people are required to carry weapons as a matter of duty, such as police officers or members of the armed forces (*Bryan* v *Mott* (1976) 62 Cr App R 71). In these circumstances, MOHAMMED could not claim this defence and answer D is incorrect.

General Police Duties, para. 4.8.3.1

Answer 8.8

Answer **A** — This offence was added to the Prevention of Crime Act 1953, and a further offence was added to the Criminal Justice Act 1988 of having a sharply pointed or bladed instrument on school premises. The definitions of weapons mirror the original offences; therefore, it follows that a flick knife-will be an offensive weapon *per se.*

Under the definition of 'school premises', the offence may only be committed on premises providing primary or secondary education, or both, whether full-time or part-time.

The offence will not be committed on land occupied solely as a dwelling by a person employed at the school. This means a caretaker's house in a school. Answer B is incorrect for this reason.

The fact that one of the people was not a resident is not relevant (which is why answer C is incorrect), and the exemption applies to both the land and the dwelling (therefore, answer D is also incorrect).

General Police Duties, para. 4.8.4

Answer 8.9

Answer **A** — Under the Criminal Justice Act 1988, an offence is committed when a person has an offensive weapon with him or her on school premises.

Under the Act, a constable may enter school premises and search those premises and any person for an offensive weapon. Note that the power under the Act only enables a constable to enter and search premises and search people on the premises. The power is not extended to searching people off school premises. The officer may, of course, use his power under s. 1 of the Police and Criminal Evidence Act 1984 to search the youths. This is why answer A is correct and answer B is incorrect.

There is no requirement for the constable to be in uniform, and therefore answer D is incorrect.

A person may commit an offence under this Act whether he or she is on the premises lawfully or not, and therefore answer C is incorrect.

General Police Duties, para. 4.8.4.2

Answer 8.10

Answer **B** — The Violent Crime Reduction Act 2006 has inserted a new s. 550AA into the Education Act 1996. Under s. 550AA(1), a member of the staff of a school who has reasonable grounds for suspecting that a pupil at the school may have with him or her or in his or her possession:

(a) an article to which section 139 of the Criminal Justice Act 1988 applies (knives and blades etc.), or
(b) an offensive weapon (within the meaning of the Prevention of Crime Act 1953),
may search that pupil or his possessions for such articles and weapons.

(Answer A is incorrect).

A pupil's possessions may not be searched under this section except in their presence and in the presence of another member of the staff. Since the pupil needs to be present, answer D is incorrect. However, the search may take place without the pupil's permission — indeed, as much force as is reasonable may be used in exercising this power (see s. 550AA(8)). Answer C is therefore incorrect.

Note that the person carrying out a search may only require the removal of outer clothing; they must be of the same sex and carry out the search in the presence of another member of staff also of the same sex as the pupil (s. 550AA(5)).

General Police Duties, para. 4.8.4.3

Answer 8.11

Answer **A** — The Violent Crime Reduction Act 2006 has inserted a new s. 550AA into the Education Act 1996. Under s. 550AA(1), a member of the staff of a school who has reasonable grounds for suspecting that a pupil at the school may have with him or her or in his or her possession:

(a) an article to which section 139 of the Criminal Justice Act 1988 applies (knives and blades etc.), or
(b) an offensive weapon (within the meaning of the Prevention of Crime Act 1953),
may search that pupil or his possessions for such articles and weapons.

Under s. 550AA(2), a search may be carried out only where the member of the staff and the pupil are on school premises; or they are elsewhere and the member of the staff has lawful control or charge of the pupil. Answer B is therefore incorrect.

A person may carry out a search under this section only if he or she is the head teacher of the school; or he or she has been authorised by the head teacher to carry out the search (see s. 550AA(3)). Answer C is therefore incorrect.

Finally, such a search may take place without the pupil's permission — indeed, as much force as is reasonable may be used in exercising this power (see s. 550AA(8)). Answer D is therefore incorrect.

General Police Duties, para. 4.8.4.3

Answer 8.12

Answer **D** — The Violent Crime Reduction Act 2006 has inserted a new s. 550AA into the Education Act 1996. Under s. 550AA(9) and (10), any article seized must be delivered to a police constable as soon as reasonably practicable, and the Police (Property) Act 1897 will apply to its disposal. Answers A, B and C are therefore incorrect.

General Police Duties, para. 4.8.4.3

Answer 8.13

Answer **D** — Under s. 8 of the Criminal Law Act 1977, a person commits an offence when they are on premises as a trespasser, having entered as one, if without lawful authority or reasonable excuse they have with them a weapon of offence.

The baseball bat may well have been a weapon of offence, because of TAYLOR's intention to use it as such. However, the offence may only be committed where a person has entered as a trespasser. TAYLOR had obviously not done so as he was a bona fide tenant when he entered, which makes answer D correct and answer A incorrect.

Answers B and C are incorrect statements because premises includes, amongst other things, any building and the site comprising any buildings with ancillary land. The offence is not restricted to a dwelling house.

General Police Duties, para. 4.8.5

Answer 8.14

Answer **A** — For an offence contrary to s. 8 of the Criminal Law Act 1977 the definition of 'weapon of offence' is the same as that for aggravated burglary, namely any article made or adapted for use for causing injury to or incapacitating a person, or intended by the person having it with him or her for that use (s. 8(2)). This is answer A; therefore answers B, C and D are incorrect.

General Police Duties, para. 4.8.5

Answer 8.15

Answer **C** — Section 141 of the Criminal Justice Act 1988 makes it an offence to manufacture, sell, hire, offer for sale or hire, expose, have in possession for the purpose of sale or hire, or lend or give to another person, any weapon listed in the schedule to the Act (knuckle dusters are included).

The offence may be committed by making an offer — the Act makes no mention of being in possession of the article when the offer is made, which is why answer C is correct (this is similar to a case of offering to supply drugs under the Misuse of Drugs Act 1971).

Although offences would be made out in answers A and B, the offence has already been committed.

Answer D would be an incorrect answer in any circumstances, as unlike the original 1953 Act, which requires a person to have the weapon with him, this offence deals with possession for the purpose of sale or hire.

General Police Duties, para. 4.8.6

Answer 8.16

Answer **A** — Under s. 141 A of the Criminal Justice Act 1988, it is an offence for any person to sell to a person under 16 a knife, blade, razor blade, axe, any article which has a blade or sharp point and is made or adapted for causing injury. The offence does not apply to a razor blade in a cartridge, where not more than 2 mm of the blade is exposed (or a folding pocket-knife with a blade of less than 3 inches).

The age of the person making the sale is not relevant (which is why answer C is incorrect). There is a defence provided for the person charged to show that they took all reasonable precautions and exercised due diligence to avoid the offence. However, since no offence took place, it is not relevant in these circumstances. If it were relevant, it would only be available to the person making the sale, as the offence only applies to that person (therefore answers B and D are incorrect). It would not apply to WENDY, as she was aware of PETER's age.

(Note that when s. 43(1), (2) of the Violent Crime Reduction Act 2006 is in force, the age will increase from under 16 to under 18.)

General Police Duties, paras 4.8.7.1, 4.8.7.2

Answer 8.17

Answer **D** — Under s. 3 of the Crossbows Act 1987, a person under the age of 17 who has with him or her a crossbow (or parts of a crossbow) capable of discharging a missile is guilty of an offence, unless accompanied by a person who is over 21 (which makes answer A incorrect).

There is no requirement for the person to be in a public place and therefore answer B is incorrect. Answer C is incorrect, as the statement is taken from the Firearms Act 1968 in relation to air weapons.

(Note that when s. 44(1)-(2)(c) of the Violent Crime Reduction Act 2006 is in force, the age will increase from under 17 to under 18.)

General Police Duties, para. 4.8.8

Answer 8.18

Answer **D** — If a constable (no mention of uniform) reasonably suspects a person is committing or has committed an offence under s. 3 of the Crossbows Act 1987, they may search the suspected person or their vehicle for the crossbow (or part of a crossbow). Answer A is therefore incorrect.

For the purposes of exercising the power of search, a constable may enter any land other than a dwelling house in order to conduct the search. Answer B is therefore incorrect.

This power of search is governed by PACE Codes of Practice, Code A, not Code B. Answer C is therefore incorrect.

General Police Duties, para. 4.8.8.1

9 | Civil Disputes

STUDY PREPARATION

After the wealth of detail covered by the previous few chapters, this one may come as something of a relief.

Although the title would tend to suggest that the police have little interest or involvement, civil disputes are nevertheless a significant feature of police patrol work. The area of domestic violence has received a great deal of political and legislative attention over recent years. A number of important changes were made to this area of the law by the Domestic Violence, Crime and Victims Act 2004.

In addition to the various statutory measures in place to govern civil disputes, it is in this area that some of the most difficult 'balancing acts' in relation to human rights issues take place. These issues should be borne in mind when addressing questions in this chapter.

QUESTIONS

Question 9.1

Inspector BHARWANI was called to the house of Constable URQUART who was accused of assaulting his wife. A criminal investigation began and evidence was gathered. This evidence was insufficient for a criminal change, however Constable URQUART stands charged with 'general conduct' misconduct.

What sanction can Constable URQUART expect if found guilty at a misconduct hearing?

A He can expect any sanction except dismissal/requirement to resign as he was not convicted of criminal offence.

B He can expect a fine higher than normal due to the aggravating factor of domestic violence.

C He can expect to be dismissed/required to resign, as this is guidance from the Association of Chief Police Officers.

D He could be dismissed/required to resign, at the presiding officer's discretion.

Question 9.2

MUSGRAVE is 15 years old and under the care of social services following an abusive home life. She wishes to take out a non-molestation order to prevent her uncle from contacting her, as he regularly approaches her to tell her that her father is sorry.

Under the Family Law Act 1996, can MUSGRAVE apply for a non-molestation order?

A No, as a non-molestation order only applies to spouses or former partners.

B No, as a person under 16 cannot apply for a non-molestation order.

C Yes, provided social services are satisfied she has sufficient understanding to make the application.

D Yes, provided the court is satisfied she has sufficient understanding to make the application.

Question 9.3

DANIELS and EVERSHAM used to share a house as friends, but not as co-habitants. Over a period of time, DANIELS became fixated with EVERSHAM. The behaviour caused EVERSHAM considerable distress and she eventually moved out. DANIELS then began following EVERSHAM home from work and she genuinely feared for her safety. EVERSHAM visited a solicitor with a view to obtaining a non-molestation order against DANIELS.

Would EVERSHAM be likely to succeed in obtaining such an order, under s. 42 of the Family Law Act 1996?

A No, DANIELS has not been made subject to a court order under this Act.

B Yes, an application may be made in these circumstances.

C No, DANIELS and EVERSHAM were not co-habitants, or spouses or related to each other.

D No, such an order may only be made to prevent the molestation of a child.

Question 9.4

DAWKINS has had a non-molestation order taken out against him by his wife, which has a power of arrest attached. DAWKINS breaches the order and is arrested at 10.30 pm on Saturday night. He arrives at the police station at 10.35 pm and detention is authorised at 10.55 pm.

By what time must DAWKINS be brought before the relevant judicial authority?

A   Sunday, no later than 10.30 pm.
B   Sunday, no later than 10.35 pm.
C   Monday, no later than 10.30 pm.
D   Monday, no later than 10.35 pm.

Question 9.5

ASHTON has been sacked from his job at an aeronautical factory. He complains to his union, who take 4 weeks to decide his case. The union eventually decides to authorise industrial action and to picket the aeronautical factory. In the intervening period, however, the firm has moved premises and no longer occupies the premises where ASHTON worked. A considerable amount of land at the new factory is private.

In relation to picketing, which of the following is true?

A   The pickets cannot enter the private land to picket.
B   The pickets could picket the new premises as it is still technically ASHTON's place of work.
C   There would be a maximum of 6 pickets allowed at any one time.
D   The right to picket outside the factory is an absolute right and cannot be overridden.

Question 9.6

Employees of a company are currently on strike; however a few have remained at work. One employee, HIGGINS, who is still working, is followed home by 2 of the 'strikers'; they call him a 'scab' and a 'strike breaker'. They also whistle and jeer at him. HIGGINS is very distressed by this behaviour. Consider the offence of intimidation or annoyance by violence or otherwise contrary to s. 241 of the Trade Union and Labour Relations (Consolidation) Act 1992.

Has this offence been committed?

A   No, because there need to be more than 2 people following HIGGINS.

B No, because they are not threatening or intimidating HIGGINS or using violence.

C Yes, provided the strikers intended to compel HIGGINS to join the strike.

D Yes, provided the strikers intended to cause the distress that HIGGINS suffered.

ANSWERS

Answer 9.1

Answer **C** — The area of domestic violence has received a great deal of political and legislative attention, bringing about important changes that affect the police. First, the Domestic Violence, Crime and Victims Act 2004 makes significant changes to the law. In addition the Association of Chief Police Officers has issued a policy document setting out the approach to be adopted where police officers are personally involved in domestic violence and advocating a 'presumption towards dismissal' where an officer is convicted of a domestic violence-related offence. In addition, any officer whose conduct is found to have fallen below the required standard in respect of domestic violence/abuse can expect to be dismissed or required to resign despite not having attracted a criminal conviction. The expectation is that he or she will have to leave the service; answers A and B are therefore incorrect. And this is not at the presiding officer's discretion; answer D is therefore incorrect.

General Police Duties, para. 4.9.2

Answer 9.2

Answer **D** — A non-molestation order under the Family Law Act 1996 does not only apply to spouses or former partners; it applies to anyone who is 'associated' with the respondent, and now includes same-sex couples (see s. 62(3)(aa) and (3)(eza)). The association also applies to relatives (s. 62(3)(d)) and therefore answer A is incorrect.

A child under the age of 16 may not apply for a non-molestation order except with the leave of the court (s. 43(1)), and therefore answer B is incorrect. The court may grant leave for the purposes of subsection (1) only if it is satisfied that the child has sufficient understanding to make the proposed application for the order. Note that it is the opinion of the court (not social services) which counts, and therefore answer C is incorrect.

General Police Duties, para. 4.9.2.3

Answer 9.3

Answer **B** — Under s. 42(1) of the Family Law Act 1996, a 'non-molestation order' means an order containing a provision prohibiting a person ('the respondent') from molesting another person who is associated with the respondent or from molesting a relevant child. Since the provisions do not only apply to children, answer D is incorrect.

Under s. 42(2)(a), the court may make a non-molestation order when an application has been made by a person who is associated with the respondent whether or not any other family proceedings have been instituted. Answer A is therefore incorrect.

Section 62 contains a long list of people who are 'associated' with the respondent, including relatives, children, spouses, co-habitants, civil partners (and people who formerly enjoyed these status). Under s. 62(3)(c), they also include people who live, or have lived in the same household, otherwise than merely by reason of one of them being the other's employee, tenant, lodger or boarder. Answer C is therefore incorrect.

General Police Duties, para. 4.9.2.3

Answer 9.4

Answer **C** — If a power of arrest is attached to a non-molestation order under s. 47 of the Family Law Act 1996 and the respondent is arrested for breaching that order, he must be brought before the relevant judicial authority within the period of 24 hours beginning at the time of his arrest. In reckoning for the purposes of s. 47 any period of 24 hours, no account is to be taken of Christmas Day, Good Friday, or any Sunday (s. 47(7)), and therefore answers A and B are incorrect. Note that it is 24 hours from the time of the arrest and not from the 'relevant' time, therefore answer D is incorrect.

General Police Duties, para. 4.9.2.4

Answer 9.5

Answer **A** — Although picketing is lawful under s. 220 of the Trade Union and Labour Relations (Consolidation) Act 1992, there are some restrictions. It is lawful to picket your former place of work if the action is as a result of the termination of your employment. However, a person's place of work does not include new premises of an employer who has moved since dismissing the people picketing (*News Group Newspapers Ltd* v *SOGAT '82 (No. 2)* [1987] ICR 181), and therefore answer B is incorrect. The 1992 Act does not place restrictions on the number of pickets; the number 6 is from the agreed Code of Practice on picketing which has no legal force, and therefore answer C is incorrect. Note, however, that if numbers are large enough, there might be a presumption that the pickets intend to intimidate others, which would make it unlawful (*Broome* v *DPP* [1974] AC 587). If there is a real danger of any offence (e.g. public disorder) being committed, the pickets have no right to attend at the factory to picket under s. 220 (*Piddlington* v *Bates* [1960] 1 WLR 162), and therefore answer D is incorrect. Section 220 does not authorise pickets to enter onto private land (*British Airports Authority* v *Ashton* [1983] 1 WLR 1079).

General Police Duties, para. 4.9.3.1

Answer 9.6

Answer **C** — This is an offence of 'specific intent', and as such there has to be an element of intention to bring about a specific outcome. It is committed by 'two or more persons' (therefore answer A is incorrect), where they follow the victim 'in a disorderly manner in or through any street or road'. There does not have to be a threat or use of violence; disorder would be sufficient, and therefore answer B is incorrect. Their intention must be to compel HIGGINS to join the strike, and not simply to cause distress, and therefore answer D is incorrect. (Note that if the circumstances were reversed and HIGGINS was on strike, the offence would still be committed by compelling him to return to work.)

General Police Duties, para. 4.9.3.3

10 | Offences Relating to Land and Premises

STUDY PREPARATION

The Criminal Justice and Public Order Act 1994 created several offences which have the effect of allowing the criminal courts to deal with offences of trespass. This chapter deals with offences such as trespassing with intent to disrupt lawful activities, trespassing with intent to reside on land, raves and residing in vehicles on land, all of which are very topical.

Each offence has several elements to it, but there are common themes throughout, such as authorising officers, offences of failing to leave land when directed to do so and returning within three months of a direction being given.

The Criminal Law Act 1977 makes up the bulk of the second part of the chapter. Offences under ss. 6 and 7 of the Act are rarely used, but remain useful pieces of legislation, especially that of using violence for securing entry to premises.

Lastly, do not ignore the offences of being found on enclosed premises and causing a nuisance on educational premises; both are useful offences to remember.

QUESTIONS

Question 10.1

A supermarket is to be built on the outskirts of a town. Vehicles belonging to the building company have been parked in a compound on land owned by the supermarket, adjacent to the building site. The night after building had started, STIG, an environmental activist, entered the compound and let down the tyres of all the vehicles, in order to disrupt work the next day.

Has STIG committed an offence under s. 68 of the Criminal Justice and Public Order Act 1994?

A No, as he was not on land where the activity was due to take place.

B Yes, he has committed an offence in these circumstances.

C Yes, but only if it can be shown that work was disrupted.

D No, people were not engaged in any activity when he acted.

Question 10.2

PARSONS, a farmer, agreed to allow a family of travellers to stay on his land for a week. Between them, the travellers had 2 caravans and 2 cars. After 2 weeks, they were still on the land and PARSONS asked them to leave. When they refused, he contacted the police.

Would the officers have the power, under s. 61 of the Criminal Justice and Public Order Act 1994, to direct the family to leave the land?

A No, because the family did not have more than 12 vehicles between them.

B Yes, they could direct the family to leave the land, with their vehicles.

C No, because the family were originally given permission to stay by the land-owner.

D No, because the family have not caused damage or used threatening/insulting behaviour.

Question 10.3

HARNEY worked as a security guard on a building site, which was due to be developed for housing. HARNEY was employed by the company which owned the land, as there had been persistent problems with travellers setting up an unofficial site. One day, O'CONNER drove onto the site in his car. He was alone at the time, and HARNEY recognised him as a traveller who had stayed at the site some time ago. HARNEY spoke to O'CONNER, who admitted that his family were due at the site in a few hours, and that they intended staying there for a while. HARNEY then contacted the police to assist.

Would the officer attending the scene have the power to direct O'CONNER to leave the land, under s. 62A of the Criminal Justice and Public Order Act 1994, in these circumstances?

A Yes, because he has at least 1 vehicle with him.

B No, because he does not have a caravan with him.

C Yes, provided there is a suitable site elsewhere for him to go to.

D No, because O'CONNER was unaccompanied at the time.

Question 10.4

Inspector YORKE attended a beach to assist officers who believed that a rave was due to take place in the area. On arrival, Inspector YORKE saw that LINCOLN had a van in the beach car park and was unloading sound equipment. LINCOLN admitted that people were attending later that night for a rave.

Would LINCOLN's presence at the scene provide a reason for a direction to be given for people to leave the land, under s. 63(2) of the Criminal Justice and Public Order Act 1994?

A Yes, because LINCOLN is preparing for a rave to take place.

B No, there must be at least 2 people making preparations for a rave and 10 people waiting for the rave to take place.

C No, there must be at least 2 people making preparations for a rave.

D Yes, there are no restrictions on how many people are present preparing for a rave, the restrictions apply to how many people are attending a rave.

Question 10.5

Section 63(1A) of the Criminal Justice and Public Order Act 1994 sets out the requirements for a rave, where 20 or more people are gathering on land.

Which of the following must be true, in order for a gathering to qualify as a rave under this section?

A They must be trespassing on land in the open air.

B They must be trespassing on any land, whether in the open air or not.

C They must be trespassing on any land, or in any building on that land.

D They must be on land in the open air, whether they are trespassing or not.

Question 10.6

DC WU was in plain clothes one evening, when he responded to an assistance call from a uniformed officer, Constable HOLMES. When he arrived, Constable HOLMES informed DC WU that a gathering was taking place 3 miles away, which had been declared as a 'rave'. Constable HOLMES had stopped 20 vehicles and was attempting to get them to turn around. Until further assistance arrived, Constable HOLMES continued to stop vehicles, while DC WU spoke to the drivers suspected of attending the rave and directed them not to proceed.

Were the directions given by DC WU lawful in the circumstances?

A Yes, he has acted correctly in these circumstances.

B No, he was outside the required radius from the rave to be able to give the directions.

C No, he was inside the required radius from the rave to be able to give the directions.

D No, he should have been in uniform when giving the directions.

Question 10.7

TOM and CAROL live together, but TOM has been violent towards her after drinking heavily. One evening, when TOM was in a pub, CAROL double locked the front door of their house to stop him getting in. When he got home, TOM lost his temper and began kicking the door to get in. CAROL was scared and called the police.

Would TOM be guilty of an offence under s. 6 of the Criminal Law Act 1977 (using violence for securing entry)?

A No, because CAROL is not a trespasser on the property.

B Yes, but he would have a defence as a displaced residential occupier.

C Yes, but he would have a defence as a protected intending occupier.

D Yes, if it can be shown that he was aware CAROL was on the premises.

Question 10.8

GREEDY is a landlord who wishes to regain possession of one of his flats, the tenant of which is refusing to leave; GREEDY is unhappy that the tenant has moved in three of her friends. GREEDY turns up at the front door for the purpose of gaining possession of the property, using violence if necessary. He threatens to kick the front door down, he then threatens to enter and use violence against any person in the house, he then specifically threatens violence against the tenant. The tenant inside is obviously opposed to this entry and GREEDY knows this is the case.

At what point is an offence contrary to s. 6 of the Criminal Law Act 1977 first committed?

A When GREEDY first attends at the premises with the purpose of using violence to gain possession.

B When GREEDY threatened violence to property i.e. the door.

C When GREEDY threatened violence to any person i.e. any of the persons in the flat.

D When GREEDY threatened violence to a specific person i.e. the tenant.

Question 10.9

TILLEY owned a printing business, which was located in a shop premises. TILLEY owned the building, and lived in a flat above the shop. Business was slow and TILLEY had to lay off his assistant, CARNE. CARNE kept his keys to the premises and while TILLEY was away on business the following week, CARNE moved into his flat. When TILLEY returned, CARNE refused to leave the flat, stating that he was homeless as a result of losing his job. TILLEY contacted the police, claiming to be a displaced residential occupier. When the police arrived, CARNE refused to leave.

Given that the flat in question is situated in a business premises, what defence is available to CARNE under s. 7 of the Criminal Law Act 1977 (person failing to leave premises)?

A None, failing to leave premises when requested in these circumstances is an absolute offence.

B None, but the prosecution must show that this part of the premises was used mainly for residential purposes.

C CARNE has a defence, unless the prosecution can show that this part of the premises was used mainly for non-residential purposes.

D CARNE has a defence if he can show that this part of the premises was used mainly for non-residential purposes.

Question 10.10

MARKS intended to frighten his neighbour KAREN on Halloween night. He wore a mask and climbed into her garden, which was enclosed on three sides by hedges. He approached the kitchen window, where KAREN was standing, and pressed his face against the glass. KAREN was frightened and screamed loudly. She was heard by other neighbours who contacted the police

Could MARKS be guilty of the offence of being found on enclosed premises in these circumstances?

A Yes, but only if it can be shown MARKS intended committing a criminal offence at that time.

B No, as MARKS was not on the premises for an unlawful purpose.

C No, as MARKS did not intend committing a criminal offence.

D Yes, MARKS could be guilty of the offence in these circumstances alone.

Question 10.11

Constable CARVER attended a call of a suspicious person at an empty warehouse. On arrival, Constable CARVER found CAHILL on the roof of the building. There were no signs of forced entry to the building, and Constable CARVER was considering whether CAHILL had committed the offence of being found on enclosed premises.

Would the warehouse amount to a 'premises' for an offence under s. 4 of the Vagrancy Act 1824?

A No, the offence applies to enclosed yards or gardens only.

B No, the offence applies when a person is *in* a building or enclosed place, not on it.

C Yes, the premises qualify for an offence under this Act.

D No, the offence only applies to dwellings, or enclosed yards or gardens attached to them.

Question 10.12

BRENT lived in a property owned by Western Housing Association. BRENT owned several abandoned cars which were in a dangerous condition and were parked in a communal parking area at the rear of the property, owned by the association. The association served a notice to remove the cars; however, BRENT refused to do so and attended the company's offices, threatening to tow the cars across the entrance of the parking area to barricade them in. The association was concerned that this action might cause distress to other residents.

Would BRENT's threats be sufficient to merit an application by the association for an anti-social behaviour injunction, under s. 153A of the Housing Act 1996?

A No, the conduct was not directed at a person living in the vicinity of the house.

B Yes, provided the company named the people likely to be affected in the injunction.

C No, as the conduct occurred in the association's offices and not in the vicinity of the house.

D Yes, regardless of where the conduct occurred, or whether the company can name the people likely to be affected in the injunction.

Question 10.13

EASTWOOD is a caretaker at a school maintained by a local authority. He received a call from teachers that some youths from a different school were on the playing fields shouting and swearing at them. EASTWOOD telephoned the police and made his way to the field. He arrived before the police to find several youths sitting next to a classroom quietly.

Which statement will be correct in relation to the youths causing a nuisance on educational premises?

A They may be removed from the premises by either EASTWOOD or the police.

B EASTWOOD has no powers to deal with the youths; he must wait for the police to arrive.

C EASTWOOD has no powers to deal with the youths, as the disturbance has ceased.

D EASTWOOD has a power to detain the youths until the police arrive at the school.

ANSWERS

Answer 10.1

Answer **B** — The offence will be committed when a person trespasses on land intending to intimidate people, or obstruct or disrupt lawful activity (s. 68 of the Criminal Justice and Public Order Act 1994).

The lawful activity may be something which people are engaged in or about to engage in, and therefore answer D is incorrect.

The offence is committed when a person trespasses on land where the activity took place or on adjoining land (which makes answer A incorrect).

There is only a requirement to prove that a person intended his or her actions to bring about the effects listed above. There is no need to show a successful outcome, and therefore answer C is incorrect.

General Police Duties, para. 4.10.4

Answer 10.2

Answer **C** — To prove the offence under s. 61 of the Criminal Justice and Public Order Act 1994, you need to show that at least 2 people are trespassing on land with a common purpose of residing there and reasonable steps have been taken to ask them to leave.

If the above conditions are apparent, you must then show that:

- they have damaged land; *or*
- they have used threatening, etc. behaviour; *or*
- they have between them *6* or more vehicles.

As none of these apply, answers B and D are incorrect. Under s. 61(2), if the people had been given permission to stay on the land but had subsequently become trespassers, the officers would have to satisfy themselves that one of the conditions in s. 61(1) had occurred after they had become trespassers.

The original 1994 Act specified 12 vehicles, but this has been amended to 6 and therefore answer A is incorrect.

(It should be noted that the Home Office has issued guidance to the police on the use of the powers under s. 61. It advises that the police must be able to demonstrate that all eviction and enforcement decisions are 'proportionate' in weighing individual harm against the wider public interest).

General Police Duties, para. 4.10.5

Answer 10.3

Answer **D** — Section 62A of the Criminal Justice and Public Order Act 1994 provides an alternative power to police officers to the one contained in s. 61 of the Act. In order to use the powers under this section, the senior officer at the scene may direct persons to leave the land and remove any vehicles if the following conditions are met:

- that the person and 1 or more others (i.e. at least 2 people) are trespassing on land;
- that they have at least 1 vehicle between them;
- that they are present with a common purpose of residing there; *and*
- that the occupier or a person acting on his or her behalf has asked the police to remove the trespassers.

Since there must be at least 2 persons present on the land, and O'CONNER was alone, the police officer attending the scene would have had no powers under this section, regardless of how many vehicles were present, which makes answer A incorrect.

If the people have 1 or more caravans in their possession or control, and there is a suitable pitch on a relevant caravan site elsewhere, there is a further condition requiring the senior officer to consult with the local authority and ascertain if there is a suitable pitch on a relevant caravan site for each of the caravans. However, this is an additional power, and s. 62A may still be used if the people do not have a caravan with them, which means that answers B and C are incorrect.

General Police Duties, para. 4.10.6

Answer 10.4

Answer **C** — Under s. 63(2) of the Criminal Justice and Public Order Act 1994, a superintendent may give a direction for people to leave land if he or she reasonably believes that 2 or more people are making preparations for a rave to take place, (answer A is incorrect) or 10 or more people are waiting for a rave to take place or 10 or more people are attending a rave. The direction may be given in any of the above situations and a two people preparing for the rave would suffice. Answers B and D are therefore incorrect.

General Police Duties, para. 4.10.7

Answer 10.5

Answer **A** — Under s. 63(1A)(a) of the Criminal Justice and Public Order Act 1994, it will be a 'gathering' if 20 or more persons are trespassing on land. Answer D is therefore incorrect. Section 63(1A)(b) goes on to say that it will be a gathering if it took place in the open air. Answers B and C are therefore incorrect.

General Police Duties, para. 4.10.7.1

Answer 10.6

Answer **D** — Under s. 65 of the Criminal Justice and Public Order Act 1994, where a constable in uniform reasonably believes a person is on his or her way to a gathering to which s. 63(2) applies (direction to leave land in respect of a rave), the officer may stop the person and direct him or her not to proceed in the direction of the gathering. Unlike other directions under this Act, a direction under s. 65 must be given by a constable in uniform, and answer A is incorrect.

The power may be exercised within 5 miles of the boundary of the site of the gathering. Answers B and C are incorrect, as the officers were inside this radius; and had DC WU been in uniform, the directions not to proceed would have been lawful.

General Police Duties, para. 4.10.7.6

Answer 10.7

Answer **D** — A person is guilty of an offence if he or she uses or threatens violence for the purpose of securing entry to premises, provided there is someone on the premises who is opposed to the entry and the person using/threatening the violence knows that this is the case (s. 6(1) of the Criminal Law Act 1977).

The person would have a defence if he or she could show that he or she was either a displaced residential occupier (DRO) or a protected intended occupier (PIO).

To be a DRO, a person would have to show that he or she was occupying premises immediately before being excluded by a person who entered those premises as a trespasser. As CAROL is not a trespasser, TOM would not be a DRO and would have no defence. Answer B is therefore incorrect.

To be a PIO, a person must have a freehold/leasehold interest in a property with 2 years to run. He or she must intend to use the property for his or her own occupation as a residence and, as above, must have been excluded by a person who has entered the premises as a trespasser. As CAROL is not a trespasser, answer C is incorrect.

The fact that CAROL is not a trespasser is the reason for TOM having no defence, which is why answer A is incorrect.

General Police Duties, paras 4.10.9.3, 4.10.9.4

Answer 10.8

Answer **B** — Section 6 the Criminal Law Act 1977 states:

(1) Subject to the following provisions of this section, any person who, without lawful authority, uses or threatens violence for the purpose of securing entry into any premises for himself or for any other person is guilty of an offence, provided that —

    (a) there is someone present on those premises at the time who is opposed to the entry which the violence is intended to secure; and

    (b) the person using or threatening the violence knows that that is the case.

It is immaterial whether the violence used/threatened is against a person or property, or whether the purpose of the entry is to gain possession of the premises or any other purpose (s. 6(4)). So the offence is complete only after violence is first used or threatened, not when it is intended; answer A is therefore incorrect. Although answers C and D would amount to an offence contrary to s. 6 the question asked at what point will the offence first be committed, and that is when the threat of violence was made against the front door; answers C and D are therefore incorrect within the confines of this question.

General Police Duties, para. 4.10.9.3

Answer 10.9

Answer **D** — The offence of failing to leave a premises when requested is covered by s. 7(1) of the Criminal Law Act 1977. The offence is complete, because CARNE entered the premises as a trespasser and refused to leave when requested by a displaced residential occupier (TILLEY).

A defence is provided under s. 7(3)(a) of the Act (and answer A is incorrect); it is for the accused to prove that the premises are or formed part of premises used mainly for non-residential purposes. Answers B and C are incorrect. (Whether CARNE would be able successfully to claim this defence is doubtful, as the flat is clearly a residential premises.)

General Police Duties, para. 4.10.9.5

Answer 10.10

Answer **D** — A person commits an offence under s. 4 of the Vagrancy Act 1824 if he or she is found in several types of places, including enclosed yards, gardens or area, for an unlawful purpose (and not for the purposes of committing a criminal offence), therefore answer C is incorrect. There is no need to show that the person intended to carry out a criminal offence at the particular time that he or she was found (or even at that particular place). Answer A is therefore incorrect.

The case of *Smith* v *Chief Superintendent of Woking Police Station* (1983) 76 Cr App R 234 dealt with the issue of 'unlawful purpose'. The defendant was convicted after being found in the garden of a house peering through a window trying to frighten the woman inside. This makes answer B incorrect.

General Police Duties, para. 4.10.9.6

Answer 10.11

Answer **C** — A person commits an offence under s. 4 of the Vagrancy Act 1824 if he or she is found in or on any dwelling house, warehouse, coach house, stable or outhouse or in any enclosed yard, garden or area for an unlawful purpose. Answer B is incorrect, as the offence may take place when a person is *on* a building. Answers A and D are incorrect, as the offence is not limited to dwellings, yards or gardens, it applies also to warehouses.

General Police Duties, para. 4.10.9.6

Answer 10.12

Answer **D** — Under s. 153A of the 1996 Act a court may, on the application of a relevant landlord, grant an anti-social behaviour injunction if:

the person against whom the injunction is sought is engaging, has engaged or threatens to engage in housing-related conduct capable of causing a nuisance or annoyance to:
(a) a person with a right (of whatever description) to reside in or occupy housing accommodation owned or managed by a relevant landlord,
(b) a person with a right (of whatever description) to reside in or occupy other housing accommodation in the neighbourhood of housing accommodation mentioned in paragraph (a),
(c) a person engaged in lawful activity in, or in the neighbourhood of, housing accommodation mentioned in paragraph (a), or

(d) a person employed (whether or not by a relevant landlord) in connection with the exercise of a relevant landlord's housing management functions.

Therefore, as the conduct can be directed at a person employed by the company, answer A is incorrect. Further, it is immaterial where conduct to which this section applies occurs (answer C is incorrect).

Finally, an injunction may be granted without a particular individual being named as someone adversely affected by the conduct referred to in the injunction, and in respect of conduct that is not described by reference to any person or persons at all. If conduct is described in an injunction by reference to a person or persons, these may be persons generally, or persons of a particular description, or a specified person. Answer B is therefore incorrect.

General Police Duties, para. 4.10.9.7

Answer 10.13

Answer **A** — Where a person has caused a nuisance, disturbance or annoyance on educational premises, a police constable, or a person authorised by the local authority, may remove that person from the premises (s. 40(3) of the Local Government (Miscellaneous Provisions) Act 1982 and s. 47(3) of the Education Act 1996). The power is to remove, not to detain, which is why answers B and D are incorrect.

Answer C is incorrect because the power to remove a person may be used even when the disturbance has ended.

General Police Duties, para. 4.10.9.8

11 | Licensing and Offences Relating to Alcohol

STUDY PREPARATION

There have been significant changes to this chapter with the introduction of the Licensing Act 2003. The whole concept of licensing and licensed premises has been brought into line with the Government's effort to place crime and disorder matters at the top of the policing agenda. Licensing justices have been replaced by the licensing authorities (made up of local authority members). In addition, there is now a requirement for a *premises* to have a licence, as well as the personal licence required by the traditional licensee.

With the introduction of 'operating schedules', emphasis is placed firmly on the holders of personal licences to run orderly premises, taking into account such matters as crime and disorder, public safety and protection of children. The concept of 'permitted hours' has been removed completely and each premises will have its own opening hours, depending on its operating schedule.

Knowledge of the different types of licences and the new system of objecting to them is critical. You should also learn the powers to enter premises and, once inside, how to deal with offences and/or drunkenness.

Ages are important, and most of the original offences of under-age drinking under the 1964 Act have remained.

When fully enacted, the Violent Crime Reduction Act 2006 will have an impact on alcohol-related violent crime.

The Confiscation of Alcohol (Young Persons) Act 1997 first introduced the concept of confiscating alcohol from young people in public places. The Criminal Justice and Police Act 2001 introduced a similar power to confiscate alcohol from people in designated public places.

You should familiarise yourself with the powers given by the courts to exclude people from licensed premises and the powers to deal with people who breach

---

such directions. Further powers of enforcement were provided under the Criminal Justice and Police Act 2001, allowing police to make an order requiring licensed premises to be closed.

Somewhat hidden at the end of the chapter are betting and gaming. These are also important areas on which to concentrate. Even though the content has been scaled down in recent years, there is still a lot to get through; in particular, the difference between the two definitions, and where betting and gaming can (and cannot) take place. When fully enacted, the Gambling Act 2005 will introduce reforms to the Betting, Gaming and Lotteries Act 1963, the Gaming Act 1968 and the Lotteries and Amusements Act 1976.

QUESTIONS

Question 11.1

Which of the following would best describe a person who 'provides late night refreshment' under Sch. 2 to the Licensing Act 2003?

He or she would be a person who supplies:
A Food and drinks to members of the public.
B Hot food and drinks to members of the public.
C Hot food or hot drinks to members of the public.
D Hot food and alcoholic drinks to members of the public.

Question 11.2

The Licensing Act 2003, sch. 2 makes provision in relation to 'late night refreshment'.

Between which hours must refreshments be supplied in order for a person to qualify as a provider of 'late night refreshment'?
A 11 pm and 5 am.
B 10 pm and 5 am.
C 11 pm and 5.30 am.
D 9 pm and 5.30 am.

Question 11.3

Constable KHAN was on duty as part of a plain-clothes team of police officers, working with LEWIS, a licensing officer from the local authority and a person authorised under the Licensing Act 2003. The team was tasked with visiting public houses in the locality to identify licensing offences. They arrived at the Royal Oak public house at 10.50 pm and identified themselves to GEORGE, the door supervisor, and asked to enter the premises. GEORGE refused, stating the premises were about to close. The operating schedule stated that the premises should close at 11 p.m.

Does either Constable KHAN or LEWIS have the power to enter the premises using reasonable force under the Licensing Act 2003?

A No, the power to enter by reasonable force is restricted to uniformed officers only.

B Constable KHAN only, LEWIS does not have a power to enter by force in these circumstances.

C Yes, both have the power to enter using reasonable force in these circumstances.

D Yes, but only if they have reason to believe that offences are being committed.

Question 11.4

Section 11 of the Licensing Act 2003 states that a 'premises licence' means a licence granted in respect of any premises, which authorises the premises to be used for one or more licensable activities.

How long will a premises licence generally last for?

A 2 years, unless it is revoked or surrendered.

B 5 years, unless it is revoked or surrendered.

C 10 years, unless it is revoked or surrendered.

D No limit, unless it is revoked or surrendered.

Question 11.5

FERDINAND has bought a public house and is applying for a premises licence. When FERDINAND appeared before the licensing authority, there were no specific representations from the responsible authorities, or interested parties. However,

FERDINAND's application did not contain a plan of the premises, which the licensing authority insisted on seeing before granting a licence.

> In respect of s. 17(4) of the Licensing Act 2003, which of the following statements is correct, regarding the licensing authority's decision?
>
> **A** As there have been no specific representations, the authority may only ask for anything covered by s. 17(4), which includes a plan of the premises.
>
> **B** As no representations have been received, the authority may not ask for the plan of the premises, as is not required as part of the operating schedule.
>
> **C** The licensing authority may impose any conditions it sees fit, regardless of any specific representations.
>
> **D** A plan of the premises is only required if any responsible authority believes it is necessary; in this case therefore, it is not required.

Question 11.6

PORTELLI is the licensee of the Golden Lion public house and holds a personal licence for the premises. PORTELLI is facing prosecution for an offence listed in sch. 4 to the Licensing Act 2003 (suspension of personal licence after being charged with, or summonsed for certain offences).

> In relation to the possible suspension of PORTELLI's personal licence, which of the following statements is correct?
>
> **A** The personal licence must be produced to the court, who may suspend it for a minimum period of six months.
>
> **B** The personal licence must be produced to the licensing authority, who may suspend it for a minimum period of six months.
>
> **C** The personal licence must be produced to the court, who may suspend it for a maximum period of six months.
>
> **D** The personal licence must be produced to the licensing authority, who may suspend it for a maximum period of six months.

Question 11.7

LEE is the licensee of the Railway Public House and has a personal licence for the premises. LEE has been charged by CID officers with attempting to rape a member of staff.

Has LEE committed an offence listed in sch. 4 to the Licensing Act 2003, which would attract a suspension of his licence?

A Yes, this offence carries a mandatory suspension of a personal licence.

B Yes, this is an offence that could attract the suspension of LEE's personal licence.

C No, this not a licensing offence, therefore LEE's personal licence cannot be suspended.

D No, only firearms offences, or those involving violence, dishonesty or drugs would attract such a suspension.

Question 11.8

The general conditions for 'qualifying clubs' are set out in s. 62 of the Licensing Act 2003. Amongst these conditions is the minimum number of members a club should have.

How many members should a 'qualifying club' have before it is entitled to claim that it is such a club?

A At least 25 members.

B At least 30 members.

C At least 35 members.

D At least 50 members.

Question 11.9

The British Legion Club has applied for a temporary variation of its club premises certificate, to allow it to extend its hours for members on a specific day due to a Remembrance Day parade. Constable BARRETT, the local licensing officer intends to enter and inspect the premises as a result of this application.

What restrictions are placed on Constable BARRETT's entry into the premises by s. 96 of the Licensing Act 2003?

A Entry must be made within 21 days of the application, provided 48 hours' notice is given.

B Entry must be made within 14 days of the application, provided 24 hours' notice is given.

C Entry must be made within 14 days of the application, provided 48 hours' notice is given.

D Entry may be made at any time between the date of the application and the date of the proposed variation, provided 48 hours' notice is given.

Question 11.10

Section 97 of the Licensing Act 2003 provides a power of entry for a constable to enter and search premises which hold a club certificate.

What restrictions are placed on this power of entry during normal opening hours?

A Entry is allowed to detect licensing offences or to prevent a breach of the peace only.

B Entry is allowed to prevent a breach of the peace only.

C Entry is allowed to detect licensing offences, to search for offences relating to the supply of drugs, or to prevent a breach of the peace.

D Entry is allowed to search for offences relating to the supply of drugs, or to prevent a breach of the peace only.

Question 11.11

Part 5 of the Licensing Act 2003 allows premises users to carry out licensable activities on a temporary basis under certain conditions.

What is the maximum permissible period for such temporary activities?

A A period not exceeding 24 hours.

B A period not exceeding 36 hours.

C A period not exceeding 48 hours.

D A period not exceeding 96 hours.

Question 11.12

GEORGES has served a temporary event notice on the local authority, indicating an intention to hold a disco in the local youth club. Within the notice, GEORGES has outlined that the club intends selling alcohol at the disco, but only to people that members of staff know to be over 18. The licensing officer, Constable LEONARD, has received a copy of the notice. Constable LEONARD intends objecting to the sale of alcohol, due to the previous history of such events, when a substantial amount of damage was caused to local shops and vehicles by youths leaving the premises.

What must Constable LEONARD do now, in order to object to the granting of the temporary event notice?

A Send a notice of objection to the local authority.

B Send a notice of objection to the local authority and GEORGES.

C Send a notice of objection to the owner of the premises, who would qualify as the premises user.

D Send a notice of objection to GEORGES.

Question 11.13

Section 107 of the Licensing Act 2003 places certain restrictions on the number of temporary events that may be held in any calendar year.

How many temporary event notices may the same holder of a personal licence give before the licensing authority issues a counter notice?

A 12 event notices in one calendar year.

B 25 event notices in one calendar year.

C 50 event notices in one calendar year.

D Any amount in the first year provided there are no more than 24 event notices in *two* calendar years.

Question 11.14

RICHARDS entered the Horse and Groom public house in an intoxicated condition and was served a pint of beer by HOPKINS. RICHARDS walked away from the bar and began abusing other customers. RICHARDS was ejected from the premises before drinking any of the beer. HOPKINS is a bar worker and is neither the holder of a premises licence nor the designated premises supervisor.

Has HOPKINS committed an offence by selling alcohol to a person who is drunk, under s. 141 of the Licensing Act 2003?

A Yes, HOPKINS would commit the offence in these circumstances.

B No, the offence will only be committed by the holder of a premises licence and the designated premises supervisor.

C No, as RICHARDS did not consume the drink.

D No, the offence will only be committed by the holder of a premises licence.

Question 11.15

HOULIE was in the Glendale public house one evening and was asked to leave by GREEN, the holder of the premises licence. HOULIE was drunk and abusive towards the bar staff. HOULIE left the premises voluntarily. However, once outside, he began banging on the door trying to get back into the pub. GREEN ignored HOULIE and contacted the police and when they arrived, HOULIE was walking away from the premises.

Has HOULIE committed an offence under s. 143 of the Licensing Act 2003 in these circumstances?

A No, because HOULIE has not actually re-entered the premises after being asked to leave.

B No, as no one has requested that he not re-enter the pub.

C Yes, as he was trying to regain entry to the pub in which he was drunk and disorderly.

D Yes, as it is an offence to be or have been drunk and disorderly on licensed premises.

Question 11.16

GOULDING was asleep in a doorway of a shop in a city centre late at night, having consumed excessive amounts of alcohol. Constable GRIFFIN was passing by on patrol and tried to wake GOULDING. Because of GOULDING's condition, the officer decided it was necessary to effect an arrest for being found drunk. While being led to the police vehicle, GOULDING became violent and disorderly towards Constable GRIFFIN.

Given that GOULDING's initial behaviour amounted to an offence of being found drunk (under s. 12 of the Licensing Act 1872), could he also be guilty of the more serious offence of being drunk and disorderly, under s. 91(1) of the Criminal Justice Act 1967, because of his conduct after being arrested?

A No, because the disorderly behaviour occurred after GOULDING's arrest.

B Yes, GOULDING was drunk before the arrest and the offence is made out.

C Yes, the disorderly behaviour can occur at any time during the arrest.

D No, because GOULDING had consumed excessive amounts of alcohol, the appropriate offence is 'found drunk'.

Question 11.17

JENKINS is a heavy drinker, and is well known for being able to handle his liquor. One night he is out drinking with his friends and as a prank one of them drops amphetamine powder into JENKINS' pint of lager. Two hours later, in the street outside the pub, JENKINS begins to shout and swear at people. JENKINS is drunk, having consumed 10 pints of lager. Police officers approach him and he shouts and physically threatens the officers. They arrest JENKINS for being drunk and disorderly. At court, it is argued that his disorderly behaviour was due entirely to the drug, of which he had no knowledge, and that he is not guilty.

In relation to this offence, which of the following statements is correct?

A He may be guilty, as alcohol is a partial cause of his intoxication.

B He is guilty, as it is immaterial what caused the intoxication.

C He is not guilty, as this offence is not made out where there are several causes of the incapacitated state.

D He is not guilty, as the cause of his intoxication was not self-induced.

Question 11.18

APPLEBY is 16 years old and in a public house which is open for the purposes of supplying alcohol for consumption on those premises. She is passing through the main area to go to the toilet as there is no other way to get into there. She is not accompanied by anyone as her parents are outside in the beer garden.

Has an offence been committed contrary to the Licensing Act 2003?

A Yes, as she is 16 and unaccompanied, the licensee commits an offence of allowing her to be in there.

B Yes, as she is 16 and unaccompanied, both APPLEBY and the licensee commit an offence.

C No, because she is 16, neither APPLEBY nor the licensee commits the offence.

D No, because she is only passing through the premises, there being no other way to get to the toilet.

Question 11.19

JABLONOWSKI is working in the Masons Arms public house. She serves TINNEY who is aged 16 and, generally speaking, looks his age. JABLONOWSKI believes he is 18 years of age, but asks for identification to impress her boss and TINNEY produces a student ID card stating he is 18; the card however is a very poor fake and should have been easily perceived as such. JABLONOWSKI, however, serves TINNEY alcohol.

Which of the following is true in relation to selling alcohol to someone under 18?

A JABLONOWSKI has a defence in that she honestly believed that TINNEY was over 18.

B JABLONOWSKI has a defence in that she asked for evidence of his age and it was produced.

C JABLONOWSKI has a defence in that she believed TINNEY was over 18 *and* she asked for evidence of his age.

D JABLONOWSKI has no defence as TINNEY produced fake evidence and it should have been obvious to her it was fake.

Question 11.20

In the Horse and Jockey public house, GILES, aged 18, went to the bar and ordered a pint of beer for himself, and another for his friend HARRISON, whom he knew was aged 17; both were consuming table meals. PARRY, who was serving at the time, provided the beer, but was not aware one of them was for HARRISON whom she knew was aged 17. HARRISON drinks his beer.

In relation to offences under the Licensing Act 2003, who of the above, if any, have committed offences?

A No offences have been committed, as HARRISON was consuming a table meal and can drink beer in such circumstances.

B Only GILES, of buying alcohol on behalf of an individual aged under 18.

C GILES, of buying alcohol on behalf of an individual aged under 18, and PARRY for serving it.

D All three; GILES for buying, PARRY for selling and HARRISON for consuming the drink, which was not cider or wine.

Question 11.21

DENNIS is the owner of an off-licence and is the responsible person for the premises. The police suspected that young people in the area were persistently buying alcohol from the premises and conducted a series of test purchase operations in a month. On 4 occasions, alcohol was sold to different young people, under the age of 18. On 2 occasions, DENNIS was responsible for the sales and on the other 2 occasions, while DENNIS was not at the premises, ASPINALL, the designated premises supervisor, sold alcohol to a person under 18.

Would DENNIS be guilty of an offence under s. 147A of the Licensing Act 2003 (persistently selling alcohol to children) in these circumstances?

A No, DENNIS was not the responsible person on each occasion.

B No, alcohol was sold to different individuals.

C Yes, regardless of the fact that alcohol was sold to different individuals.

D Yes, regardless of the fact that DENNIS and ASPINALL were both responsible for the sales.

Question 11.22

Section 147A of the Licensing Act 2003 creates an offence of persistently selling alcohol to children under the age of 18.

On how many occasions must alcohol be sold to young persons, in order to attract a prosecution for this offence?

A 3 or more occasions in 2 consecutive months.

B 3 or more occasions in 3 consecutive months.

C 3 or more occasions in 4 consecutive months.

D 4 or more occasions in 3 consecutive months.

Question 11.23

The police have conducted a series of test purchase operations over a period of a month at the Railway public house, due to suspected under-age drinking. The officers conducting the exercise have reported that GREEN, the premises licence holder, served alcohol to 5 under-age drinkers during this period. The duty inspector considers that an offence has been committed under s. 147A of the Licensing Act 2003, and a closure notice should be served on GREEN, to prevent further sales to young people.

Which of the following statements is correct, in relation to such a notice, under s. 169A of the Act?

A The inspector may authorise a closure notice, provided GREEN accepts responsibility for the offence under s. 147A.

B The inspector may authorise a closure notice in these circumstances alone.

C A superintendent may authorise a closure, provided GREEN accepts responsibility for the offence under s. 147A.

D A superintendent may authorise a closure, provided there is a realistic prospect of prosecuting GREEN for an offence under s. 147A.

Question 11.24

FABIEN, aged 21, was entering an off-licence one evening when a group of young people were standing outside. One of the group asked FABIEN to buy 4 cans of lager for them. FABIEN suspected that the young people were under age, but agreed to buy the cans. However, the conversation was overheard by the owner of the off-licence, who refused to sell the lager to FABIEN.

Does FABIEN commit an offence under s. 149 of the Licensing Act 2003, in these circumstances?

A No, because the shop owner refused to sell the alcohol to FABIEN.

B No, the alcohol was not intended for consumption on relevant premises.

C No, both because the shop owner refused to sell the alcohol to FABIEN *and* it was not intended for consumption on relevant premises.

D Yes, regardless of whether the shop owner refused to sell the alcohol to FABIEN, or where it was to be consumed.

Question 11.25

GARDINER is 17 years old and works for ASDA as a temporary worker. His supervisor is YANCEY. Whilst on the tills GARDINER checks through a four-pack of Fosters Ice bottles. YANCEY is at the till next to GARDINER but does not notice that the sale of alcohol has happened and she did not tell GARDINER he was not allowed to sell alcohol.

In relation to the sale of alcohol by GARDINER, which of the following statements is correct?

A YANCEY has committed an offence as she failed to supervise the sale of alcohol properly.

B YANCEY has committed an offence as she failed to train GARDINER in the sale of alcohol.

C GARDINER has committed an offence of selling alcohol whilst under 18 years of age.

D Neither has committed an offence in these circumstances.

Question 11.26

Constable SINGH was walking through a park when he came across two young people, who were intoxicated. He discovered they were 15 years old and that they had been given drink by HAWKINS. Constable SINGH intercepted HAWKINS, who was walking away from the park, and saw that he was in possession of a can of lager from which he was drinking. HAWKINS is over 18 years old.

What are Constable SINGH's powers to deal with HAWKINS in these circumstances?

A He has the power to confiscate the alcohol from HAWKINS and demand his name and address.

B He has no powers, as HAWKINS did not intend to supply the alcohol to a person under 18.

C He has no powers, as HAWKINS is not under 18.

D He has no powers, as HAWKINS is not in the company of a person under 18 to whom he intends to supply the alcohol.

Question 11.27

Section 1(6) of the Confiscation of Alcohol (Young Persons) Act 1997 outlines the definition of a 'relevant place' for the purposes of confiscating alcohol.

Which of the following places would *not* qualify as a 'relevant place' for the purposes of the Act?

A A cinema.

B A school playing field during the summer holiday.

C An off-licence.

D A railway station platform.

Question 11.28

Constable PARIS was on patrol in a public park, which the local authority has designated as an area where alcohol may not be consumed. Constable PARIS saw BELL sitting on a park bench with 4 unopened cans of lager. BELL was intoxicated, but did not consume alcohol from the cans in the officer's presence.

What power is available to Constable PARIS to deal with BELL under the Criminal Justice and Police Act 2001 (alcohol consumption in designated places)?

A Constable PARIS had a power to direct BELL not to drink from the cans.

B None, Constable PARIS did not see BELL drinking from the cans.

C None, as the cans were unopened.

D Constable PARIS had a power to confiscate the cans, but not to dispose of them.

Question 11.29

The Albion public house is situated in the middle of a residential estate. The premises has live bands playing on weekend evenings. One Saturday afternoon, Constable TELFORD was called to speak to several residents in the area, who were complaining about the noise that had come from the live band the night before.

They all stated that there was another live band booked for that evening, and that the excessive noise was causing a serious disturbance in the area. As a result of speaking to the neighbours, Constable TELFORD contacted her inspector, who attended the scene. The inspector was considering whether or not to type out a closure order to serve on the licensee.

In the circumstances, would the inspector be able to implement a closure order under s. 161(1)(b) of the Licensing Act 2003?

A No, because the disturbance was not ongoing at the time.

B Yes, provided the noise was actually coming from the premises itself.

C No, closure orders are designed for disorder at licensed premises, not noise complaints.

D Yes, provided the noise was coming either from the premises, or from the vicinity of the premises.

Question 11.30

Inspector CARROLL was working a late shift when she received information that several disturbances had taken place in the Admiral public house during the evening. Inspector CARROLL was aware that the police had dealt with a number of public order situations at the Admiral in the previous week and that the owner, HALL, had a reputation of being unable to control his customers. The inspector typed out a closure order for the premises, which she intended serving on HALL; however, she was called away to deal with a firearms incident in another area before she could serve the notice.

Could Inspector CARROLL delegate the serving of the notice to another officer?

A No, the order must be served by the inspector making it.

B Yes, the order may be served by any other inspector.

C Yes, the order may be served by any other officer.

D Yes, the order may be served by the senior officer on duty in the area.

Question 11.31

Inspector CLINTON was working late shifts on a Sunday. During the weekend, he had dealings with PARKS, the licensee of the Ship public house. The police were called to the premises several times on Friday evening because of fighting and persons were arrested. Intelligence suggested on the Saturday evening that further trouble was likely, and Inspector CLINTON served a closure order on PARKS at 8 pm. There was no court on the Sunday and Inspector CLINTON visited the Ship again at

5 pm that evening. PARKS said that he was going to open the pub again that night, because it was costing him too much money to stay closed.

What powers would be available to Inspector CLINTON, if he reasonably believed there was likely to be further disorder at the premises on the Sunday evening?

A None, the closure order has expired; he must wait until Monday to report the matter to the court.

B He may extend the closure order by serving a notice on PARKS when the existing one expires at 8 pm.

C He may extend the closure order, provided he serves a notice on PARKS before 8 pm.

D He must serve a new closure order on PARKS, and attend court on Monday to report the matter.

Question 11.32

WILKINS is manager of a betting office, and one day BELL entered the premises in a drunken condition. Seeing his condition, WILKINS asked him to leave. BELL became abusive and started shouting. Constable GREEN was walking past as the incident occurred and heard the disturbance.

In relation to the Betting, Gaming and Lotteries Act 1963 only, what powers does Constable GREEN have in these circumstances?

A Authority to enter the premises, in order to assist WILKINS to expel BELL under the Act.

B Authority to enter the premises, but only if the constable suspected offences were being committed against the Act.

C Authority to enter the premises, in order to expel BELL under the Act.

D Authority to enter the premises to deal with offences, but only upon the request of WILKINS.

Question 11.33

JENNINGS has recently taken over as personal licence holder of the Bluebell public house. The premises are frequented by a small group of locals, who enjoy a game of cribbage in their lunch hours. These people have queried with JENNINGS whether they can continue with their games, which involve a certain amount of betting.

In order to comply with the Gaming Act 1968, can JENNINGS allow them to continue?

A Yes, there are no restrictions on gaming in a public house.

B No, gaming on premises covered by a premises licence is illegal.

C No, the only gaming allowed on premises covered by a premises licence is dominoes.

D Yes, provided the game does not involve high stakes.

ANSWERS

Answer 11.1

Answer **C** — A person 'provides late night refreshment' under the Licensing Act 2003 if he or she supplies hot food or hot drinks to the public at any time between the hours of 11 pm and 5 am. This is not a licence to sell alcohol, therefore answer D is incorrect. The person may either sell food or drink, provided either one is hot; therefore answers A and B are incorrect.

General Police Duties, para. 4.11.2

Answer 11.2

Answer **A** — A person 'provides late night refreshment' under the Licensing Act 2003 if he or she supplies hot food or hot drinks to the public at any time between the hours of 11 pm and 5 am. Answers B, C and D are incorrect.

General Police Duties, para. 4.11.2

Answer 11.3

Answer **C** — Under s. 179 of the Licensing Act 2003, where a constable or an authorised person has reason to believe that any premises are being, or are about to be, used for a licensable activity, they may enter the premises with a view to seeing whether the activity is being, or is to be, carried on under and in accordance with an authorisation (s. 179(1)). A person exercising the power conferred by this section may, if necessary, use reasonable force (s. 179(3)). Since the power under this section is not restricted to police officers, answer B is incorrect. Also, there is no requirement for a police officer to be in uniform, therefore answer A is incorrect.

There is a separate power, under s. 180 of the Act, for a constable to enter premises in order to investigate offences. A constable may enter by reasonable force under this section. However, s. 179 above shows that a constable or authorised person may enter premises using reasonable force simply to make sure that licensing activities are being carried out within the law. Answer D is therefore incorrect.

(Note that an authorised person exercising the powers conferred on them must, if so requested, produce evidence of their authority to exercise the power.)

General Police Duties, para. 4.11.2.3

Answer 11.4

Answer **D** — Under s. 26 of the Licensing Act 2003, a premises licence lasts until it is either revoked or surrendered. There is no specific time limit attached to this licence, therefore answers A, B and C are incorrect.

General Police Duties, para. 4.11.4.1

Answer 11.5

Answer **A** — When a person applies for a premises licence, under the Licensing Act 2003, the application must be accompanied by an operating schedule. The operating schedule will describe how the licensee intends operating his or her premises, and will include such things as how the licensee intends promoting the licensing objectives and the times during which the premises will be open to the public (s. 17(4)). The schedule must also include a detailed plan of the premises. Answers B and D are therefore incorrect.

Where an application for a licence under s. 17 gives rise to no relevant representations from responsible authorities or interested parties, an applicant is entitled to the grant of a licence without the imposition of conditions beyond those consistent with the content of the operating schedule referred to in s. 17(4) of the Act and any mandatory conditions under the Act, (which includes a plan of the premises), (*(1) British Beer and Pub Association (2) Association of Licensed Multiple Retailers (3) British Institute of Innkeeping* v *Canterbury City Council* (2005) 169 JP 521). Answer C is therefore incorrect.

General Police Duties, para. 4.11.4.1

Answer 11.6

Answer **C** — If a person is charged with a 'relevant offence', as laid out in sch. 4 to the Licensing Act 2003, they have a duty to produce their personal licence to the court. Answers B and D are therefore incorrect. The court may order the licence to be forfeited or suspended for a period not exceeding six months. Answer A is incorrect as this is a maximum period (not a minimum period). (Answer B is incorrect for this reason also.)

General Police Duties, para. 4.11.4.4

Answer 11.7

Answer **B** — Schedule 4 to the Licensing Act 2003 lists a number of offences, which would attract the suspension of a personal licence. The offences include licensing offences, but also offences of dishonesty (such as theft), misuse of drugs, firearms, sexual and violent offences, and offences involving drink driving (answers C and D are therefore incorrect). Under s. 129 of the Act, a person's licence may be suspended when a person is charged with an offence listed in sch. 4. This is not a mandatory suspension, therefore answer A is incorrect.

General Police Duties, para. 4.11.4.4

Answer 11.8

Answer **A** — The general conditions for 'qualifying clubs' are set out in s. 62 of the Licensing Act 2003. Amongst these conditions is the minimum number of members a club should have, which is 25 members. Answers B, C and D are therefore incorrect.

There are other conditions listed in s. 62, such as the requirement that new members are denied the privileges of the club for a period of at least two days, between nomination for membership and admission. These conditions — among other things — prevent sham 'clubs' being set up whereby instant membership allows the provisions of the framework to be circumvented.

General Police Duties, para. 4.11.5

Answer 11.9

Answer **C** — Where a club applies for a club premises certificate, for variation of a club premises certificate or an application is made for a review of such a certificate in respect of any premises, a constable authorised by the chief officer of police (on production of their authority) may enter and inspect the premises (see s. 96(2)).

> Any entry and inspection under this section must take place at a reasonable time on a day —
> (a) which is not more than 14 days after the making of the application in question, and
> (b) which is specified in the required notice served with at least 48 hours' notice on the club.

(s. 96(3) and (4))

Answers A and B are therefore incorrect. Since Constable BARRETT has a specific timescale in which to conduct this visit, answer D is incorrect.

It should be noted that obstructing a constable or other authorised person in the exercise of this power is a summary offence (s. 96(5)).

General Police Duties, para. 4.11.5.1

Answer 11.10

Answer **D** — Under s. 97 of the Licensing Act 2003, where a club premises certificate has effect in respect of any premises, a constable may enter and search the premises if he/she has reasonable cause to believe —

(a) that an offence under section 4(3)(a), (b) or (c) of the Misuse of Drugs Act 1971 (supplying or offering to supply, or being concerned in supplying or making an offer to supply, a controlled drug) has been, is being, or is about to be, committed there, or

(b) that there is likely to be a breach of the peace there.

This section does not allow a constable to enter the premises to detect licensing offences; therefore answers A and C are incorrect. Entry is allowed (using reasonable force if necessary) in order to detect offences under the Misuse of Drugs Act 1971, or if a breach of the peace is likely to occur in the premises. Answers A and B are incorrect for this reason.

General Police Duties, para. 4.11.5.2

Answer 11.11

Answer **D** — Part 5 of the Licensing Act 2003 allows premises users to carry out licensable activities on a temporary basis under certain conditions. Such temporary activities can only be carried out for a period not exceeding *96 hours* (see s. 100). Answers A, B and C are therefore incorrect.

General Police Duties, para. 4.11.6

Answer 11.12

Answer **B** — Under s. 104(1) of the Licensing Act 2003, the premises user must give a copy of any temporary event notice to the relevant chief officer of police no later than 10 working days before the day on which the event period specified in the notice begins.

Where the chief officer is satisfied that allowing the premises to be used in accordance with the notice would undermine the crime prevention objective (mentioned in s. 4(2)(a)), he or she must give a notice stating the reasons why he or she is so satisfied (an 'objection notice') to the relevant licensing authority, and the premises user (see s. 104(2)). Answers A and D are incorrect.

Section 100(2) of the Act states that the 'premises user', in relation to a temporary event notice, is the individual who gave the notice. Answer C is therefore incorrect.

General Police Duties, paras 4.11.6.1, 4.11.6.2

Answer 11.13

Answer **C** — These restrictions are set out in s. 107 of the Licensing Act 2003 and generally apply where the applicant has exceeded the relevant limits applied to temporary events. The limits apply either to the individual premises licence holder, or to the premises itself. In relation to the individual, where the premises user has a personal licence and has already given 50 notices in the same calendar year as the specified temporary event, the licensing authority may issue a counter notice. Answers A, B and D are therefore incorrect.

In relation to the premises, the same restrictions apply where at least 12 notices have been given in respect of the same premises in that year.

General Police Duties, para. 4.11.6.3

Answer 11.14

Answer **B** — The Licensing Act 2003, s. 141 states:

(1) A person to whom subsection (2) applies commits an offence if, on relevant premises, he knowingly —
   (a) sells or attempts to sell alcohol to a person who is drunk, or
   (b) allows alcohol to be sold to such a person.

This subsection applies:

(2) (a) to any person who works at the premises in a capacity, whether paid or unpaid, which gives him authority to sell the alcohol concerned,
   (b) in the case of licensed premises, to —

(i) the holder of a premises licence in respect of the premises, and

(ii) the designated premises supervisor (if any) under such a licence...

Under s. 141(2)(a) above, the offence may be committed by any person who works on the premises, whatever their capacity. However, on licensed premises (which is the case in this question) the offence is covered by s. 141(2)(b), which restricts liability to the holder of a premises licence and/or the designated premises supervisor. Answers A and D are therefore incorrect. It is irrelevant that RICHARDS did not consume the drink — the offence is complete when the alcohol is sold to a person who is intoxicated. Answer C is therefore incorrect.

General Police Duties, para. 4.11.8.6

Answer 11.15

Answer **B** — Under s. 143(1)(a) of the Licensing Act 2003, a person who is drunk or disorderly commits an offence if, without reasonable excuse he or she *fails* to leave relevant premises when requested to do so by a constable or by a person to whom subs. (2) applies (the holder of a premises licence in respect of the premises, and/or the designated premises supervisor). Since HOULIE left when requested by GREEN, no offence was committed under this subsection; answer D is therefore incorrect.

Under s. 143(1)(b) of the Act, a further offence is committed if a person enters or attempts (answer A is therefore incorrect) to enter relevant premises after a constable or a person to whom subs. (2) applies has requested him or her not to enter. GREEN was not so requested and therefore would also not commit this offence; answer C is therefore incorrect.

General Police Duties, para. 4.11.8.8

Answer 11.16

Answer **A** — Under s. 91(1) of the Criminal Justice Act 1967, a person commits an offence if, in a public place, he or she is guilty, while drunk, of disorderly conduct. To prove this offence, you must show that the person has consumed excessive amounts of alcohol. Answer D is incorrect, as drunk and disorderly may be the appropriate charge if someone has consumed so much alcohol.

However, the offence is not committed when a person does not commit a disorderly act until after their arrest (*H* v *DPP* (2006) 170 JP 4). Answers B and C are therefore incorrect.

General Police Duties, para. 4.11.8.9

Answer 11.17

Answer **A** — For this offence the drunkenness must be caused by excessive amounts of alcohol; where this is not the case and his state is caused by some other intoxicant, e.g. a drug, the offence is not made out (*Neale* v *RMJE* (*a minor*) (1985) 80 Cr App R 20) and therefore answer B is incorrect. In *Neale*, Goff LJ held that 'drunkenness' means taking intoxicating liquor to an extent that affects steady self-control. However, where there are several causes of a person's intoxicated state, one of which is alcohol, a court can find the person was in fact drunk even though some other intoxicant had an effect on this 'steady self-control' and therefore answer C is incorrect. Answer D is a defence from the Public Order Act 1986 and has no impact on this offence and is incorrect.

General Police Duties, para. 4.11.8.9

Answer 11.18

Answer **C** — Section 145 of the Licensing Act 2003 states that it is an offence for a person holding roles in public houses that would allow them to take appropriate action to prevent the presence of children in the way prohibited to allow unaccompanied children on those premises. This applies to licensees, staff working in the pub, etc.; the children themselves commit no offence by just being in there. Answer B is therefore incorrect.

No offence is committed if the unaccompanied child is on the premises solely for the purpose of passing to or from some other place to or from which there is no other convenient means of access or egress (s. 145(5)).

However, by virtue of s. 145(2)(a), 'child' means an individual aged under 16, and APPLEBY is 16. No offence is committed as she is not an 'unaccompanied child' as defined by the Act and not because she is passing through; that exception to the legislation applies only to unaccompanied children. Answers A and D are therefore incorrect.

General Police Duties, para. 4.11.9.1

Answer 11.19

Answer **D** — The new legislation has greatly expanded the responsibility of persons selling alcohol to ensure they do not sell it to persons under 18. There are a lot of 'ors' and 'ands' in the legislation so it has to be read carefully. First it is an absolute offence to sell alcohol to someone who is under 18, but there are defences available.

To begin with, the person selling the alcohol must believe the person is aged 18 or over; lack of this belief loses the defence immediately. However this belief must then be supported by either of the following circumstances:

- nobody could reasonably have suspected from the individual's appearance that he was aged under 18; *or*
- all reasonable steps to establish the individual's age had been taken.

JABLONOWSKI's belief is not enough on its own; answer A is therefore incorrect.

In the scenario TINNEY did not look over 18, so JABLONOWSKI would have to follow the reasonable steps route to establish identity.

The Licensing Act 2003 further defines what 'reasonable steps' are in relation to establishing identification. They are:

- the individual was asked for evidence of his age; *and*
- the evidence produced would have convinced a reasonable person.

Producing identification does not negate the offence if such identification is obviously fake (as it was in the scenario). Answers B and C are therefore incorrect.

In summary then, for the defence to succeed, the person selling must believe the individual buying to be 18 or over. If it is not obvious to everyone else that this individual, by appearance, is over 18 then proof of age is required; such proof has to be convincing.

General Police Duties, para. 4.11.9.4

Answer 11.20

Answer **A** — The offences referred to in this question relate to various sections of the Licensing Act 2003:

- s. 147, allowing the sale of alcohol to children;
- s. 149, purchase of alcohol by or on behalf of children;
- s. 150, consumption of alcohol by children.

They all relate to selling and consumption of alcohol by a person aged under 18, and if the person is indeed under 18 then the offences are complete. However offences under ss. 149 and 150 do not apply where a person is 16 or 17, provided they are accompanied at a table meal by someone aged 18 or over. In these circumstances they can have bought for them and consume beer, wine and cider (although hopefully not all in the same glass!).

In the scenario the buying and consumption of the beer was lawful and in consequence the selling was also lawful and no one commits an offence. Answers B, C and D are therefore incorrect.

General Police Duties, paras 4.11.9.5, 4.11.9.9, 4.11.9.10

Answer 11.21

Answer **A** — Under s. 147A(1) of the Licensing Act 2003, a person is guilty of an offence if:

(a) on 3 or more different occasions within a period of 3 consecutive months alcohol is unlawfully sold on the same premises to an individual aged under 18;
(b) at the time of each sale the premises were either licensed premises or premises authorised to be used for a permitted temporary activity; and
(c) that person was a responsible person in relation to the premises at each such time.

The 'responsible person' in relation to licensed premises means:

- the holder of a premises licence in respect of the premises, *or*
- the designated premises supervisor (if any) under such a licence, or
- any individual aged 18 or over who is authorised by such a holder or supervisor.

Therefore, under s. 147A(1)(c) above, the offence is committed when the same person is the responsible person on each occasion and since DENNIS was not the responsible person on each occasion, this offence is not committed. Answers C and D are incorrect.

The individual aged under 18, to whom the sale is made, can be the same person or different people (subs. (5)), therefore answer B is incorrect.

General Police Duties, para. 4.11.9.6

Answer 11.22

Answer **B** — Under s. 147A(1) of the Licensing Act 2003, a person is guilty of an offence if:

(a) on 3 or more different occasions within a period of 3 consecutive months alcohol is unlawfully sold on the same premises to an individual aged under 18;

Answers A, C and D are therefore incorrect.

General Police Duties, para. 4.11.9.6

Answer 11.23

Answer **D** — Section 169A of the Licensing Act 2003, inserted by Violent Crime Reduction Act 2006, provides that a senior police officer (of the rank of superintendent or higher), or an inspector of weights and measures, may give a closure notice where there is evidence that a person has committed the offence of persistently selling alcohol to children at the premises in question. Answers A and B and are therefore incorrect.

A further condition exists under s. 169A — the superintendent must consider that the evidence is such that there would be a realistic prospect of conviction if the offender was prosecuted for it. Answer C is incorrect.

General Police Duties, para. 4.11.9.16

Answer 11.24

Answer **D** — Under s. 149(3)(a) of the Licensing Act 2003, a person commits an offence if he or she buys or attempts to buy alcohol on behalf of an individual aged under 18. The offence is complete when the person attempts to purchase the alcohol; therefore answers A and C are incorrect.

There is a separate offence under s. 149(4) of the Act, of a person buying or attempting to buy alcohol for consumption by a person under 18, for consumption on relevant premises — however, since the offence may be committed in either of the above circumstances, answers B and C are incorrect.

General Police Duties, para. 4.11.9.9

Answer 11.25

Answer **D** — Clearly selling alcohol in premises like ASDA has to be controlled and there is an offence under s. 153(4) of the Licensing Act 2003 of unsupervised sales by children (those under 18). The offence is committed by 'a responsible person' allowing an individual aged under 18 to make on the premises any sale of alcohol, a responsible person being defined as:

- the holder of a premises licence in respect of the premises;
- the designated premises supervisor (if any) under such a licence; or
- any individual aged 18 or over who is authorised for the purposes of this section by such a holder or supervisor.

(s. 153(4) of the Licensing Act 2003)

Only the responsible person commits this offence not the person under 18; answer C is therefore incorrect. The offence, however, is perpetrated 'knowingly' and as such there has to be such conscious awareness of what was happening. Answer A is incorrect because YANCEY has no such knowledge.

It is not committed by omission or error in training; answer B is therefore incorrect.

General Police Duties, para. 4.11.9.13

Answer 11.26

Answer **A** — Under s. 1(1) of the Confiscation of Alcohol (Young Persons) Act 1997, a constable who reasonably suspects that a person who is in a relevant place (public place, etc.) is in possession of alcohol, may confiscate the alcohol and demand a person's name and address if either:

(a) the person is under 18; *or*
(b) the person intends that any of the alcohol shall be consumed by a person under 18 in a relevant place; *or*
(c) the person is with *or* has recently been with a person under 18 and that person has recently consumed alcohol in the relevant place.

Under subs. (c) above, as HAWKINS has recently been with a person under 18 who has consumed alcohol, regardless of whether he intends to supply more alcohol to the children, the officer will have the power to confiscate the alcohol he is in possession of and demand his name and address. Answers B and D are therefore incorrect.

Also, alcohol may be confiscated from a person who is over 18 if he or she has committed an act mentioned under subsections (b) and (c) above — the power is designed to prevent alcohol either being consumed by, or supplied to, people under 18. Answer C is therefore incorrect.

General Police Duties, para. 4.11.9.14

Answer 11.27

Answer **C** — A 'relevant place' under s. 1(6) of the Confiscation of Alcohol (Young Persons) Act 1997 would include:

• any public place, *other* than licensed premises (which includes an off-licence);

- any place other than a public place, to which the person has unlawfully gained access.

The first bullet point would include a place to which the public has access on payment. It would not include licensed premises. The second would not apply where a person gained access lawfully and later became a trespasser. (However, a person would presumably be a trespasser on school premises during the summer holiday.)

Since answer C is the only place which would not qualify as a relevant place, answers A, B and D are incorrect.

General Police Duties, para. 4.11.9.14

Answer 11.28

Answer **A** — Under s. 13 of the Criminal Justice and Police Act 2001, local authorities may identify and designate public places within their areas as 'alcohol free zones', provided they are satisfied that nuisance, annoyance or disorder has occurred as a result of consumption of intoxicating liquor in those areas. Section 12 of the Act provides a constable with powers to deal with people who contravene orders, if he or she reasonably believes that a person is or has been consuming, or intends to consume alcohol in that place. Answer B is therefore incorrect.

A constable is provided with three distinct powers:

- to require the person not to consume alcohol;
- to require the person to surrender the alcohol;
- to dispose of anything surrendered in a manner he or she considers appropriate.

Answer D is incorrect, because the officer may exercise any of the above powers and dispose of anything surrendered in such a manner as he or she considers appropriate. The fact that the cans were unopened is not relevant and they may be confiscated utilising the powers described above. Answer C is therefore incorrect.

General Police Duties, para. 4.11.10.2

Answer 11.29

Answer **A** — There are two general powers to serve closure orders under s. 161 of the Licensing Act 2003. First, when a senior police officer (an officer of at least the rank of inspector) has reason to believe that there is disorder on, or in the vicinity of and related to the premises, or there is likely to be disorder on, or in the vicinity of and related to the premises, and in either case he or she reasonably believes that the order is necessary in interests of public safety (s. 161(1)(a)).

Secondly, a closure notice may be served when it is reasonably believed that a disturbance is being caused to the public by excessive noise emitted from the premises and a closure order is necessary to prevent the disturbance. Since a closure order may be served in relation to noise only (s. 161(1)(b)) answer C is incorrect.

However, this power is restricted to ongoing incidents and may be used only where a disturbance is occurring, which means that answers B and D are incorrect. Lastly, the senior police officer must be satisfied that the excessive noise is actually being emitted from the premises (unlike the power to deal with disorder, which may occur in the vicinity of the premises). Answer D is also incorrect for this reason.

General Police Duties, para. 4.11.11.2

Answer 11.30

Answer **C** — Under s. 161 of the Licensing Act 2003, a senior police officer (an inspector) may make an order requiring the relevant licensed premises to be closed if it is necessary in the interests of public safety, where disorder is occurring or where it is likely to occur, either on the premises or in the vicinity. Past conduct of the licensee may be taken into consideration.

The closure order must be a written notice and comes into effect when a constable serves notice on the holder of the premises licence or the designated premises supervisor in respect of licensed premises (s. 161(5)). Because another police officer of any rank may actually serve the written notice on the relevant person, the senior police officer making the order need not be present on the premises when the order is served. Answers A, B and D are therefore incorrect. Note that the power to order the closure cannot be delegated to a person below the rank of inspector.

General Police Duties, para. 4.11.11.2

Answer 11.31

Answer **C** — Under s. 164(1) of the Licensing Act 2003, where a closure order has been made, the responsible officer must apply to the relevant justices for them to consider the order as soon as reasonably practicable after the order was made, so that the court may consider the order and any extension to it. The responsible officer must also notify the relevant licensing authority.

However, a closure order will expire 24 hours after the notice was served on the relevant person. The legislators have allowed for the fact that most areas do not have a court sitting on a Sunday by allowing the senior police officer to extend the existing closure order by serving a new written notice on the relevant person (s. 162). This extension will last for another 24 hours, allowing the responsible officer to attend court on the Monday. Answers A and D are therefore incorrect.

The original closure order in the question expired at 8 p.m. on the Sunday. The further extended period of 24 hours commences when the previous order expires; however, the written notice must be served on the relevant person before the existing closure order expires (see s. 162(3) and (4)). Answer B is incorrect.

Note that in order to extend a closure order the senior police officer would still reasonably have to believe that it is necessary in the interests of public safety or to prevent excessive noise. Therefore, if the inspector in the question had no reason to suspect that there would have been further problems on the Sunday, he could not have closed the premises down. He would still have to attend court on the Monday to report on the facts of the closure order served on the Saturday.

General Police Duties, paras 4.11.11.3, 4.11.11.4

Answer 11.32

Answer **A** — Under s. 10(2) of the Betting, Gaming and Lotteries Act 1963, the licensee may refuse to admit or may expel any person who is drunk, violent or quarrelsome. Under s. 10(3) of the Act, a constable may, on request of the licensee, help to expel such a person. Force may be used as necessary. There is a further power under s. 10(4) to enter premises to detect offences, but this is in addition to the power under s. 10(3); these relate to offences under s. 10(1) of the Act and do not rely on an invitation from the licensee or any servant or agent of the licensee; answers B and D are therefore incorrect. As the power amounts to assisting the licensee only answer C is therefore incorrect.

General Police Duties, para. 4.11.13.4

Answer 11.33

Answer **D** — Gaming is defined as the playing of a game of chance for winnings in money or money's worth (s. 52(1) of the Gaming Act 1968). There are restrictions placed by the Gaming Act 1968 as to where gaming can take place. It is a summary offence to take part in gaming in the street or in a public place (s. 5). However, gaming on licensed premises is permitted in certain circumstances, and therefore answers A and B are incorrect.

Customers may play cribbage, dominoes and other games (and answer C is therefore incorrect) approved by the licensing authority, provided the games do not involve high stakes or the games are not used as an inducement to people to frequent the premises. In the given scenario, the games are played by local customers for low stakes; therefore such gaming would be permissible.

General Police Duties, para. 4.11.13.6, 4.11.13.7

12 | Offences and Powers Relating to Information

STUDY PREPARATION

The management — and mismanagement — of information is an area of increasing importance to the police generally and therefore to its supervisors, managers, trainers and examiners.

The key issues here are the statutory restrictions on who can access what type of information and for what purpose. Much accessing of information involves the use of computers and it is necessary therefore to understand the relevant aspects of the Computer Misuse Act 1990.

This chapter now contains the provisions of the Regulation of Investigatory Powers Act 2000, which covers the interception of communications and the covert acquisition of information about people.

QUESTIONS

Question 12.1

Section 1 of the Computer Misuse Act 1990 makes provision in relation to unauthorised access to computer material.

Where a person is not authorised and they have the required intent and knowledge, at which point would an offence under this section first be committed?

A When the computer is switched on.

B When the 'log on screen' is filled out.

C When they are successfully logged onto the system.

D When the actual program is accessed.

Question 12.2

Constable BROWN has been asked by his neighbour to check the Police National Computer (PNC), as the neighbour wants to know if his future son-in-law has a criminal record. Constable BROWN agrees and conducts a PNC check on the person, and notices he has a record for offences of violence. Fearing the consequences, the officer does not want to tell the neighbour the truth, so he tells the neighbour that there is no criminal record. Constable BROWN is an authorised PNC operator, but realises he is not authorised to carry out a private check on behalf of his neighbour.

When does Constable BROWN first commit an offence contrary to s. 1 of the Computer Misuse Act 1990?

A When he agrees to carry out the check.
B When he carries out the PNC check on the computer.
C When he views the data on the screen.
D When he gives the neighbour false information.

Question 12.3

DAWLISH is a Crown Prosecution Service employee and is the prosecutor in a case of 'hacking' (under s. 1 of the Computer Misuse Act 1990). DAWLISH received the papers from the police on Monday. On Friday, DAWLISH decided that the evidence produced by the police amounted to sufficient evidence to warrant prosecutions.

Within what period may proceedings for an offence under s. 1 above be brought?

A 6 months from the Monday.
B 6 months from the Friday.
C 12 months from the Monday.
D 12 months from the Friday.

Question 12.4

DAVIDSON is a computer programmer who has been asked by JELLIS to assist in a crime. JELLIS wants him to access the computer records of a Ferrari dealership's new customers' accounts and add JELLIS' details as a bona fide customer. This will, he believes, enable him to test drive a Ferrari. He intends not to return the car but take it for a 'joy-ride', amounting to an offence under s. 12(1) of the Theft Act 1968 (taking a motor vehicle or other conveyance without authority, etc.). DAVIDSON 'hacks' into the company's computer and makes the changes. However, in reality, JELLIS will not be able to carry out his plan as the company always sends a representative on the test drive.

Has DAVIDSON committed an offence under s. 2 of the Computer Misuse Act 1990 (unauthorised access with intent to commit or facilitate commission of further offences)?

A Yes, even though the commission of the offence intended was impossible.
B Yes, even though he was merely facilitating the crime.
C No, as the intention to commit the crime lay with JELLIS.
D No, as the offence intended is not covered by s. 2.

Question 12.5

TURLEY has made an unauthorised modification of a computer program. In order to prove an offence of unauthorised modification of computer material contrary to s. 3 of the Computer Misuse Act 1990, it is necessary to show that the person had the 'requisite knowledge'.

What is that 'requisite knowledge'?
A That the modification will affect the operation of the program.
B That the modification will affect the operation of the computer.
C That the modification will prevent access to the program.
D That the modification was unauthorised.

Question 12.6

The Data Protection Act 1998 sets out data protection principles and schedules, which must be complied with.

In relation to a particular police force and its responsibility under principle 4 ('personal data shall be accurate, and where necessary, kept up to date'), which of the following people have direct responsibility for this principle according to s. 4 of the Act?
A The chief officer.
B The data protection officer.
C The data controller.
D The person who puts the data on the computer.

Question 12.7

Officers intend to use a covert human intelligence source (CHIS) to further an ongoing operation. The CHIS will be used to attend a meeting of the target criminals which is being held in a public house, to record their conversations on tape and to return the tapes to the officer in the case.

In relation to surveillance, would this operation need to be authorised, beyond the authorisation of the CHIS?

A Yes, as this is directed surveillance.

B No, as the surveillance involves an authorised CHIS.

C Yes, as this is intrusive surveillance.

D No, as the surveillance is not in a private house.

Question 12.8

Police strongly suspect that pupils from a local high school are dealing in Class A drugs, and wish to use a juvenile covert human intelligence source (CHIS); however, the information is that the dealing is going on at the moment, and it is urgent that the CHIS be authorised. Due to his being unavailable, it is not reasonably practicable for the local superintendent to authorise the application at this time.

Which of the following statements is correct?

A In these circumstances an inspector may give the relevant authorisation, and this can be oral.

B The relevant authorisation in this case will have to wait until the local superintendent can give it.

C In these circumstances an inspector may give the relevant authorisation, and this must be in writing.

D In these circumstances the assistant chief constable can give the relevant authorisation.

Question 12.9

Section 43(3)(a) of the Regulation of Investigatory Powers Act 2000, in urgent cases, allows an inspector to authorise the use of a covert human intelligence source (CHIS).

How long would such an urgent authorisation last before it would have to be renewed?

A 72 hours.
B 24 hours.
C 12 hours.
D 48 hours.

Question 12.10

The use and conduct of a covert human intelligence source (CHIS) must be author-ised by a designated officer.

In relation to the prevention of crime, what must the designated officer believe to authorise a CHIS?
A It is reasonable to prevent a crime.
B It is suspected that it will prevent a crime.
C It is reasonable in the circumstances to prevent a crime.
D It is necessary to prevent a crime.

Question 12.11

Officers received information that JOHNSON was dealing drugs while sitting in his car in a car park on the outskirts of town. After some research, the officers dis-covered that a new closed circuit television (CCTV) camera had been installed in the area, overlooking the car park, which was powerful enough to see inside parked cars. The officers considered using the CCTV office as an observation point, in an operation to catch JOHNSON handing over the drugs and collecting his money in-side his vehicle.

Would the use of the CCTV camera to look inside JOHNSON's vehicle amount to intrusive surveillance?
A No, intrusive surveillance applies to residential premises only.
B Yes, this would amount to intrusive surveillance and would require the appro-priate authorisation.
C No, this would amount to directed surveillance and would require the appropri-ate authorisation.
D No, it would be intrusive surveillance only if the vehicle was on residential property.

Question 12.12

Police officers wish to use directed surveillance on a newspaper office with a view to obtaining material that is of a journalistic nature that will be used in the investigation of an offence of murder.

Who can grant authorisation for this directed surveillance?

A An officer of at least the rank of superintendent only.
B An officer of at least the rank of superintendent, or an inspector in cases of urgency.
C The chief officer only.
D Any Association of Chief Police Officers (ACPO)-ranking police officer.

Question 12.13

Section 5(3) of the Regulation of Investigatory Powers Act 2000 allows for the application for a warrant to intercept communications, for the purpose of safeguarding the economic well-being of the United Kingdom, where the relevant acts or intentions relate to people outside the United Kingdom.

For how long is such a warrant valid?

A 1 month.
B 2 months.
C 3 months.
D 6 months.

Question 12.14

Section 5 of the Regulation of Investigatory Powers Act 2000 allows for the application of a warrant to intercept communications.

Who may authorise such a warrant?

A Only the Secretary of State.
B The Secretary of State or an authorised senior official.
C An assistant chief constable or assistant commissioner for police.
D An assistant chief constable or assistant commissioner for police, but in cases of urgency, a superintendent may perform this function.

Question 12.15

Undercover police officers have infiltrated a large gang which is organising armed robberies in banks and building societies throughout the country. It is estimated that the gang is responsible for 30 crimes which have so far yielded over £500,000. The investigating officers believe that the investigation would be assisted by obtaining a warrant to intercept communications between the various members of the gang.

Would the authorising officer be able to agree to such a warrant under s. 5 of the Regulation of Investigatory Powers Act 2000?

A Yes, provided the information would prove valuable to the investigation.

B No, the case is not one which affects the interests of national security.

C No, the case is not one which affects the interests of national security or which would affect the economic well-being of the United Kingdom.

D Yes, provided the information would prove necessary to the investigation.

Question 12.16

PRIESTLEY is employed by the police as an analyst in a police staff role, in a force intelligence bureau. He goes home one evening and, as a matter of conversation, he tells his wife, a serving police officer, that he saw an interception warrant issued in relation to a local company, but does not mention which company it is.

In relation to unauthorised disclosures, contrary to s. 19 of the Regulation of Investigatory Powers Act 2000, which of the following is true?

A PRIESTLEY cannot commit the offence as he is a member of the support staff.

B PRIESTLEY does not commit the offence as he does not name the company.

C PRIESTLEY commits the offence simply by mentioning it to his wife.

D PRIESTLEY commits the offence, but has a defence that he did not disclose it outside the police service.

ANSWERS

Answer 12.1

Answer **A** — An offence under s. 1 of the Computer Misuse Act 1990 is committed by causing a computer to perform a function, and all the above answers would amount to 'functions'. As you were asked at which point an offence would first be committed, answer A is the correct answer. Although answers B, C and D all may fall under the section, they are incorrect, as switching the computer on is the first function that would amount to the offence.

General Police Duties, para. 4.12.2.1

Answer 12.2

Answer **B** — A person commits an offence under s. 1 of the Computer Misuse Act 1990 when they 'cause a computer to perform any function with intent to secure access to any program or data held in any computer'. This involves more than an agreement, and therefore answer A is incorrect, and more than simply looking at material on a screen, and therefore answer C is incorrect. It does relate to an act completed on a computer and not on supplying personal information from such, whether true or false, and therefore answer D is incorrect (although this may be an offence under other legislation governing data). In addition, the access to the data needs to be unauthorised, and the defendant must know it to be unauthorised, which it clearly is.

General Police Duties, para. 4.12.2.2

Answer 12.3

Answer **A** — The period in which proceedings must be brought is 6 months, and therefore answers C and D are incorrect. Time begins to run once evidence comes to the knowledge of the prosecutor and not when the prosecutor comes to the opinion that the evidence is sufficient to warrant proceedings (*Morgans* v *DPP* [1999] 1 WLR 968). This amounts to the Monday, and therefore answer B is also incorrect.

General Police Duties, para. 4.12.2.1

Answer 12.4

Answer **D** — Section 2 of the Computer Misuse Act 1990 requires intent on the part of the defendant; and this is either intention to commit an offence to which s. 2 applies, or the intention to facilitate the commission of such an offence. DAVIDSON has this intention, as he knows the purpose of his actions and is aware that it will facilitate the taking and driving away (TADA), and therefore answer C is incorrect. Section 2 applies to the particular classes of offences set out in s. 2(2) of the 1990 Act. Section 12(1) of the Theft Act 1968 (taking a motor vehicle or other conveyance without authority, etc.) is such a summary offence and therefore does not fall within offences outlined in s. 2(2), and therefore answer B is incorrect. As to impossibility, s. 2(4) of the 1990 Act makes clear that a person may be guilty of an offence even though the facts are such that the commission of the further offence is impossible; but as the offence intended is not covered by s. 2 of the 1990 Act this is immaterial, therefore answer A is incorrect.

General Police Duties, para. 4.12.2.3

Answer 12.5

Answer **D** — To prove an offence under s. 3 of the Computer Misuse Act 1990, you have to show that the person had the requisite intent and the requisite knowledge. The knowledge is defined in the section as the 'knowledge that any modification [the defendant] intends to cause is unauthorised'. This makes answer D the correct answer. The other three answers refer to the intent or *mens rea* the person has to have, which is defined in s. 3(2) as follows:

> ...the requisite intent is an intent to cause a modification of the contents of any computer and by so doing —
>
> (a) to impair the operation of any computer;
> (b) to prevent or hinder access to any program or data held in any computer; or
> (c) to impair the operation of any such program or the reliability of any such data.

Answers A, B and C are incorrect as they refer to the requisite intent and not the requisite knowledge.

General Police Duties, para. 4.12.2.4

Answer 12.6

Answer **C** — A crucial element in the Data Protection Act 1998 is the data protection principles set out in sch. 1. As well as introducing the principles, s. 4 of the Act makes it clear that principle 4 is the duty of the relevant 'Data Controller'. Answer C is the only correct option, and therefore answers A, B and D are all incorrect.

General Police Duties, para. 4.12.3.2

Answer 12.7

Answer **B** — Generally, the action of covertly recording conversations will amount to some form of surveillance, which will be subject to authorisation. However, authorisation is not required where a covert human intelligence source (CHIS) is involved (s. 48(3) of the Regulation of Investigatory Powers Act 2000). So although the action of covertly recording conversations in this way would amount to directed surveillance (answer D is incorrect), which would normally need to be authorised, here it does not need to be as a CHIS is involved (answer A is incorrect). Intrusive surveillance is broadly what it says it is, and is that which would intrude on someone's personal life. This would not include a public house, and therefore answer C is incorrect.

General Police Duties, para. 4.12.4.4

Answer 12.8

Answer **D** — The people who can give authorisations for a covert human intelligence source (CHIS) are prescribed by s. 30 of the Regulation of Investigatory Powers Act 2000. In the case of police services in England and Wales, the relevant rank is superintendent and above, not necessarily the local superintendent; therefore, answer B is incorrect. However, where it is not reasonably practicable to have the application for authorisation considered by someone of that rank, and having regard to the urgency of that case, an inspector may, in general, give the relevant authorisation. As with other parts of the Act, the Codes of Practice do constrain this power, and where the CHIS is a juvenile, or where he or she is likely to obtain confidential material, the Code does not allow an inspector to give the relevant authority, orally or in writing, therefore answers A and C are incorrect.

General Police Duties, para. 4.12.4.4

Answer 12.9

Answer **A** — An urgent authorisation given by an inspector under s. 43(3)(a) of the Regulation of Investigatory Powers Act 2000 will cease to have effect 72 hours later, unless it is renewed. Answers B, C and D are therefore incorrect.

General Police Duties, para. 4.12.4.4

Answer 12.10

Answer **D** — A designated person must not authorise any activity by a covert human intelligence source (CHIS) unless he or she believes it is necessary, and that to do so is proportionate to what is being sought. It is not enough to believe it was reasonable to prevent a crime (answer A is incorrect), nor that it is reasonable in the circumstances to prevent a crime (answer C is incorrect), nor that it was suspected that it would prevent a crime (answer B is incorrect). It can be authorised only if the designated officer believes that it is both necessary and proportionate to the legitimate objective of the operation.

General Police Duties, para. 4.12.4.4

Answer 12.11

Answer **B** — Normally, the use of closed circuit television (CCTV) to prevent and detect crime will not amount to covert surveillance. However, if CCTV is used for a planned operation, it may amount to covert surveillance, which will require authorisation. Under s. 26(3) of the Regulation of Investigatory Powers Act 2000, if surveillance is covert and is carried out in relation to anything taking place on any residential premises, or in any private vehicle, and it involves the presence of an individual on the premises or in the vehicle, or is carried out by means of a surveillance device, it will generally be intrusive surveillance. Since the officers in the scenario were seeking to monitor activities inside a private vehicle, the operation would amount to intrusive surveillance, and answers A and D are incorrect. Note that the use of a surveillance device will be 'intrusive' if that device consistently provides information of the same quality and detail as might be expected from a device that was actually present on the premises or in the vehicle (s. 26(5)). Surveillance will be either 'directed' or 'intrusive', it cannot be both; therefore answer C is incorrect.

General Police Duties, para. 4.12.4.5

Answer 12.12

Answer **C** — In general, directed surveillance can be authorised by an officer of at least the rank of superintendent, or an inspector in cases of urgency, making answer A incorrect. However, the Codes of Practice again restrict this practice. For instance, where the material sought by the surveillance is subject to legal privilege, or is confidential personal information or journalistic material, the only person who can authorise it is the chief officer; therefore, answers B and D are incorrect.

General Police Duties, para. 4.12.4.5

Answer 12.13

Answer **D** — An interception warrant is normally valid for three months. However, where such a warrant is applied for as being necessary under s. 5(3) of the Regulation of Investigatory Powers Act 2000 (safeguarding the economic well-being of the United Kingdom) the warrant is valid for six months from the date of issue. Answers A, B and C are incorrect.

General Police Duties, para. 4.12.4.8

Answer 12.14

Answer **B** — The power to authorise a warrant to intercept communications, under s. 5 of the Regulation of Investigatory Powers Act 2000 is given to the Secretary of State. Because of the higher level of intrusion on the individual, responsibility for the authorisation is taken away from the police. Answers C and D are therefore incorrect. However, in urgent cases an interception may be signed by a senior official who has been expressly authorised to do so by the Secretary of State (s. 7). Answer A is therefore incorrect.

General Police Duties, para. 4.12.4.8

Answer 12.15

Answer **D** — Section 5 of the Regulation of Investigatory Powers Act 2000 allows the Secretary of State to issue interception warrants under certain, very stringent, conditions. Section 5(2) says that the Secretary of State must not issue an interception warrant unless he or she believes that the warrant is necessary:

- in the interests of national security;

- for the purpose of preventing or detecting 'serious crime', e.g. offences for which a person aged 18 or over could reasonably expect to be sentenced to at least three years' imprisonment on his or her first offence, or offences resulting in substantial financial gain, involving the use of violence or a large number of people pursuing a common purpose;
- for the purpose of safeguarding the economic well-being of the United Kingdom (where the relevant acts or intentions relate to people outside the United Kingdom);
- for the purpose of 'international mutual assistance'.

Therefore, although a warrant may be issued when it is necessary in the interests of national security or for the purpose of safeguarding the economic well-being of the United Kingdom, one may also be issued where the offence is one in which people commit offences resulting in substantial financial gain and involve the use of violence or a large number of people pursuing a common purpose. Answers B and C are incorrect.

It is not enough that the Secretary of State 'suspects' that these threats or needs exist, nor that he or she considers that an interception warrant might be useful, valuable or effective. The Secretary of State must believe that the warrant is necessary for one of the purposes set out. Answer A is therefore incorrect.

General Police Duties, para. 4.12.4.8

Answer 12.16

Answer **C** — This offence applies to police officers and police staff alike, and would apply to anyone involved in an investigation (answer A is incorrect). It deals with interception warrants, and requires those to whom it applies to keep secret any knowledge they have in relation to that warrant. The offence would be committed by simply mentioning the warrant's existence, irrespective of whether any individual or company was named (answer B is incorrect). Although there is a defence, it relates to the accused taking steps to prevent the disclosure; in the circumstances of the question this is clearly not the case and PRIESTLEY has no defence (answer D is incorrect). Note that there are other defences available to s. 19, but they relate to communication with legal advisers and the Interception of Communications Commissioner.

General Police Duties, para. 4.12.4.9

13 Diversity, Discrimination and Equality

STUDY PREPARATION

At last, the final chapter!

Although it would be easy to dismiss this area as merely a bit of political correctness, this chapter contains some of the most relevant and important legislation for supervisors and managers.

It is essential that all public servants understand their legal obligations in relation to the equal and/or fair treatment of others. In order to do so you need to know what will amount to discrimination, how to distinguish between direct and indirect discrimination, and which groups of people are protected therefrom.

It is also as important to understand the concept of victimisation and to recognise when and where it can arise.

When dealing with this area, it is worth remembering that in some circumstances you have to treat everyone in the same way, while in others treating everyone in the same way is discriminatory — and if you don't understand this point, you need to revise this chapter!

QUESTIONS

Question 13.1

Constable HEAL failed to attend a call for assistance from a colleague, and as a result the other officer suffered injuries. The injured officer, Constable STANLEY, who is African-Caribbean, believes that Constable HEAL did not attend the incident because of Constable STANLEY's ethnic background. Constable STANLEY intends to pursue a legal remedy.

Who may be liable in any future claim for discrimination on grounds of race?
A The chief officer only.
B HEAL only.
C Both HEAL and the chief officer.
D Neither, as the officer has not been discriminated against.

Question 13.2

Constable STUBBS is currently suing her employers for discrimination in the workplace. She has cited several instances of inappropriate sexual behaviour towards her by her line managers in work. Constable STUBBS has also included evidence in her statement of inappropriate sexual behaviour towards her by work colleagues while they were at a social Christmas function in a nearby public house.

Would Constable STUBBS be able to rely on *all* of this evidence in her claim of discrimination against her employers?
A Yes, she may rely on evidence of any inappropriate behaviour, inside or outside the workplace.
B No, but she would have been able to if the behaviour had taken place at an off-duty function at her actual workplace.
C No, her employers cannot be held liable for the behaviour of her colleagues outside the workplace.
D Yes, she may be able to rely on this evidence because the function was an extension of the workplace.

Question 13.3

The Chief Constable of Westshire Police is being sued under the Race Relations Act 1976 by a member of the public, SHAH. SHAH has claimed that he suffered racial discrimination by members of the force who were investigating a serious assault upon him. His allegation is that officers failed to investigate the offence correctly, and that their failure was due to their prejudice against SHAH because of his ethnic background.

Would the chief constable be able to claim a statutory defence in these circumstances, that he was *not* vicariously liable for the officers' actions?
A Yes, if he could show he took all reasonable steps to prevent the acts of discrimination complained of.
B There is no need; police officers will be liable for their own actions under the Act and not the chief officer.

C There is no need; police officers are not employees, which means they cannot be sued under this Act.

D Yes, if he could show he provided sufficient training to the officers to prevent such acts of discrimination.

Question 13.4

FLINT is a school teacher at a high school and is openly gay. The teachers in FLINT's school regularly take children on camping expeditions in the school holidays and a pre-requisite for teachers attending this trip is that they must have attended a Health and Safety in the Workplace course. FLINT has applied for this course on several occasions to become eligible to go on the camping trips; however, he has been unsuccessful each time. FLINT has found out that his employers are preventing him from attending this course because he is gay and they do not want him to have contact with the children outside the school environment.

Would FLINT be able to make a legal claim of discrimination against his employers in these circumstances?

A No, this is not sexual discrimination and therefore FLINT has no claim.

B Yes, FLINT has been discriminated against because of his sexual orientation.

C No, although FLINT has been discriminated against, vocational training is not covered.

D Yes, he will have to claim sex discrimination against his employers.

Question 13.5

A force motor cycle section has advertised a vacancy. One of the criteria is that the police officer must be able to pick up a Honda Pan European motor cycle (a large, heavy machine) from being on its side, and put it on its stand.

Is this a lawful selection condition?

A Yes, it is a legitimate expectation of the job and must be able to be performed by all successful applicants.

B Yes, provided the condition is the same for all applicants.

C No, any condition other than one related to performance of duties is unlawful.

D No, this is not a fair condition and could disadvantage some groups.

Question 13.6

Constable HUGHES has been asked out on a date by her sergeant on several occasions. She always declines. Her sergeant also makes several inappropriate and unwelcome comments to her of a sexist nature. Since Constable HUGHES has refused her sergeant's advances, she always has to perform foot patrol and gets asked by the sergeant to deal with all the menial tasks.

Is this victimisation as defined by s. 3 of the Sex Discrimination Act 1975?

A Yes, simply because HUGHES is being treated less favourably by the sergeant.

B Possibly, but only if the sergeant suspects that HUGHES intends to make a complaint about the treatment.

C Possibly, but only if the sergeant knows for a fact that HUGHES has made a complaint about the treatment.

D No, as HUGHES is expected to perform any lawful duty when instructed by her sergeant.

Question 13.7

Constable THORNE resigned from the service 14 months ago due to her dissatisfaction at the way her sexual harassment complaint was dealt with. She has been offered and accepted a support staff post with CENTREX; however, prior to starting, the job offer was withdrawn. THORNE has found out that this is because Superintendent CHANG told the CENTREX management team that THORNE was a rebellious person and not to be trusted.

Could Constable THORNE take action against the police service for discrimination by way of victimisation?

A Yes, but only because her new employers are connected to the police service.

B Yes, as her former employer had deliberately set out to spoil her subsequent employment.

C No, victimisation cannot extend to post-employment.

D No, as more than one year has passed since she resigned.

Question 13.8

The officer in charge of the Family Support Unit has a vacancy, and would like the replacement to be a female officer. The officer has noticed that children or female victims seem to respond more positively to female officers. The officer wishes to place the following words in the advertisement of the post: 'On this occasion only female officers can apply for this post.'

In relation to these words, which of the following is true?

A This is a case of a genuine occupational qualification and is not unlawful.

B This is direct discrimination and is unlawful.

C This is indirect discrimination and is unlawful.

D This is positive action and is lawful.

Question 13.9

The Armed Response Unit has advertised a 'familiarisation day for female officers only'. This is with the intention of recruiting female officers for a forthcoming fire-arms course, as they are underrepresented in the department and below the Home Office target for minority officers. The selection process will remain the same as usual, and is open to all staff. Constable BRYAN, a male officer, is keen to join the Unit and claims that he is being discriminated against, and that being able to attend this day advantages female officers.

Is the officer the victim of discrimination in these circumstances?

A Yes, female officers would be disproportionately advantaged by this day and this is positive discrimination.

B Yes, male officers are disadvantaged by this day and this is direct discrimination.

C No, police forces are allowed to use affirmative action to target minority groups to reach target numbers.

D No, police forces are allowed to discriminate in limited circumstances and this is one such occasion.

Question 13.10

GOODE worked in the post room in the offices of a large company. He had slight learning difficulties, but was perfectly able to carry out his work, which consisted of sorting and distributing internal mail. GOODE applied for a job in another part of the company, which involved filing paperwork. The pay was the same, but it would have meant working in a larger office, with more people for company. GOODE's application was turned down, on the grounds that his learning difficulties would mean that he could not sort the files as quickly as his co-workers. GOODE subsequently made a claim of discrimination under the Disability Discrimination Act 1995.

Would his employer's actions be justified in these circumstances?

A No, they would not be able to justify their actions and have acted unlawfully.

B Yes, they would be able to show that their reasons were material to the circumstances and substantial.

C Yes, they would be able to show that the decision was made in the best interests of the company.

D No, employers will never be able to justify discrimination in the workplace.

ANSWERS

Answer 13.1

Answer **C** — Under the Race Relations Act 1976, the actions (or in this case in-action) of a fellow officer can attract liability to that individual under a claim for discrimination in addition to any claim that the victim might have against the relevant chief officer (see *AM* v *WC* [1999] ICR 1218). Both the chief officer and HEAL are potentially liable, and therefore answers A and B are incorrect. Discrimination is treating one group of people less favourably than others based on their sex, racial origin or marital status. There appears to have been discrimination and answer D is therefore incorrect.

General Police Duties, para. 4.13.1.1

Answer 13.2

Answer **D** — Where acts amounting to discrimination take place outside the workplace, the employer and employees may still be caught within the framework of the legislation. So, for instance, where police officers engage in inappropriate sexual behaviour towards a colleague at a work-related social function, a tribunal may be entitled to hold that the function was an extension of the workplace and so hold the chief officer liable for the acts of his/her officers at that function (see *Chief Constable of Lincolnshire* v *Stubbs* [1999] IRLR 81). Answer C is therefore incorrect.

This case deals with a specific example of behaviour where the officers were at a work-related function, which was an 'extension of the workplace'. The decision therefore does not mean that any behaviour can be included in such a claim (although it is worth noting that discrimination and victimisation are included in the Code of Conduct for police officers, which may include the conduct of an off-duty officer). Answer A is therefore incorrect. Lastly, the above case did not specify that the location of the function was important, merely that it was an off-duty function and an extension of the workplace. Answer B is therefore incorrect.

General Police Duties, para. 4.13.1.1

Answer 13.3

Answer **A** — The Race Relations (Amendment) Act 2000 has changed the situation in respect of claims against the police when it comes to discriminatory acts. The original 1976 Act made employers vicariously liable for the actions of their employees; however, as police officers were not classed as employees, the legislation did not apply to either chief officers or their staff.

The 2000 Act makes it unlawful for a public authority to discriminate against a person on the grounds of race while carrying out their functions (which would include investigating offences). The fact that police officers are not employees is no longer relevant as they work for a 'public authority', and answer C is incorrect. Further, since it is unlawful for a 'public authority' to commit acts of discrimination, the chief officer will be liable, and not his or her staff (answer B is incorrect).

However, whereas the new legislation now allows for the police to be sued under the Race Relations Act, it also provides a statutory defence for a chief officer (under s. 32) if he or she shows that he or she took all reasonable steps to prevent the acts of discrimination complained of. Providing training may represent part of the reasonable steps taken by the chief officer, but other efforts must be made, such as publishing Race Equality Schemes and regular assessments of those schemes. Answer D is therefore incorrect.

General Police Duties, para. 4.13.4.2

Answer 13.4

Answer **B** — The issue of discrimination on grounds of sexual orientation is covered by the Employment Equality (Sexual Orientation) Regulations 2003 (SI 2003/1661). The Regulations, which came into force in December 2003, implement Council Directive 2000/78/EC. This issue has kept the courts busy for many years until the latest decision of the House of Lords in *Pearce* v *Governors of Mayfield School* [2003] IRLR 512. One of the main legal difficulties created by this controversial subject was that applicants were forced to bring their claims under the general headings of sex discrimination. Because of the above Regulations, this is no longer necessary (and answers A and D are incorrect).

The Regulations make it unlawful to discriminate on grounds of sexual orientation in employment and vocational training and apply to direct and indirect discrimination and also victimisation and harassment. Since vocational training is covered, answer C is incorrect. Sexual orientation means a sexual orientation towards people of the same sex, people of the opposite sex or to both people of the same sex and the opposite sex (reg. 2). Specific provision is made for police constables (reg. 11).

General Police Duties, para. 4.13.8

Answer 13.5

Answer **D** — There is nothing inherently unlawful about setting legitimate conditions for a job vacancy (e.g. must have two 'A' levels), and therefore answer C is incorrect as it is too broad. However, any criteria must not disadvantage a significant proportion of people from a protected group. Simply setting the same condition for all does not make it lawful (e.g. 'applicants must be able to climb stairs' is the same for all, but would disadvantage wheelchair users) and therefore answer B is incorrect. Given the size and weight of the machine in the question, it is likely that fewer women than men could comply with the condition, and it is this that potentially makes the requirement discriminatory and unlawful. Even if only one female officer could not comply with a condition of employment (as in *London Underground Ltd* v *Edwards (No. 2)* [1998] IRLR 364), it could still be indirect discrimination. As far as answer A is concerned, is it a legitimate requirement of the job? Imposing this requirement on all applicants appears to be far too broad, wholly unreasonable and, in relation to the differences in relative strength of male and female applicants, appears disproportionately to disadvantage the latter, and therefore answer A is incorrect.

General Police Duties, para. 4.13.10.2

Answer 13.6

Answer **B** — In proving victimisation, the person must show that they suffered less favourable treatment as a result of their involvement in some form of action applying the 'but for' test (see *Aziz* v *Trinity Street Taxis Ltd* [1989] QB 463). This means that 'but for' the action taken by the victim, they would not have been given less favourable treatment. The action that the officer takes relates to any of the 3 main Acts in this area of legislation (Race Relations Act 1976, Sex Discrimination Act 1975 and Disability Discrimination Act 1995), and covers:

- bringing any proceedings under these Acts;
- giving evidence in proceedings under these Acts;
- any act with regard to a person under these Acts, e.g. providing advice;
- making an allegation about a person who may have contravened any of these Acts.

If the discriminator knows or suspects that the person has done any of these actions, or intends to, then less favourable treatment of that person amounts to victimisation. As the sergeant's actions appear to amount to sexual harassment (which is covered by Sex Discrimination Act 1975), it is possible HUGHES could be being victimised. In the question outlined, there is no evidence that the sergeant is treating her differently simply because she has taken one of the actions, therefore answer A is incorrect. Answer D is incorrect in that, even where the officer was expected to perform certain tasks, if she was treated differently using the 'but for' test, then it would be discrimination. So we are left with a possibility of victimisation, and that does not necessarily have to be based on the knowledge of the sergeant. Suspicion that Constable HUGHES might complain would meet the 'but for' test and could be victimisation, and therefore answer C is also incorrect.

General Police Duties, para. 4.13.10.4

Answer 13.7

Answer **B** — The test to be applied in assessing whether or not victimisation has taken place is, 'was the real reason for the victim's treatment the fact that he/she had carried out a protected act?' (see the House of Lords' decision in *Chief Constable of West Yorkshire Police* v *Khan* [2001] 1 WLR 1947). Those protected acts are that the victim has:

- brought proceedings against any person under any of the discrimination Acts;
- has given evidence or information in connection with proceedings brought by any person under any of those Acts;
- otherwise did anything under or by reference to the Acts with regard to any person (e.g. provided advice to someone as to his or her rights);
- has alleged that any person has done anything which would amount to a contravention of those Acts (whether or not the allegation specifically so states); or
- because the discriminator knows or suspects that the person victimised has done or intends to do any of the things set out above.

In proving victimisation, the person must show that less favourable treatment occurred as a result of his/her involvement in the protected action described, that is, applying the 'but for' test (see *Aziz* v *Trinity Street Taxis Ltd.* [1989] QB 463).

An employment tribunal has held that, notwithstanding that a person was no longer employed by another, a claim of discrimination by reason of victimisation contrary to s. 6(2) of the Sex Discrimination Act 1975 could still be laid (see *Metropolitan Police Service* v *Shoebridge* [2004] ICR 1690), however long after the previous employment had ceased. Answers C and D are therefore incorrect.

In *Shoebridge* the EAT held that the words 'subjecting [him] to any other detriment' in s. 6(2)(b) of the Sex Discrimination Act 1975 were to be broadly construed to include detriment which occurred post-employment, whether or not it was of a similar kind to that which would have occurred during the employment. There is no restriction on former/new employer relationship and provided a former employer had deliberately set out to spoil an employee's subsequent employment, or so acted knowing of the likely consequences of its actions, there would be sufficient proximity and a sufficiently close connection with the employment to establish *prima facie* liability. Answer A is therefore incorrect.

General Police Duties, para. 4.13.10.4

Answer 13.8

Answer **B** — Answer D is incorrect because positive action amounts to an encouragement of particular groups to apply for certain posts, under certain strict conditions, and here the officer's actions go way beyond simple encouragement. Answer A is also incorrect as a genuine occupational qualification (GOQ) is where there is a legitimate reason (such as grounds of decency) to state that only certain groups may apply. Here there are no such grounds. An attempt to recruit female officers into a specialist department by excluding male applicants has been held to be unlawful in *Jones* v *Chief Constable of Northamptonshire Police*, The Times, 1 November 1999. It is direct discrimination because it is treating one group of people less favourably than others based on their sex. Answer C is incorrect because indirect discrimination involves setting the same criteria for a job, but the criteria are such that a significant proportion of people from a protected group are less likely to be able to achieve the criteria because of their membership of that group (e.g. a height restriction, which would affect female and some minority ethnic groups).

General Police Duties, paras 4.13.11.1, 4.13.11.2

Answer 13.9

Answer **D** — Positive discrimination involves selecting people in preference to others based on their membership of a minority group. The circumstances of the question do not amount to positive discrimination because the selection process is open to all staff, and therefore answer A is incorrect. As positive discrimination is unlawful in this country, answer C is incorrect. Direct discrimination is treating one group of people less favourably than others based on their sex, and here the male officer has the same opportunity to apply for the post and there is nothing to suggest selection will be on anything other than merit (therefore answer B is incorrect). Did the term 'discriminate' in answer D put you off? Positive action, which this is, is a form of discrimination, but is lawful. An employer may discriminate if within the preceding 12 months there are no people, or only a small number of people, from a particular racial group or of a particular sex doing that work (in this case on the Unit) in a specific locality.

General Police Duties, para. 4.13.11.2

Answer 13.10

Answer **A** — Under the Disability Discrimination Act 1995, the definition of discrimination contains a reference to the inability of the discriminator to 'justify' its treatment. However, on limited occasions, employers will be able to use 'justification' as a defence, to take into account the operational and practical realities of the workplace. Answer D is therefore incorrect.

Less favourable treatment of a disabled person will be justified only if the reason is both material to the circumstances and substantial (or in other words, significant and considerable). Answer B contains the appropriate wording contained in the defence; however, the Codes of Practice issued list specific case studies where the employer would not be able to justify its actions. The scenario mirrors a case study from the Codes of Practice, which advises that in these circumstances, the employer's actions would be unlawful. Answers B and C are therefore incorrect.

General Police Duties, para. 4.13.11.3

Question Checklist

The checklist below is designed to help you keep track of your progress when answering the multiple-choice questions. If you fill this in after one attempt at each question, you will be able to check how many you have got right and which questions you need to revisit a second time. Also available online, to download visit www.blackstonespolicemanuals.com.

	First attempt Correct (✓)	Second attempt Correct (✓)
1 Police		
1.1		
1.2		
1.3		
1.4		
1.5		
1.6		
1.7		
1.8		
1.9		
1.10		
1.11		
1.12		
1.13		
1.14		
1.15		
1.16		
1.17		
1.18		
1.19		
1.20		
1.21		

	First attempt Correct (✓)	Second attempt Correct (✓)
2 Extending the Policing Family		
2.1		
2.2		
2.3		
2.4		
2.5		
2.6		
2.7		
2.8		
2.9		
2.10		
3 Human Rights		
3.1		
3.2		
3.3		
3.4		
3.5		
3.6		
3.7		
3.8		
3.9		
3.10		

	First attempt Correct (✓)	Second attempt Correct (✓)
3.11		
3.12		
3.13		
3.14		
3.15		
4 Policing Powers		
4.1		
4.2		
4.3		
4.4		
4.5		
4.6		
4.7		
4.8		
4.9		
4.10		
4.11		
4.12		
4.13		
4.14		
4.15		
4.16		
4.17		
4.18		
4.19		
4.20		
4.21		
4.22		
4.23		
4.24		
4.25		
4.26		
4.27		
5 Harassment, Hostility and Anti-social Behaviour		
5.1		

	First attempt Correct (✓)	Second attempt Correct (✓)
5.2		
5.3		
5.4		
5.5		
5.6		
5.7		
5.8		
5.9		
5.10		
5.11		
5.12		
5.13		
5.14		
5.15		
5.16		
5.17		
5.18		
5.19		
5.20		
5.21		
5.22		
5.23		
5.24		
5.25		
5.26		
5.27		
6 Public Disorder and Terrorism		
6.1		
6.2		
6.3		
6.4		
6.5		
6.6		
6.7		
6.8		
6.9		
6.10		
6.11		

	First attempt Correct (✓)	Second attempt Correct (✓)
6.12		
6.13		
6.14		
6.15		
6.16		
6.17		
6.18		
6.19		
6.20		
6.21		
6.22		
6.23		
6.24		
6.25		
6.26		
6.27		
6.28		
6.29		

7 Firearms and Gun Crime

7.1		
7.2		
7.3		
7.4		
7.5		
7.6		
7.7		
7.8		
7.9		
7.10		
7.11		
7.12		
7.13		
7.14		
7.15		
7.16		

8 Weapons

8.1		
8.2		

	First attempt Correct (✓)	Second attempt Correct (✓)
8.3		
8.4		
8.5		
8.6		
8.7		
8.8		
8.9		
8.10		
8.11		
8.12		
8.13		
8.14		
8.15		
8.16		
8.17		
8.18		

9 Civil Disputes

9.1		
9.2		
9.3		
9.4		
9.5		
9.6		

10 Offences Relating to Land and Premises

10.1		
10.2		
10.3		
10.4		
10.5		
10.6		
10.7		
10.8		
10.9		
10.10		
10.11		
10.12		
10.13		

	First attempt Correct (✓)	Second attempt Correct (✓)
11 Licensing and Offences Relating to Alcohol		
11.1		
11.2		
11.3		
11.4		
11.5		
11.6		
11.7		
11.8		
11.9		
11.10		
11.11		
11.12		
11.13		
11.14		
11.15		
11.16		
11.17		
11.18		
11.19		
11.20		
11.21		
11.22		
11.23		
11.24		
11.25		
11.26		
11.27		
11.28		
11.29		
11.30		
11.31		

	First attempt Correct (✓)	Second attempt Correct (✓)
11.32		
11.33		
12 Offences and Powers Relating to Information		
12.1		
12.2		
12.3		
12.4		
12.5		
12.6		
12.7		
12.8		
12.9		
12.10		
12.11		
12.12		
12.13		
12.14		
12.15		
12.16		
13 Diversity, Discrimination and Equality		
13.1		
13.2		
13.3		
13.4		
13.5		
13.6		
13.7		
13.8		
13.9		
13.10		

ESSENTIAL—EFFECTIVE—PRACTICAL

Fully updated for the 2008 syllabus

*Indispensable **ONLINE** study-aids for all police officers sitting the Part I promotion examinations*

Blackstone's Police Manuals 2008 Online

FULLY UPDATED for the 2008 syllabus as of 21 September 2007

- Fast, desktop access to the complete text of all four Blackstone's Police Manuals
- Find the information you need quickly and easily by using the powerful search engine via the table of contents or the consolidated A–Z index
- Extensive cross-referencing ensures you can easily revise all relevant subject areas together

Subscriptions: **£78.00** (12 months) | **£58.00** (8 months)

Blackstone's Police Q&As 2008 Online*

- An online Multiple Choice Questions database—the essential study-aid for all police officers sitting the Part 1 promotion examinations
- Over 1500 questions—all of the same format and difficulty as the actual exam
- Choose the number of questions from a single subject or a mixture of all four
- Study questions from a single subject or a mixture of all four
- Get detailed feedback on your performance and a full user history
- Answers are fully explained and cross-referenced to the Blackstone's Police Manuals so you can easily go back and revise the relevant subject area

Subscriptions: **£95.00** (12 months) | **£75.00** (8 months) | **£50.00** (3 months)

Blackstone's Police Manuals 2008 and Q&As 2008 Online*

- The essential integrated study package for all police officers sitting the Part 1 promotion examinations
- The ONLY service to provide direct links from the detailed answers in Blackstone's Police Q&As Online to the relevant section of the Blackstone's Police Manuals Online

Subscriptions: **£150.00** (12 months) | **£120.00** (8 months)

* Please note: the Blackstone's Police Q&As Online service is not endorsed by the NPIA

ALBQ&AA08